Guests at God's Wedding

Guests at God's Wedding

Celebrating Kartik among the Women of Benares

Tracy Pintchman

State University of New York Press

Published by
State University of New York Press, Albany

Printed in the United States of America

For information, address State University of New York Press
194 Washington Avenue, Suite 305, Albany, NY 12210-2384

Production by Judith Block
Marketing by Anne M. Valentine

Library of Congress Cataloging-in-Publication Data

Pintchman, Tracy.
Guests at God's wedding : celebrating Kartik among the women of Benares / Tracy Pintchman.
p. cm.
Includes bibliographical references and index.
ISBN 0-7914-6595-0 (alk. paper) — ISBN 0-7914-6596-9 (pbk : alk. paper)
1. Hindu women—India—Vārānasi (Uttar Pradesh)—Social life and customs. 2. Hindu women—India—Vārānasi (Uttar Pradesh)—Religion. 3. Special months—India—Vārānasi (Uttar Pradesh). 4. Fasts and feasts—India—Vārānasi (Uttar Pradesh). 5. Pājā (Hinduism)—Indian—Vārānasi (Uttar Pradesh). 6. Hinduism and culture—Indian—Vārānasi (Uttar Pradesh). 7. Vārānasi (Uttar Pradesh, India)—Religious life and customs. 8. Vārānasi (Uttar Pradesh, India)—Social life and customs. I. Title.

HQ1173.P55 2006
294.5'36'09209542—dc22 2004065684

10 9 8 7 6 5 4 3 2 1

For my husband, William French,
who makes it all worthwhile

Contents

Illustrations

Table

Figures

Acknowledgments

First and foremost, I wish to thank all the female Kartik votaries of Benares who welcomed me into their Kartik *pūjā* circles, taught me their traditions, invited me to their homes, fed me, dressed me, introduced me to their families, helped me navigate life in Benares, and supported my interest in their culture and religious customs in so many other ways. Without them, needless to say, this book would not exist. Very special thanks are owed especially to the handful of women who spent a great deal of time with me reviewing song and story texts and offering me their interpretations of Kartik *pūjā* traditions. I have chosen to disguise the identities of all informants in this book by using only pseudonyms, so I cannot thank them here by name, but I owe these fabulous women a profound debt of gratitude. Sunita Singh, my research associate in this project, was a highly skillful and deeply loyal research partner, and I greatly appreciate all her hard work.

Several other individuals in Benares also provided invaluable assistance to my work and to me. I would like to thank Virendra Singh for all that he has done over the years to nurture my interest in Hinduism and Benares. I would like also to express my gratitude to Kashika Singh Samarth, Sushila Singh, Gita Tripathi and her family, and Shashank Singh for their ongoing friendship and support. Vidhhu Shekhar Caturvedi helped me with some text translation, and Dr. Madhavendra Prasad Pandey reviewed all my song transcriptions and helped me translate the songs into Modern Standard Hindi. Here in the United States, Professor Rakesh Ranjan of Emory University reviewed all my final song transcriptions and translations and made several helpful suggestions. I owe him enormous thanks for his generous help.

Financial support for this project was supplied by the American Institute of Indian Studies, the National Endowment of the Humanities, the American Academy of Religion, Loyola University of Chicago, and Harvard University, which granted me a position as research associate and visiting lecturer in the Women's Studies in Religion Program in 2000–2001 so that I could work on this project. I am deeply grateful to all these organizations for their support. At Harvard, Ann Braude, Sidnie Crawford, Sue Houchins, Oyeronke Olajabu, and Traci West read over portions of this manuscript and suggested ways to improve it. Nancy Ellegate at State University of New York Press has been steadfast in her support of my work during the last decade, and I am very grateful for her assistance. Judith Block and Kay Butler provided superb editorial help in bringing this book into print, and Carol Inskip prepared a draft of the index. My sister, Lisa Pintchman Rogers, came to spend time with me in Benares at just the right time, bearing coffee, chocolate, and other wondrous goodies. She took to India like a duck to water, and her excitement and interest in Benares helped keep me going. My children, Molly and Noah, kept me laughing and nurtured my spirit during the years I was finishing this book, and I can never thank them enough for all the joy they have brought into my life.

Finally, I owe the largest debt of gratitude to my wonderful husband, William French. He came to India with me several times during the years I was conducting research on this project, took numerous photos to help me out, and functioned as my camera crew (along with Sunita Singh) when I was filming in 1998. He has supported me through thick and thin, and I can never repay him for all that he has given me. This book is dedicated to him.

Portions of this manuscript have been published previously in the following articles and book chapters and are reproduced here with permission: "Domesticating Krishna: Friendship, Marriage, and Women's Experience in a Hindu Women's Ritual Tradition," in *"Alternative" Krishna Traditions: Krishna in Folk Religion and Vernacular Literature*, ed. Guy Beck (New York: State University of New York Press, 2005), 43–63; "Courting Krishna on the Banks of the Ganges: Gender and Power in a Hindu Women's Ritual Tradition," in *Comparative Studies in South Asia, Africa, and the Middle East,* 24/1 (Spring 2004): 18–28; "Women's Songs for the Marriage of Tulsi and Krishna in Benares," *Journal of Vaiṣṇava Studies* 12/1 (Fall 2003): 57–65; "The Month of Kartik and Women's Ritual Devotions to Krishna," in *The Blackwell Companion to Hinduism* (Oxford: Blackwell, 2003), 327–42; "The Month of Kārttik as a Vaiṣṇava *Mahotsav:* Mythic Themes and the Ocean of Milk," *Journal of Vaiṣṇava Studies* 7/2 (March 1999): 65–92; and "Celebrating Karttik in Benares," *Dak: The Newsletter of the American Institute of Indian Studies* (Summer 1999): 8–11.

Introduction

Every autumn in the Hindi-speaking belt of North India, the hot and humid season of monsoon rains comes to an end, and the weather begins to turn cooler, dryer, and more pleasant. The change in temperature also ushers in what is for North Indian Hindus a religiously vital time of year. Schools and universities close for days or weeks on end; trains are filled with families traveling to visit relatives; each day of the calendar is thickly filled in with the names of feasts, fasts, and rituals to be observed, and a sense of excitement and anticipation is in the air.

In the city of Varanasi, more popularly known outside of India as Benares,[1] many members of the Hindu community spend the first part of October preparing for the numerous religious celebrations that fall during the lunar autumn month of Kartik.[2] Benares is a major Hindu pilgrimage center, and many Hindus would say that it is one of the most sacred cities, if not the most sacred city, in all of India. The month of Kartik, one of twelve traditional months recognized as the basis of the Hindu calendar, also holds special religious significance.

For many Hindu Benarsis, time is measured by weekly, monthly, or yearly rhythms prescribed by the traditional Hindu calendar and differentiated by religious practices dictated by those rhythms. Of particular significance in this regard are the lunar months, which Philip Lutgendorf notes are "complete units of time in a ritual sense, as the 'profane' (for Hindus) months of the Christian calendar—used for government and business purposes—can never be" (1991, 64). Book stalls all over Benares stock manuals describing the religious significance of each month and various aspects of individual holidays, including specific narratives, ritual practices, and even foods that devout individuals ought to cook or eat on particular days. Traditional Hindu months are especially important for women, who are responsible for a great deal of the nonpriestly religious work in Benares. I recall a conversation with one Benarsi woman who knew exactly what day it was in relation to traditional Kartik dates but had no idea it was the month of October according to the "profane" calendar. I often heard women say things like, "Well, this is Kartik, so we worship this way right now, but in Shravan we will worship this other way."

This book explores the nature of Kartik as a sacred month. It examines important attributes that Hindu texts and religious practitioners ascribe to Kartik, and it investigates relationships between Kartik's perceived natural, astrological, and mythic-historical dimensions and patterns of religious observance unique to the month. In particular, however, this book highlights Kartik-related rituals, stories, songs, and experiences particular to women. When Hindu women living in and around Benares celebrate Kartik, they undertake ritual practices in which men do not participate, meeting daily to enact a form of ritual worship, or *pūjā*, unique to this month. Participants in this *pūjā* ritually raise the Hindu deity Krishna from childhood to adulthood throughout the month, marrying him off to the plant-goddess Tulsi toward the end of Kartik. This book aims to show that women who perform Kartik *pūjā* understand and celebrate Kartik and Krishna in ways that are linked to the desires, hopes, fears, and social realities that tend to be characteristic of many Hindu women living in the rather conservative social milieu of Eastern Uttar Pradesh and Western Bihar.

Two currents within contemporary scholarship on religion inform my approach. The first is a turn toward greater consideration of "vernacular religion," that is, religion as it is actually lived, or "as human beings encounter, understand, interpret, and practice it" (Primiano 1995, 44). This book engages seriously textual descriptions and prescriptions pertaining to Kartik, since these are important to those who celebrate the month. But it also considers how devotees not just implement, but also disregard and deviate from, textual formulae. Second, my approach is informed by a number of recent studies that have focused on women's everyday religious lives and have begun to take seriously women's agency in interpreting, appropriating, and shaping religion in ways that resonate with their own preoccupations and interests (e.g., Pearson 1996, Sered 1992, Brasher 1998). The women whose traditions and lives I explore in this book are generally pretty conventional Hindu housewives who are not highly educated and do not hold any notable social, political, or economic power. They tend not to challenge predominant Hindu gender ideologies or patterns of gender segregation. Yet these women exercise autonomy and initiative in creating and sustaining female-centered traditions and practices that are uniquely meaningful to women's experience in Hindu culture.

Prelude to a Book

I began the research on this project quite by accident while I was in Benares on a sabbatical leave during the fall of 1995. I had spent five weeks traveling in the Himalayas and conducting research for a project that I had begun on pilgrimage and asceticism. Armed with several hours of taped interviews, I returned to Benares to get some assistance in translating the tapes from a native Hindi speaker. I had spent ten months in Benares in 1989–1990 while I was a graduate student, so I knew the city and knew I could get help there with my project. I began to work on the translations with a Benarsi assistant just as the month of Kartik began.

Several days into our work, this assistant mentioned to me that during the month of Kartik, Benarsi women gather at the platforms or *ghāṭ*s that line the banks of the Ganges River before sunrise to conduct a special *pūjā* unique to the month. My curiosity was piqued, and I asked him to introduce me to someone who had participated in this special Kartik *pūjā,* which he did. This first contact was an elderly woman named Lilavati.[3] Lilavati told me about the *pūjā* in great detail, and I asked her if she would accompany me the next morning. She herself no longer participated in Kartik *pūjā* due to ill health, but she agreed to introduce me to the group of women who performed the *pūjā* on Tulsi Ghat, which was close to her home. She informed me that all the women who do the *pūjā* first bathe in the Ganges, so I would have to either accompany them or bathe at home before leaving the house. I opted to bathe at home.

The next day I appeared freshly scrubbed at the door of my assistant at four in the morning. He took me to Lilavati's home, where he banged on the door for five minutes before Lilavati finally appeared. Apparently having forgotten her promise to me and visibly annoyed at being woken so early, she gesticulated forcefully in the direction of Tulsi Ghat and closed the door in our faces. My sleepy assistant, happy that his gender excluded him from participating in this early-morning ritual, went home to go back to bed. I had no choice but to go on by myself and hope that the women doing the *pūjā* would not mind having a foreigner join them.

Figure 1. The Ganges River flowing at the edge of Benares *(photo by William C. French)*

I climbed down the stairs at Tulsi Ghat, sat down on a step, and waited. A group of women was forming, and I noticed that they were gathering around some figures they had made out of the clay lining the banks of the river. All of a sudden they began to sing, and the group became very busy; women began to reach into *pūjā* baskets to pull out flowers, vials of sugar and flour, sandalwood powder, and other *pūjā* items. I reached into my bag and pulled out my tape recorder, which I turned on and then slipped halfway back into the bag. I realized later this was a mistake; I should have waited and asked the women's permission before attempting to record. But at the time, I was thinking that before deciding whether or not I wanted to engage in scholarly work on this tradition, I would sit down with the tape to figure out exactly what the whole thing seemed to be about. Feeling too shy to simply join in, I sat at a small distance and watched. The women, however, were well aware of both my presence and my curiosity, and they kept looking over at me and smiling. At a break between songs, one of the women caught my eye and yelled, "*āvā*!" ("come!"). She then moved over and pushed another woman away to make room for me in the circle.

I shuffled over and slipped awkwardly into the space that the women had made for me. The next song began, and the woman who

Figure 2. Women performing Kartik *pūjā* on Assi Ghat

had called me over started slipping *pūjā* offerings into my hand, motioning when and where I should place the offerings. Spotting the tape recorder in my bag, she cried out, "She has a tape recorder, so sing louder!" Embarrassed at my own clumsiness, I pulled the recorder out and held it up for all to see. The women laughed and poked me; chastened, I grinned back at them. During the period of storytelling that came after the *pūjā,* one of the women grabbed the recorder from my hand and held it next to the mouth of the storyteller, who was quite cooperative, so I guessed I had probably not offended sensibilities too much. After the *pūjā* and storytelling ended, several of the women invited me to come the next day. I asked them if I could continue to record; not only did they assure me that that would be fine, but they asked me to play back for them what I had recorded that day, crowding close around me. Hearing their own voices on the tape, they laughed gleefully, and there was much teasing and playful banter.

I continued to participate in the *pūjā* for the rest of the month of Kartik, although I had missed the first twelve days. I began to learn what items to offer when, and I tried to learn some of the *pūjā* songs. Many of the women were curious about me and came to me after the *pūjā* to talk to me and ask me questions. Although many foreigners visit Benares and many foreign scholars and students live there for long periods of time, most of the women I worked with had never spoken to a foreigner. Not only is language a barrier, but traditional mores in Benares also dictate that married women should be modest in public and should not speak to strangers on the street, especially male strangers but also female ones. Through our interactions surrounding our mutual participation in Kartik *pūjā,* I gradually got to know several of the women.

By the end of my stay in Benares in 1995, I had begun to understand a bit about what Kartik meant to the women with whom I had celebrated it. I had also collected a number of songs and stories from the *pūjā* and had conducted several interviews with participants. My project on pilgrimage and asceticism fell to the wayside, and I became more absorbed and interested in the world of Kartik *pūjā.* I had to leave India and go back to the United States in December of 1995, but this book project was starting to take form in my mind. Several grants allowed me to return to Benares in 1997 and 1998 to complete my field research.

In 1997, I began to rely heavily on the help of Sunita Singh, a young Benarsi woman whom I met through my Hindi instructor, Virendra Singh. Sunita became not only my partner in research, but also a dear friend. She has come to visit me in the United States, and we remain in close contact. Taking a cue from Elaine Craddock (2001, 145, 168n.1), I will refer to Sunita in this book as my research associate, not research assistant, because she was more partner than assistant. I could not have written this book without her help, and she deserves a great deal of credit for whatever contributions this book might make.

Confessions of an Inexpert Ethnographer

The time that I spent doing field research in Benares for this book provided me with many friendships I continue to cherish and numerous moments of shared emotional warmth and loving connection with the many women who generously opened up to me their homes and their hearts. It also made me painfully aware of the many limitations I was unable to overcome. I realize now that I had naively assumed my training in Hindu studies and the gender identity my fellow *pūjā* participants and I shared as women would accord me a sense of comfort and belonging that, in fact, I never fully attained nor was granted. Judith Stacey observes that feminist ethnographers (and I count myself as such) who study women may be more apt than others to suffer from what she calls "the delusion of alliance," that is, a tendency to be overconfident about one's empathy for and identification with one's ethnographic subjects (1988, 25–26). It is my desire to try and avoid perpetuating such a delusion by sharing with readers some sense of the limitations and frustrations I encountered in the course of conducting my research. I also want to reflect on what these may reveal about the ethnographic process and power relations in the field.

To begin with, language was always a problem for me. I speak Hindi and my language abilities were much better in 1997 and 1998 than in 1995, but I am not fluent. In addition, all the songs and stories sung and recited during the *pūjā* are not in Modern Standard Hindi but largely in Bhojpuri, which is spoken in and around Benares, often with words from Braj Bhasha (spoken in the region of Mathura-Vrindavan) or other languages thrown in. While the women I worked with could usually understand my stodgy textbook Hindi, they would usually reply using the colloquial mix with which they were most familiar but which I often found close to incomprehensible. I was able to familiarize myself with some basic Bhojpuri while I was in Benares, but I never arrived at a point where I was really comfortable with it. This meant that my informal interactions with the women were sometimes stifled by communication problems. Furthermore, I was unable to translate the songs and stories I collected without assistance from native speakers, who had to explain the Bhojpuri to me in Hindi before we could work together to translate materials into English. Since I could not verify the translations from Bhojpuri myself, I felt it necessary to check translations several times over with not only knowledgeable *pūjā* participants, but other native speakers as well, which was a very time-consuming process.

In addition to participating in the daily *pūjā* and other religious activities throughout the month, I also conducted thirty-six interviews of Kartik *pūjā* participants as well as a number of other interviews of both male and female individuals knowledgeable about Kartik, including astrologers, pundits, religious leaders, and university professors. Interviewing *pūjā* participants posed special challenges. When I first started conducting interviews, I had clear expectations regarding how the process would work. I anticipated that I would go to a woman's house, spend a few minutes making chitchat, conduct the interview, thank her profusely, and leave. I quickly realized that this modus operandi was not only unrealistic, but also rude. Most of the women I interviewed were from the *pūjā* groups in which I participated, so we saw each other frequently during the month of Kartik. When they invited me to their homes to interview them, they did so with the expectation of friendship, not information exchange. So on several occasions, the first time I went to an informant's home I simply sat with her—and usually other family members as well—to talk, drink tea, nibble on snacks, and give both of us a chance to get to know the other. I would conduct the interview on the second visit and try to return for at least one more social visit after that when possible, often bringing some token of appreciation. It was impossible for me to meet the expectations of friendship that some women brought to our relationship, however, and the process seemed to bewilder and even anger many of the *pūjā* participants I interviewed. I sometimes felt overwhelmed by requests and demands women made, asking me to attend family functions, find jobs for relatives, get them things from abroad, and so forth.

With only one exception, I went to my informants' homes to interview them or ask them questions. Although I would have been happy to have them come to my home, they usually did not wish to do so. In 1998, when my husband accompanied me to Benares for just under a month, we rented a private apartment, but in 1995 and 1997–1998, I stayed with a Benarsi family that rents out rooms to foreign scholars studying or doing research in Benares. Not only were there single young men around in my household, but most of the girls and women in my *pūjā* groups had to rush home after morning devotions to get ready for school, prepare food for family members, or fulfill other household responsibilities. To make a special trip to my house in the afternoon would have been difficult and inconvenient for them. Interviewing women in their homes, however, had one great disadvantage: if mature male family members were around—husbands, fathers-in-law, or adult sons—then it was sometimes difficult to interview the women, who would not always speak openly in front of adult male family members. In such cases, too, the men's agenda would often take precedence, and I would end up answering questions about myself and my country or sitting through elementary lectures on Hinduism, Indian culture, and the like while the woman I had come to see sat there quietly or retreated to the kitchen to prepare tea and snacks. Once I caught on, I tried to plan interviews to coincide with times that men were most likely to be out of the house, but I was not always successful. Furthermore, during the formal interview process, women tended to wander in and out; sometimes other household women would enter the room and also begin to respond to my questions during the course of the interview, and sometimes the subject I had targeted would leave the room halfway during the interview allowing another female family member to complete it.

In 1995 and 1997, I used both a tape recorder and camera to help me in my research. While my tape recorder never caused trouble for me, my camera was a different story. In 1995 I brought my camera along to the *pūjā* on a few occasions and took several roles of pictures, having obtained permission to do so from *pūjā* participants. I also brought my camera with me when I went to women's homes to interview them, and on several occasions I presented pictures to informants who had helped me as a way of thanking them. Cameras are pretty expensive by Indian standards, and most of the women I worked with did not have cameras in their families, or if they did have a camera, it was not a very good one. I had purchased an expensive camera of excellent quality just before coming to India, and I wanted my informants to benefit from it.

Although my desire to offer something to those who had given me their time was, I would maintain, well intentioned, the photos were a source of tension and conflict. I did not give photos to all my informants—there were occasions when I simply forgot to do so—and in some cases I caved into pressure to shoot numerous photos of family members while I was in someone's home. I soon found that those who felt they had been short shrifted were angry not only with me, but also with neighbors to whom I had given more generously. Women whom I had not interviewed asked me to come to their homes for a photo shoot, and a number of women I had interviewed asked me to return to their homes to take more shots. I could think of no simple way to resolve the tensions I had caused, so I resorted to saying that I was out of film and could no longer take pictures. When I returned in later years, I shot only black-and-white film, which was not appealing to most of the *pūjā* participants, so the same problems did not arise.

My conspicuousness as a foreigner sometimes affected the research process in ways that were difficult for me. To most Benarsis, I appeared to be just another foreign tourist, and I was treated accordingly. Walking downtown with Indian friends, I would be approached to buy silk, Benarsi crafts, or other objects. When I was participating in the *pūjā,* people often gathered around to stare at me. One day while I was sitting in the *pūjā* circle with the women doing *pūjā,* a boatman came up to me and whispered in my ear, "Madam, Boat?" I felt rage welling up inside me: couldn't he tell that I was there not as a tourist, but as a scholar of Hinduism engaged in serious research?

The women who invited me to do *pūjā* with them also worried that I would break the rules. When I did something wrong in the *pūjā,* it was often the object of playful ridicule or public correction. Some of the *pūjā* participants were especially concerned that I know not to perform *pūjā* while menstruating and reminded me about this repeatedly. While other women discreetly refrained from participation during their menstrual periods, my period became an object of public discussion and comment. When I returned to the *pūjā* circle after several days of nonparticipation, my hair was checked to make sure I had washed it properly, and I was quizzed about how I had handled my personal hygiene.

In Benares the conventions of dress and adornment that dictate what married women should wear are pretty strict, and I was not in the habit of conforming to them when I began to work on this project in 1995. On the day that I first participated in the *pūjā,* one of the women approached me and asked me if I was married. When I told her that I was, she reached into her bag and pulled out a tin of *sindūr,* a bright red (or orange) powder that married women place in the part of their hair, and applied it to my hair part. This gesture was accompanied by an explanation about how married women should dress and adorn themselves, and I took the hint. I was used to wearing a *salvār-kamīz,* a long tunic over a pair of baggy, drawstring pants, but in Benares many people consider this outfit to be proper only for unmarried girls; married women must wear saris. When I came to the *pūjā* a few days later dressed in a sari, several of the women expressed their approval, so from then on I would wear saris while participating in religious events. I also adopted more of the customs regarding married women's dress in Benares: I began to wear *sindūr,* a sari, and a *bindi* (the decorative "dot" placed on the forehead) every day, and with the women's help I eventually added toe rings, ankle bracelets, earrings, bangles, and *mangal sūtra,* a type of necklace worn by married women. These items constitute the married women's "uniform" in Benares. My dressing this way seemed to make my fellow *pūjā* participants happier, but it also meant that my dressing habits became part of the public domain and subject to public scrutiny. Women were constantly untying and retying my sari, adjusting my *bindi,* commenting on my bangles, and so forth.

These and other experiences I had while conducting field research drove home to me the lesson that, no matter how long I study Hinduism and Indian culture, and no matter how much time I spend in India, I will never be an "insider," even among women. I knew this intellectually, of course, from my training as a student of religion and Indian culture, but being in the field and working on this project drove the point home in visceral, concrete ways that felt very personal. It is one thing to know that one is an outsider; it is quite another to experience it in numerous ways day in and day out over an extended period of time. During the three years in which I conducted research in the field, both my own actions and those of the *pūjā* participants I was there to observe and share worship with spoke constantly of my status as a culturally bumbling, ritually inexpert social outsider.

In an essay that explores the relationship between Western expatriates living in India and their domestic servants, Louise H. Kidder notes that the relationship between these two groups "do not lie simply on an axis of domination and subjection. . . . The hierarchy is not simply linear. The servant's knowledge and the master's ignorance, the servant's mastery and the master's dependence, complicate the picture and contradict colonial assumptions of worth" (Kidder 2000, 208). I would argue that relationships between ethnographers and the populations they study "in the field" may be equally complicated in this regard. I have no desire to minimize or deny the asymmetrical relations of privilege or the colonial history in which the whole project of ethnography is grounded, nor do I wish to deny that peoples all over the world have been subject to the type of objectifying gaze that characterizes much of the Western ethnographic process. But it is very clear to me that the situation in the field is far more complex than powerful ethnographer vs. powerless natives.[4]

Contours of the Book

There are three primary goals of this book: to highlight some of the most significant dimensions of Kartik as a religiously important month; to describe female-specific Kartik worship practices undertaken by Benarsi women; and to interpret these practices in light of available research on Krishna traditions, women's religiosity, Hinduism and Indian culture, and related fields. There is a good deal of information I have chosen to leave out, although some readers will undoubtedly feel I have included too many details as it is. I never had time to investigate some aspects of the month I heard about (e.g., I was told that Marwaris have their own unique Kartik-related practices), and I am sure there are many texts, beliefs, and practices that I simply failed to discover during the course of my research. In order to make this book more accessible to nonspecialists, I have tried to minimize the use of Sanskrit and Hindi terms, and I have chosen not to use diacritical marks on proper names or terms derived from proper names (e.g., Vishnu, Vaishnava).

Together chapters 1 and 2 explore the broad religious significance of Kartik to both male and female Hindus, taking into account textual and ethnographic evidence. Chapter 1 contextualizes Kartik in relation to larger spheres of concern in Hinduism and explores important textual sources, narratives, and practices associated with the month as a whole. Many Benarsis consider Kartik to be highly auspicious, and the second chapter investigates the particular nature of Kartik's auspiciousness through the Hindu sacred narrative of the churning of the ocean of milk, a cosmogonic event that some Benarsi Hindus claim took place during Kartik. Chapter 2 also details connections between Kartik and Krishna, the deity who is central to the practice of women's Kartik *pūjā*.

Brahmanical traditions, including authoritative religious texts, play a large role in these first two chapters because they play a large role in many Hindus' lives. Both men and women read authoritative Hindu texts or listen to them being recited, use Hindu texts or parts thereof in Kartik ritual practices, and engage in Kartik-related practices grounded in Sanskritic Hinduism. The female-specific traditions surrounding Kartik *pūjā*, on the other hand, appear to be largely folk traditions. I turn to these in the third chapter. Exploring Kartik's broader significance before turning to female-specific traditions helps highlight how such traditions comment on, add to, and depart from Sanskritic materials shared across gender lines. Taken together the first three chapters attempt to offer a thick description of what I consider to be the three primary layers of Benarsi Hindu women's encounter with Kartik, all different yet all important and meaningful: the month as a whole, its individual festival celebrations, and women's Kartik *pūjā* traditions.

Chapters 4 and 5 constitute the analytic core of the book. Chapter 4 analyzes how Kartik *pūjā* appropriates and transforms predominant Kartik and Krishna traditions in ways that reflect women's this-worldly concerns and desires. One major issue that comes to the fore in this chapter is the mixing of maternal and erotic imagery in relation to Krishna, a mixing that takes place throughout Kartik *pūjā*. Some scholars have applied psychoanalytic frames of interpretation to forms of Krishna devotion that conflate maternal and erotic relationality and argue that this conflation signals an inherently pathogenic sexual attraction between mother and son. Chapter 4 explores the conflation of maternal and erotic sentiments in Kartik *pūjā* from a woman-centered perspective, leading to a very different interpretation of these materials.

Chapter 5 takes up issues concerning women's religious empowerment in relation to Kartik *pūjā*. A good amount of contemporary postcolonial scholarship has grappled with ways of assessing, in a postcolonial context, women's power in non-Western cultures. All the discussion, however, has not resulted in consensus; instead, it has exposed clear fault lines. Some scholars prize cultural and religious pluralism and are suspicious of Western feminist discourse as a type of hegemonic "discursive colonialism" that simply continues the colonial project in measuring all cultures against Western values (Mohanty 1988). Others emphasize the need for feminist universals that can be applied cross-culturally, fearing that too much talk of women's power especially in traditional contexts tends to disregard the reality of the material oppression that women face (e.g., Nussbaum 2000). What might we say about Kartik *pūjā* in this regard? Is it empowering to the women who take part in it? If so, how?

Chapter 1

Kartik as a Sacred Month: The Kartik *Vrat* in Text and Context

> The month of Kartik is the most excellent of all months. It is the most meritorious. It sanctifies all sanctifying things. . . . There is no month on par with Kartik.
>
> —Kartik Mahatmya of the Skanda Purana 1.27–36

A group of sages is asking about the religious importance of Kartik. This question has been asked and answered many times before, we are told, most notably in a conversation that took place in ancient times between Brahma, generator and grandfather of the universe, and the sage Narada. That conversation is repeated to the curious sages, and we, as readers of the Skanda Purana, get to eavesdrop. Brahma sings the praises of Kartik, lauding it as the most excellent of months, greater than all the pilgrimage spots (*tīrthas*), sacrifices (*yajña*), and acts of monetary donation (*dāna*) combined (1.21). The translator, G. V. Tagare, notes that this is a typical example of exaggeration (*atiśayokti*) found in the Puranas (Skanda Purana vol. 6, 51, n. 2). That is certainly true; but there is also a grain of truth in this exaggeration. As any Benarsi will tell you, there is indeed something very special about the month of Kartik.

When measured against the solar calendar commonly used in the West, the first day of Kartik usually falls sometime in mid-October, although this varies from year to year.[1] To understand what the coming of Kartik might mean to a Benarsi on a gut level, it is helpful to have spent the hot and rainy seasons in Benares. In April the temperature begins to climb higher and higher, usually reaching above a hundred degrees before the month is out. The air is intensely hot and dry, and fewer and fewer people head out into the streets during the harsh midday heat. As temperatures soar even higher through May and into early June, bodies already drained by the heat become more vulnerable to heat stroke. When the monsoon rains finally break, usually around the end of June, they bring a welcome drop in temperature, but daytime temperatures in July and August still remain in the nineties. Now soaring humidity added to the heat brings new forms of discomfort. By September many people feel weak and feverish.

It is no wonder that many Benarsis look forward to the coming of Kartik and the drop in temperature that it brings. From the perspective of traditional Indian medicine (Ayurveda), the change of season that occurs at this time of year is unhealthful and leaves the body vulnerable to illnesses. In Benares, I frequently heard people attribute all kinds of medical problems to the change in the weather. Yet many also declared that autumn is the best season, and that during Kartik the climate is more favorable than at any other time of the year. It is during this period that nature is at its best: the sky clears, the temperature is moderate, the land is lush and green from the monsoon rains, ripening crops mature, and food becomes abundant as harvesting begins.

In addition to being welcomed for the change of seasons that it marks, Kartik is celebrated in Benares as a deeply sacred month. It is principally concerned with the worship of Vishnu and therefore is most meaningful to Vaishnavas, those whose devotional orientation centers on Vishnu. At least in Benares, however, non-Vaishnavas also participate in month-long observances that take place during Kartik, although my own research indicates they are outnumbered by Vaishnavas. Distinctive narratives, practices of text recitation, and month-long ritual observances bring the month to life in Benares in people's homes, in temples, and along the platforms, or *ghāṭ*s, that line the banks of the Ganges River at the edge of the city. The numerous religious practices and celebrations that occur at different points during the month—festivals, fasts, the giving of donations (*dāna*), and so forth—mark the cadence of the month's rhythms and give shape to the devotional spirit that permeates the month.

Kartik and the Hindu Calendar

Kartik is defined within larger systems of time calculation in the Hindu tradition. The traditional Hindu calendar consists of twelve months divided into pairs that constitute six seasons. Spring (*vasanta*) encompasses the months of Chaitr (March–April) and Vaishakh (April–May); summer (*grīṣma*) includes Jyesht (May–June) and Ashadh (June–July); the monsoon or rainy season (*varśa*) comprises Shravan (July–August) and Bhadrapad (August–September); autumn (*śarad*) consists of Ashvin (September–October) and Kartik (October–November); winter (*hemanta*) includes Margashirsh (November–December) and Paush (December–January); and the cool season (*śiśira*) embraces Magh (January–February) and Phalgun (February–March).

Kartik derives its name from the constellation called Krittika, a group of stars known in English as the Pleiades. The names of all twelve months of the Hindu calendar are based on the placement of each month's full moon in relation to twenty-seven or twenty-eight minor constellations (*nakṣātra*) often referred to in English as "asterisms" or "lunar mansions." The different asterisms are unevenly spaced apart, but they are assigned fixed positions in the sky (Pugh 1981, 80). Because of the earth's rotation, each month the full moon occupies a different part of the sky, which means that it appears to be in conjunction with a different asterism every month. Kartik's full moon generally appears in conjunction with the Krittika asterism.[2]

Each Hindu month comprises two fortnights: the "dark" or "waning" fortnight (*kṛṣṇa pakṣa*), lasting from full moon to new moon; and the "light" or "waxing" fortnight (*śukla pakṣa*), which lasts from new moon to full moon. Months may be calculated from new moon to new moon or from full moon to full moon.[3] In Uttar Pradesh, the state in which Benares is located, the latter system prevails, so the full-moon night of Ashvin, the month that precedes Kartik, marks the onset of Kartik month in Benares. Each fortnight consists of fifteen lunar days or *tithi*s. *Tithi*s are named according to the position they occupy in the sequence of *tithi*s during the fortnight in which it falls. So, for example, the second *tithi* of either fortnight is called "the second" (*dvityā*) of that fortnight, the third is called "the third" (*tritiyā*), and so forth, up to the fifteenth *tithi*, which is identified by the state of the moon, either new (*amāvāsya*) or full (*pūrṇimā*). The following day marks the beginning of the next fortnight, and the sequence of *tithi*s from one to fifteen begins again. Although *tithi* is often translated as "day," it is not the same as a solar day. A solar day lasts from one sunrise to the next sunrise, but a *tithi* is defined as the time it takes for the moon to move twelve degrees around the earth. *Tithi*s can last anywhere from twenty-two to twenty-six hours, and a cycle of thirty *tithi*s may take more or less than thirty solar days to complete (cf. Pugh 1981, 50–51). The Hindu calendar harmonizes lunar and solar calculations by proclaiming any given solar day as the *tithi* that is current at the time of sunrise on that day. The result is that *tithis* may drop out of the calendar or be repeated.

The yearly cycle of traditional Hindu months marks not just climatic processes, but ritual and cultural process as well (Wadley 1983, 54; cf. Vaudeville 1986). Each month has its own specific religious and cultural characteristics, and these are addressed in Hindu texts.

Textual Sources and Kartik

The most important Sanskrit sources pertaining to the months, including Kartik, are the Puranas, which form the most recent scriptural layer of the Brahmanical Hindu canon. Recorded over several centuries, the Puranas encompass narrative, ritual, philosophical, and other materials drawn in from many different historical periods. There are eighteen major and eighteen minor Puranas, but the most important ones pertaining to Kartik in its entirety as well as individual celebrations that take place during the month are the Padma and Skanda Puranas. The Narada Purana also contains one chapter that focuses on the importance of Kartik, and other Puranas, such as the Bhavishya, include some discussion of religious observances or narrative materials connected with the month. Significant Kartik-related materials also appear in the Dharma-Nibandhas, encyclopedic digests of religious prescriptions that date from about the twelfth to eighteenth centuries. The Nibandhas draw upon scripture to elucidate Hindu laws and customs and even preserve lost verses from the Puranas and other Hindu scriptures (McGee 1987, 41). Two of the most important Nibandhas with respect to Kartik observances are the Dharmasindhu (18th c.) and the Nirnayasindhu (17th c.). These two texts contain lengthy sections devoted to Kartik and its many religious observances.

Most of the individuals with whom I spoke tended to learn more about Kartik and its rituals from one another than from any textual source. But they also relied on ritual functionaries who work on the *ghāṭ*s, family and temple priests, gurus, and other religious authority figures to answer their questions about ritual observance, and these religious specialists were often steeped in Sanskrit sources. Hence the Sanskrit sources are important, for they help shape the devotional attitudes of many Kartik celebrants in Benares and guide their ritual practices.

Religious manuals written in Hindi are also widely available in Benares. These manuals tend to draw on the Puranas and Nibandhas as well as popular tradition, and they detail narrative and ritual traditions associated with the religious observances and festivals of the entire year.

They are usually organized on a month-by-month basis and include sections on each of the twelve months, including, of course, the month of Kartik. In Benares, women tend to use these ritual manuals more than men do, and when women I interviewed pulled out a text to consult regarding Kartik-related religious observances, they relied more on these manuals than on any other text. Also available in Benares are local vernacular sources on Kartik, including newspaper articles and materials about the month published by Vaishnava temples in the city.

The Texts of the Kartik Mahatmya

Set back behind the area of downtown Benares known as Godauliya are numerous narrow, meandering alleyways known as *gali*s that wind through one of the most colorful sections of the city. This is the area around Vishvanath Gali where pilgrims come to visit the famous Vishvanath Temple, dedicated to Shiva in his capacity as "Lord of All." This is also the most touristy part of the city, and numerous foreigners wander through the area to enjoy the sights and shop for silk and other items. If one happens to be browsing through one of the many bookstalls that line the alleys in downtown Benares beginning in late September, one will inevitably come across devotional pamphlets that contain a rendition in Hindi of a text called the Kartik Mahatmya, "Glorification of Kartik." These are translations of Sanskrit materials excerpted from the Puranas, and Sanskrit editions are also widely available. During Kartik, the Kartik Mahatmya is read, recited, translated, and preached in Vaishnava temples, monasteries (*maṭh*s), and households all over Benares.

The version of the Kartik Mahatmya most widely sold in Benares, both in Hindi and in Sanskrit, is a section of text from the Padma Purana. It includes twenty-nine continuous chapters from Padma Purana 6.88 to 6.117 along with another Kartik-related Puranic chapter or section included as a thirtieth chapter or as an addendum. Puranic texts borrow heavily from one another, however, and sections of one Purana sometimes reappear in a similar form in another Purana, so it is not too surprising that a section of another Purana, Skanda Purana 2.4.1–36, also goes by the title "Kartik Mahatmya." Although I was told that some of the Hindi pamphlets sold in Benares as the Kartik Mahatmya are translations of the Skanda Purana's section of text, I never came across such a pamphlet myself. But devotees engage both versions of the text in both public and private venues all over Benares throughout the month.

The two versions of the Kartik Mahatmya, that of the Padma Purana (hereafter KMPP) and that of the Skanda Purana (hereafter KMSP), are not exactly the same, but they do share a good deal of content. Significant portions of material appear in both texts in identical or nearly identical form, and some narrative sections that are elaborated at length in the KMPP are recounted in abbreviated form in the KMSP. Some portions of the KMSP that are not reproduced in the KMPP are found elsewhere in the Padma Purana, and vice versa.

Relevant sections of the Puranas are often recited publicly for important religious occasions. During the month of Kartik, it is considered highly meritorious to recite daily a portion of the Kartik Mahatmya in the original Sanskrit, have it recited by a Brahmin priest, or at least listen to it being recited. Of the two versions, the KMPP is the one most popularly recited in Benares, and it is also the one most familiar to the women with whom I participated in Kartik-related religious observances during the month. Both the KMPP and the KMSP include passages glorifying Kartik, explanations of its religious importance, descriptions of ritual practices that should be undertaken during Kartik, narrative material related to the month and its observances, and passages lauding those who recite the text or listen to its recitation.[4]

Kartik and Auspiciousness

Much has been written about the auspicious (*śubh, maṅgal*) and the inauspicious (*aśubh, amaṅgal*) in Hindu culture (e.g., Marglin 1985a; Carman and Marglin 1985). Generally speaking, auspiciousness, which is embodied in the goddess Lakshmi, is a desired value that connotes well-being and happiness; inauspiciousness embraces all opposing values. While a good deal of scholarship on auspiciousness in Hindu culture has emphasized values generally associated with householdership and worldly pursuits, Vasudha Narayanan ramifies the discussion by calling for a clear recognition of two levels of auspiciousness: one that has to do with everyday life and householder values and pertains to things like prosperity, happiness, or the longevity of a husband; and another that encompasses the pursuit of spiritual liberation (*mokṣa*) and is allied with renunciant values (Narayanan 1985, 62). This second level pertains to the achievement of spiritual advancement, renunciation of the world, and pursuit of the divine. Kartik exemplifies auspiciousness on both these levels. Many Kartik-related practices can be viewed as conducive to either worldly or spiritual boons, or both, depending on the devotee, and the line between the two is quite fluid. Many auspiciousness-related images, themes, and practices that permeate the month are not unique to Kartik, but during the month they assume unique forms while embodying more general themes of auspiciousness in Hindu culture.

Many of those whom I encountered in Benares described Kartik as not only auspicious, but also pure (*śuddh*), since it is a month for cleansing oneself of spiritual defilements. Scholarly discourse about auspiciousness has made much of the distinction between the values of auspiciousness and purity in Hindu culture (e.g., Carman and Marglin 1985), and such a distinction is unquestionably important and helpful in many contexts. However, while auspiciousness/inauspiciousness and purity/impurity represent different axes of value, they are not mutually exclusive. Ritual activities that establish purity may also promote auspiciousness (Khare 1976, 109). Many of the Benarsis with whom I spoke also thought of Kartik as pure, although they tended to emphasize the month's auspiciousness.

Judy Pugh notes that forms of auspiciousness related to periods of time in the Hindu calendar tend to cluster around two poles: one pole is related to fertility and reproductive auspiciousness and reflects climatic cycles, and a second pole marks moral, affective, and aesthetic dimensions of auspiciousness and is mediated by celestial cycles unrelated to climatic conditions (Pugh 1983, 47). While the former category includes such things as proper times to sow seeds, for example, the latter has more to do with appropriate times to meditate, conduct particular rituals, undertake a pilgrimage, and so forth. There is some correlation between the two levels of auspiciousness that Narayanan articulates and those that Pugh articulates. Reproductive auspiciousness, which Pugh identifies with certain climatic conditions, is analogous to the "this-wordly" values typical of householder life. Not only does agricultural fertility serve as a metaphor for abundance in other domains, but the same goddess, Lakshmi, is thought to bring wealth and abundance in progeny as well as agricultural success. Certain moral and affective states, on the other hand—for example, wisdom or peacefulness—connote spiritual attainment, especially spiritual liberation. In the Hindu tradition spiritual attainments are pursued in ascetic life through celibacy, fasting, and other ascetic activities, although householders may also engage in ascesis in temporally limited ways.

Kartik is popularly perceived to be both materially and spiritually auspicious. Scholars of Hindu astrology who spoke with me about Kartik, however, insisted that prevailing astrological conditions during the month are actually detrimental to those pursuing spiritual advancement. Those unfamiliar with popular Hinduism might find an appeal to astrology surprising, but astrology plays an important role in the religious lives of traditional Hindus all over India. Major universities in Benares boast entire departments dedicated to Hindu astrology (Jyotish), and many Hindus consult astrologers before they undertake a marriage, major purchase, pilgrimage, or other serious activity.

From the perspective of astrology, the transition of the sun into the Libra (*tulā*) constellation at this time of year makes spiritual progress difficult. The Hindu calendar takes into account not just lunar rhythms, but solar movements as well, especially with respect to the position of the sun in relation to the twelve constellations (*rāśi*) that form the basis of the zodiac. The sun is in conjunction with Libra for roughly the duration of the month of Kartik.[5] According to Hindu astrology, certain constellations can exalt the effect of a particular planet or can debilitate its effect, and Libra is held to be the Sun's debilitating constellation (*nīc rāśi*). Hence, while the sun is in Libra, its influence is extremely weak. From the perspective of Hindu astrology, the debilitated position of the sun creates an inauspicious situation with regard to spiritual life.

The passage of the sun into Libra calls for caution for other reasons as well. The Hindu calendar counts the transition of the sun into the Libra constellation as the autumnal equinox.[6] All transitions of the sun from one constellation to the next are considered precarious, but the equinoxes and solstices are particularly so. It is probably no coincidence that many of the ritual activities prescribed for Kartik are also prescribed for Magh (January–February), the month of the winter solstice, and Vaishakh (April–May), the month of the vernal equinox. Textual sources often cite these three months together. Many informants in Benares compared Kartik not only to these months, but also to Shravan (July–August), the month of the summer solstice, which is a religiously important month comparable to Kartik in several ways. For Benarsis actively engaged in calendrical cycles of devotional religious practice, these four months are closely linked by the religious practices they necessitate.

In Hindu astrology a planet rules every constellation. Libra is ruled by Venus (Shukra), a planet that connotes beauty, women, sexuality, and the production of sexual fluids. In explaining Venus's influence on people and other living creatures during the month, some astrologers with whom I spoke noted that Venus's effect during Kartik would be different for different people depending on the astrological influences at work in each person's life. Others, however, did not make the same distinctions, emphasizing in a more universal way Venus's influence on sexuality. A professor in the Astrology Department at Sampuranand Sanskrit University in Benares, explained Venus's influence during Kartik in this way:

> PROFESSOR: In this month, everyone has increased sexual tendencies because the sun enters its debilitated constellation (*nīc rāśi*) and Venus becomes very powerful. Libra is Venus's constellation. And this month, sperm increases. When the sun becomes weak, then other planets become stronger, and in Kartik the sun is very weak. That is why in Kartik, sexual inclinations rise.
>
> QUESTION: Is this influence only on humans?
>
> PROFESSOR: No. Every living thing is affected by it. . . . If you look on the street, you will see that all the female animals are pregnant in the month of Kartik. Everything is affected by the influence of Venus. In Kartik, all the dogs, monkeys, cows—they are all pregnant. The sun is not very strong, and the sex drive becomes stronger.

The belief that sexual desire increases during Kartik is also current on the popular level. When I directly asked informants about this issue, several of them agreed that Kartik was the best time of the year for lovemaking. Most informants, however, attributed this characteristic not to astrological conditions, but to favorable weather and moderate temperatures.

While astrologers tend to describe astrological conditions during Kartik as inauspicious when it comes to spiritual advancement, most other Benarsis with whom I spoke clearly considered Kartik to be spiritually auspicious. Such thinking seems to be shaped not by astrological knowledge, but rather by engagement in practices that are observed during the month, the values that these practices promote, and their perceived outcomes. Since Kartik is a time for engaging in ritual activities that lead to spiritual advancement, it is broadly considered to be a spiritually auspicious month. Illustrative in this regard is the importance attached to maintaining a votive observance known as the Kartik *vrat.*

The Kartik *Vrat*

A *vrat* (Sskt. *vrata*) is a religious vow or votive observance. Central to the practice of *vrat*s in contemporary India is an emphasis on practices that inculcate self-discipline and restraint of the senses (McGee 1987,

50, 93–95). The major consitituent parts of *vrats* include a declaration of intention (*saṅkalpa*), ritual bathing (*snāna*), some form of worship (*pūjā*), the recitation of some kind of mantra (*japa*), an all-night vigil (*jāgaraṇa*), the sacrifice of oblations into a fire (*homa*), observation of a fast (*upavāsa*) and breaking of the fast (*pāraṇa*), "gifting" or giving donations (*dāna*), performance of a concluding rite (*udyāpana*), and the telling or hearing of a *vrat* story (*kathāśrāvaṇa*). For any given *vrat* one, or sometimes two, of these rites is designated the principal rite (*pradhāna*), whose performance is absolutely central to the *vrat* (McGee 1987, 124–25).

The month-long Kartik *vrat* includes a number of injunctions for actions and behaviors that votaries are supposed to uphold throughout the entire month and that focus on disciplines and restraints pertaining to the mind, body, and personal conduct. Many Benarsis, for example, maintain that some form of sexual continence is necessary for those performing the Kartik *vrat*. Textual traditions advocate that votaries maintain celibacy (*brahmacarya*) for the whole month (e.g., KMPP 7.9), but I encountered a diversity of opinions among married, sexually active female Kartik votaries about what type of sexual restraint was appropriate. Although some informants held month-long celibacy to be the ideal, few thought it was really necessary. Instead, many understood the injunction to remain celibate as applying only to the period of five days at the end of the month, known as the Bhishmapancak (which I discuss toward the end of this chapter), and they strongly advocated abstaining from sexual activity during that five-day period. Still others emphasized the nature of Kartik as a particularly good month for husband and wife to enjoy sexual relations. Indeed, the religious injunction to remain celibate during the month clashes with popular views of Kartik as a month particularly good for lovemaking, and one in which sexual desire runs high. Some insisted that only individuals not observing the Kartik *vrat* should enjoy the pleasures of lovemaking at this time of year, since the undertaking of any *vrat* usually requires sexual restraint. Others, however, made no such distinction, insisting that Kartik was the best month of the year for the sexual enjoyment of all human beings whether they observe the *vrat* or not. In any case, for women, maintaining celibacy requires cooperation from husbands, who may or may not go along with their wives' wishes. For this reason, some of the younger married women who spoke openly with me about such matters did not see maintaining sexual continence for the entire month as practical even if it were required. As one informant put it to me, "If it were for the whole month, the men would not allow us to observe the *vrat*! No man would allow this." Another informant exclaimed, "You should do the *vrat*, but you should also take care of your husband!"

The Kartik Mahatmyas also stipulate a number of rules regarding abstention from a variety of foods, a practice that is included in the Hindu tradition under the rubric of fasting.[7] Fasting is an important component of *vrat*s, and many Benarsis use the term *vrat* specifically to mean "religious fast." In general, foods permitted during *vrat*s are considered more conducive to purity than other foods and share certain features. Some, for example, are considered inherently pure or conveyers of purity; others are bland and hence unlikely to excite the senses, or are covered by an outer husk or shell that prevents invasion of polluting substances (McGee 1987, 97–99). The Kartik Mahatmyas state that during Kartik one should forgo such food and drink as meat, honey, eggplant, liquor, various kinds of pulses, burnt rice, food polluted by tears, bad thoughts, or bad words, other people's foods, and so forth (KMPP 7.2–8; KMSP 6.2). Many of the Benarsis with whom I spoke also advocated observance of food restrictions throughout the entire month, but there seemed to be a rather wide variation in terms of how this rule is interpreted and applied. Many women told me they abstain from specific forbidden foods, especially eggplant, white radish, onion, garlic, and certain kinds of pulses (primarily *dvidāl*, pulses that split down the middle and fall into two parts), throughout the entire month. Several informants also cited as forbidden any consumption of "outside" food—food not prepared in one's own home—during the month. Others reported that they do not abstain from any particular foods during the month as a whole that they did not normally abstain from at all times, such as meat and liquor, but instead fast for shorter periods of time during some of the important *vrat*s that take place during the month. In general, observances of rules concerning food during Kartik are considered much less crucial than bathing and devotional observances.

Some laxity in the observation of rules concerning food is probably due at least in part to practical considerations. As one votary put it, to prepare or have prepared special *vrat* foods for religiously observant family members is not terribly inconvenient if the *vrat* lasts just a day or even a few days, but requiring special foods for an entire month would require a lot more work from the family cook and would inconvenience the entire household.

In Benares, votaries clearly consider the observance of Kartik ritual bathing or *snān* (Sskt. *snāna*) undertaken early in the morning on a daily basis throughout the entire month to be the central observance (*pradhāna*) of the Kartik *vrat*. A few informants, in fact, who equated the term *vrat* with "fast" insisted that there was no such thing as a Kartik *vrat*, only injunctions regarding daily bathing and worship throughout the month.[8] The Benarsis with whom I spoke also tended to insist that Kartik bathing is most meritorious and cleansing when undertaken in Benares. A few claimed that people come to Benares from all over North India to celebrate the month. Although I was unable to confirm this claim, I did meet people from Madhya Pradesh, Punjab, Bihar, and other parts of Uttar Pradesh who had come to the city specifically to undertake Kartik ritual bathing or to participate in other Kartik-related activities.[9]

In Benares the Ganges River is the goal for Kartik bathers. The Ganges is considered to be a goddess in liquid form and is held to be eternally pure and purifying.[10] Bathing in the Ganges River at any time of year is thought to be meritorious, but Kartik, Magh, and Vaishakh are all recognized as especially auspicious months for daily Ganges bathing. It is considered particularly meritorious to undertake Kartik bathing at the Pancaganga ("five rivers"), the place in the Ganges River, located at Pancaganga Ghat in Benares, where five cleansing rivers are said to flow together: the Ganges, Yamuna, Sarasvati, Kirana, and Dhutapapa rivers.[11]

A number of prescriptions for Kartik bathing are outlined in the two Kartik Mahatmyas, but one of the most important injunctions for all Kartik votaries is that one bathe in the hour before sunrise during the period known as the *brahma muhūrta* (KMPP 6.1; KMSP 4.1). All of the Kartik votaries I interviewed were aware of this injunction, although they did not always observe it faithfully. The reasons for bathing before sunrise are not detailed in the Kartik Mahatmyas, but many of the women I interviewed had clear, though diverse, opinions about the reason for the regulation. A few women noted that early-morning rising and bathing were conducive to good health and mental peace, but most of those who offered opinions gave more explicitly religious explanations for the practice. A few described the early-morning period just before sunrise as the time when the gods (*devatā*) themselves bathe, rendering this time most auspicious for humans to bathe as well. Two informants specifically cited the nature of early-morning bathing as physical austerity (*tapasya*), which is generally linked in the Hindu tradition to spiritual advancement. The meritorious nature of early-morning bathing as physical austerity was also implied in the responses of many others. Several informants claimed, for example, that God (Bhagavān) himself comes to the *ghāṭ*s at that time to see who is there, and devotees who are up and bathing get more religious merit than those who have slept in.

Many Hindus think of practices like sexual continence, fasting, and ritual bathing as having to do more with the cultivation of purity than with the cultivation of auspiciousness. But, as noted earlier, these two values are not mutually exclusive. A good deal of Hindu ritual activity at inauspicious times, including purifying practices like fasting or bathing, is geared toward a disarticulation of inauspiciousness (Raheja 1988). The practices cited above in connection with the Kartik *vrat* both purify the practitioner and lead to spiritual advancement. Rivers also promote values broadly encompassed under the rubric of auspiciousness, and individuals may bathe in rivers specifically to attain auspicious goals, including this-worldly ones (cf. Feldhaus 1995, 65–69, 86n.6). In Benares, the Ganges appears in many Benarsi women's stories as a granter of boons, especially sons. Water connotes fertility; the rains of the monsoon are fertile rains, and at this time of year the Ganges River is swollen with them, accentuating imagery of the Ganges' waters as fertile and life bestowing.

Precepts concerning the observance of the Kartik *vrat* also pertain to devotional attitudes and forms of worship in which one is supposed to engage during the month, especially with respect to Vishnu. The Kartik Mahatmyas enjoin devotees to eulogize Vishnu daily, honor him with singing and playing on musical instruments, recite his thousand names, read Vaishnava scriptures, or listen to stories of Vishnu recounted in the Puranas (KMSP 5.2, 5.23, 6.19–20, 33.30; KMPP 6.30). The KMSP also advocates special worship during the month of Krishna, an incarnate form (*avatāra*) of Vishnu, along with Krishna's consort Radha (KMSP 3.27–29).

Also of special importance throughout Kartik is the lighting of traditional lamps (*dīpa*) in homes and temples and along the *ghāṭ*s at the edge of the Ganges River. These lamps consist of a cotton wick soaked in ghee or oil and placed in a small receptacle made of clay. The KMSP is especially expansive in its praise of lamp lighting, proclaiming that lighting and offering lamps during the month yield exceedingly meritorious fruits (7.33). Of particular note with respect to lamp offerings are the sky lamps (*ākāśa dīpa* or *vyoma dīpa*) that line the *ghāṭ*s of the Ganges. These sky lamps, which are sponsored both by institutions and by individuals from around the city, consist of wicker baskets that hold lamps and are hoisted onto poles at the edge of the river. During the entire month of Kartik, the baskets are lowered at dusk, the lamps are lit, and the baskets are then hoisted back up to the tops of the poles holding them.

The importance of lamps during this month may well be related to the weak position of the sun in the Libra constellation during Kartik

Figure 3. Woman and sky lamp on a Benares *ghāṭ (photo by William C. French)*

and the danger that such a position represents. The KMSP proclaims that lamps are born of parts of the sun (9.10), and the Nirnayasindhu marks the transition of the sun into Libra as the starting point for the lighting of sky lamps (292). Hence the lighting of lamps seems to function as a way of compensating for the sun's weak state and encouraging its safe emergence from the debilitated place that it occupies during this time. But light is also a form of Lakshmi and embodies her auspicious blessings, usually understood in terms of worldly boons. The Dharmasindhu proclaims that by offering sky lamps during Kartik, one obtains Lakshmi, meaning the auspicious boons that Lakshmi confers, such as wealth, good health, and abundance (205; cf. Nirnayasindhu 292–93). The KMSP describes the sky lamps as offerings to one's ancestors, whose path to heaven is illuminated by the lights, or to Vishnu along with his wife Lakshmi, and it claims that Lakshmi herself comes to view these lamps throughout the month (KMSP 7.101–102, 106–107, 118–20). Although light is important throughout the month, it plays an especially important role in some of

Kartik's major celebrations, including two of Kartik's most light-intensive holidays, Diwali and Kartik Purnima. It illuminates paths, such as Ram's path home after his period of exile, Lakshmi's path to individuals' homes, or souls' paths out of hell and into heaven.

Light also has esoteric connotations and can be interpreted as symbolic of spiritual processes. One finds such an interpretation of the sky lamps, for example, in a 1995 issue of the booklet *Ramanand Prakash*, "The Light of Ramanand," published at Shri Math, a Vaishnava monastery located at the Pancaganga Ghat in Benares. Shri Math is home to a number of monks of the Ramananda tradition, a Vaishnava religious order. Shri Math is very active during Kartik and is a major organizational and financial power behind many of Benares's public Kartik celebrations. *Ramanand Prakash* attributes to the sky lamps a spiritual meaning:

> These lamps hidden inside wicker baskets hanging from bamboo have probably been lit for gods. They have become a mediator between people "down below" and "people" "up there." . . . But heaven is nowhere up there, nor do the gods reside somewhere "up there." . . . Hanging the lamp in the sky means awakening consciousness in one's mind. . . . These sky lamps are nothing but an effort to elevate this consciousness. The gods reside only inside us, and whatever good there is in the outside world is nothing but an expansion of this inner divinity. (32)

Hence the religious significance of the lights offered throughout the month is interpreted in a variety of ways. Some informants even insisted to me that the real purpose of the sky lamps is to lure insects, which are especially numerous at this time of year, to flame and hence to their deaths, ridding the city of as many of them as possible during this buggy month. One informant gave a slightly different spin to the insect issue, insisting that bugs drawn to the flame get auspicious sight, or *darśan,* of the lights in the process of self-immolating and hence attain the merit that insures them a better rebirth.[12] No matter what the interpretation, in all the places that Kartik is celebrated, it is a month of light.

Daily worship of Tulsi, the basil plant, is also requisite in high-caste Vaishnava households throughout the month of Kartik. Tulsi, considered a highly purifying herb, is specifically worshiped in conjunction with Vishnu, and Vaishnavas are bid to maintain a Tulsi plant in their homes during the month, honoring it every evening by burning a small lamp at its base. The Kartik Mahatmyas are quite effusive in lauding the many merits of Tulsi, claiming, for example, that those who plant a grove of Tulsi escape the clutches of Yama, the Host of Death, and that Tulsi removes the effects of sins committed by body, mind, and speech from those who plant, water, see, or touch Tulsi (KMPP 18.9–10–12). There are several other passages throughout the Padma Purana as well that praise Tulsi at length.[13] In Benares, daily early-morning bathing and the offering of lights at the base of a Tulsi plant seem to be the month-long practices most widely observed and most highly valued by female votaries undertaking the Kartik *vrat*.

Eulogy and Narrative in the Kartik Mahatmyas: Glorifying Kartik and the Kartik *Vrat*

A Mahatmya or "glorification" is a type of Puranic literature that dedicates itself primarily to praising the merits of a particular deity, place, religious activity, period of time, and so forth. The numerous Mahatmyas that one finds throughout the Puranas, while diverse, tend to share certain characteristics (Eck 1980, 81–82; Rocher 1986, 70–71). Above all, they tend to stress the absolute superiority of the deity, place, religious activity, and so forth, that is the chosen object of veneration. This superiority is often declared repeatedly in a variety of ways and is also underscored in narrative materials found in such environments. It is questionable, however, to what extent the claims of ultimate superiority that one finds in Mahatmyas should be taken as genuine claims and to what extent they function as hyperbolic conventions for conveying the perceived excellent qualities of their objects of veneration, similar to a restaurant's claims to serve "the best food in the world."[14] In any case, the Kartik Mahatmyas of both the Padma and Skanda Puranas employ laudatory language similar to that found in other Mahatmyas.

The Kartik Mahatmyas devote much energy to exalting both the month of Kartik itself and the Kartik *vrat*. The KMPP, for example, claims that all the pilgrimage places (*tīrthas*) on the earth come to dwell in the house of one who observes the Kartik *vrat*, which it declares to be superior to a hundred sacrifices, and it describes the merits of the *vrat* as being so numerous that nobody could possibly speak them all (7.22–23, 7.27). Among the most engaging materials in the Kartik Mahatmyas, however, are the many narratives recounted in the texts that describe the benefits attained from observing the Kartik *vrat* or particular practices subsumed under the *vrat*. The KMSP includes more such stories, although they are often told in abbreviated form. The benefit of offering lamps during the month is underscored in this text by a story of an immoral woman married to a Brahmin named Buddha. Traditional Hinduism upholds for married women the ideal of the *pativratā,* the chaste, devoted wife. Proper wifely conduct accrues to a woman not only moral virtue, but also supernormal power, including the power to extend the life of her husband; improper conduct does the opposite, and in this story, Buddha's wife falls far short of the wifely ideal. Buddha's life is shortened because of his wife's evil ways, and he dies. After his death, the wife continues to lead a sinful, irreligious, and unchaste life. One day a righteous Brahmin named Kautsa comes upon her. Seeing her immoral ways, he instructs her to perform the Kartik *vrat* to remove the effects of her sins. In particular, he admonishes her to offer lamps to Vishnu, exclaiming that this practice liberates even a great sinner. She follows his instructions and attains heaven and eventual spiritual liberation (*mokṣa*) because of the merit gained from her lighting of lamps. The text declares that devotees who light lamps during Kartik and hear this story will attain liberation as well (KMSP 7.7–34). The story of Buddha's wife forms an interesting commentary on gender, for Buddha's wife attains spiritual fulfillment not through the power accumulated through proper wifely behavior, but through religious devotion, bypassing the cultural ideal. In this case, devotion to Vishnu supplants wifely devotion to the husband.

Other stories communicate the extraordinarily meritorious nature of the Kartik *vrat* by describing benefits gained by sinners who come somehow to share in the merit gained by a faithful Kartik votary. One such story is that of a Brahmin named Dharmadatta, a faithful observer of the Kartik *vrat*, and a demonness named Kalaha (KMPP 19–20). One night during the month of Kartik, Dharmadatta is on his way to a Vishnu temple to observe all-night worship (*jāgaraṇa*) in honor of Vishnu when he encounters the demoness. Terrified, the good Brahmin strikes her with the materials that he is carrying in his hands, which happen to be items used in ritual worship, including water with Tulsi leaves in it. When these meritorious items strike her, her sins are destroyed, and she suddenly remembers her former existence and the reason that she has attained her current hideous form, which she narrates to Dharmadatta.

The demoness recounts that in her former life she had been a woman named Kalaha and had been married to a Brahmin. She was a very cruel and evil wife who quarreled with her husband, fed him badly, and was consistently harsh with him. The bad treatment he suffered at her hands led Kalaha's husband to consider taking another wife. Learning of this, Kalaha killed herself. Because of her sinful behavior, Kalaha had come to be born as a ghost. Feeling sorry for her, Dharmadatta donates to her half the merit that he has earned over the course of his life through observing the Kartik *vrat*, and Kalaha becomes liberated from her horrific form.

Another narrative found in both versions of the text but in more condensed form in the Skanda Purana underscores the glory of the *vrat* by recounting how even casual contact with faithful Kartik votaries can result in the accidental transfer of enough merit to liberate a great sinner from having to suffer the consequences of his sinful deeds. This is the story of the evil Brahmin Dhaneshvara (KMPP 26–27; KMSP 29). Dhaneshvara is a wicked man with many evil habits, including drinking, stealing, gambling, and soliciting prostitutes. One Kartik he happens upon the banks of the Narmada River. He notices that men come there every morning to bathe as part of the Kartik vow, so he decides to remain there for the month to sell his wares. As he is wandering by the side of the river on the last day of Kartik, a deadly black snake bites him. He falls dying to the ground and is surrounded by a group of righteous Kartik votaries of Brahmin caste, gathered at the riverbank, who sprinkle water mixed with Tulsi leaves on his face.

When Dhaneshvara dies, the servants of Yama, the Host of Death, bind him and carry him off to Yama's netherworldly city to face his fate. The scribe Citragupta recites to Yama the bad deeds that Dhaneshvara has committed all of his life, and Yama orders his servants to throw Dhaneshvara into the hell of boiling oil (*kumbhīpāka*). But when Dhaneshvara is thrown into this hell, it suddenly becomes cool. Yama is puzzling over this turn of events when the sage Narada appears on the scene and tells Yama that because Dhaneshvara was in contact with righteous observers of the Kartik *vrat* over the course of a month, he therefore shares a portion of their religious merit; the power of this merit means he has escaped his hellish fate. Yama's servants then take Dhaneshvara to see all the hells, which are described in the text in horrific detail, and to contemplate the terrible fate that should have awaited him in each one, had he not inadvertently absorbed the religious merit of the Kartik votaries he encountered at the river.

Such stories underscore the extraordinary power of Kartik religious observances to obliterate bad karma and promote spiritual auspiciousness. But the Kartik Mahatmyas describe the *vrat* as capable of bringing worldly boons (*bhukti*) as well as spiritual liberation (*mukti*). In Benares, the *vrat* is clearly perceived to be conducive to worldly auspiciousness and to provide fruits of everyday householder life as well.[15] Most of my female informants, in fact, emphasized such worldly boons as the primary benefit reaped from observing the Kartik *vrat*.

The Bhishmapancak and the Bhishmapancak *Vrat*

Although the Kartik *vrat* is meant to be maintained for the entire month, the last five days of the month leading up to and including the full moon (*pūrṇimā*) are the most important and are treated in many ways like a microcosm of the month. This period is known as the Bhishmapancak, "the five (days) of Bhishma," and is named after the character Bhishma of the great Hindu epic, the Mahabharata. In the epic, the Ganges gives birth to Bhishma, but his father, King Shantanu, raises him. Bhishma's royal father falls in love with a woman whom he can wed only under the condition her children, not Bhishma or Bhishma's progeny, inherit his throne. To ensure that there will be no impediment to his father's marriage, Bhishma takes a vow of lifelong celibacy, which he maintains faithfully. In exchange, his father grants Bhishma the ability to choose the time of his own death. Bhishma's name, which means "terrible" (*bhīṣma*), refers to the terrible vow of celibacy to which he is bound.

The Bhishmapancak is not discussed at length in the KMPP. It is described elsewhere in the Padma Purana, however, for example, in 4.23, where it is called the Vishnupancak, and in 6.124, a chapter that closely follows on the heels of the Kartik Mahatmya section. The KMSP, on the other hand, dedicates one entire chapter (chapter 32) to discussion of the Bhismapancak vow. Bhishma was shot in the great Mahabharata war, but he chose to postpone his death to wait for auspicious astrological conditions. In the KMSP, it is said that as Bhishma lay dying on a bed of arrows, he expounded the duties of a king, duties concerning gifting, and actions conducive to liberation. Pleased with Bhishma's words, Vishnu dedicated the last five days of the Kartik month to a *vrat* done in Bhishma's name. Arjuna is said to have brought Ganges water to Bhishma on the eleventh (*ekādaśi*) of Kartik's bright fortnight to quench his thirst, and contemporary worshipers are enjoined to follow Arjuna's example by propitiating Bhishma and offering him libations during the five days of the Bhishmapancak (KMSP 32.1–5). The etymology of the *vrat* is explained differently a bit further in the text, where its name is attributed alternatively to the fact that Vishnu transmitted it directly to Bhishma or to its very difficult or terrible (*bhīṣma*) nature (32.15–21). It is declared, "If a man is incapable of performing or has no means to perform the Kartik *vrat*, he can perform the Bhishmapancak and obtain the merit of Kartik *vrat*" (32.8).

The stipulations for the observance of the Bhishmapancak as described in this chapter are similar to those of the Kartik *vrat*. One is enjoined to bathe in the early morning, for example, and offer libations to one's ancestors and to Bhishma. Celibacy is strongly advocated during this period, as is worship of Vishnu and Lakshmi, burning lights, and making donations. The text urges the abstention from all foods during this *vrat* except fruit, the five products of the cow (*pāñcagavya* : milk, yogurt, ghee or butter, urine, and dung), and food that is offerable during a fire sacrifice (*haviṣya*). During these five days many Benarsis do in fact maintain a similar type of fast, known as a *phalahār* fast.

Padma Purana 4.23.17–33 also describes the merits gained through performing the Bhishmapancak *vrat* in terms quite similar to those of the Kartik *vrat*. The text recounts the story of a villainous, sinful, and cruel low-caste man (Shudra) named Dandakara. Abandoned by his kinsmen, who get fed up with his behavior, Dandakara goes to live in a forest, where he joins forces with other villainous types. One day, oppressed by hunger, they stumble upon a group of Brahmins seated at the root of an Amla tree.[16] Dandakara asks them for food but is rebuffed by the Brahmins, who are fasting for the Bhishmapancak. Dandakara confesses that he is filled with all types of sin and asks how he can be emancipated from them. The Brahmins tell him that he too should observe the *vrat*, which he does. He gains so much merit that upon his death he becomes liberated from rebirth.

In Benares, those who have not been undertaking Kartik ritual bathing for the whole month turn out in droves to bathe in the Ganges River for at least some of these last five days. Of these, the first (the eleventh of Kartik's bright fortnight) and the last (Kartik's full moon, or Purnima) days are the most important, and many individuals bathe just on these two days, although of the two Kartik Purnima is considered more important. Much of the devotional activity spread all along the *ghāṭ*s during the rest of the month shifts for these five days over to Pancaganga Ghat and the Bindu Madhava temple, a Vaishnava temple that sits atop the stairs that tower above this *ghāṭ*, although votaries who are unable to go to Pancaganga continue to bathe and perform their devotions at other *ghāṭ*s as well. On the morning of Kartik Purnima Pancaganga Ghat gets so thickly crowded that it becomes almost impenetrable.[17]

In the KMSP, devotees are instructed to worship different parts of Vishnu's body on different days of the Bhishmapancak. On the first day, one is to worship his feet; on the second day, his knees; and thereafter, the head (32.44–45). The text claims that whoever performs this *vrat* will attain great spiritual merit. Some contemporary *vrat* manuals describe a similar process of worshiping Vishnu's body, stipulating a different body part for each of the five days, namely, the feet, knees, navel, chest, and head. In Benares, however, it is not Vishnu's body that is worshiped, but that of Bhishma. Enormous images of Bhishma are constructed along the *ghāṭ*s out of Ganges clay, and votaries circumambulate the body during these five days, making offerings and worshiping a different part of the body each day. It is said that by touching the foot, one gets the merit of having undertaken a pilgrimage; by touching the hand, the merit of giving donations (*dāna*); touching the stomach makes poverty and hunger disappear; touching the chest brings one a grandson; and touching the head assures one a place in Vishnu's heaven, Vaikunth. The most popular offerings made are sugar cane, which represents the new autumn harvest, and foods that have been renounced during the month, such as eggplant and white radish.

Many informants insisted to me that the clay images represent not Bhishma but Bhima, also called Bhimsen, who is the most physically powerful of the Mahabharata's five heroes, the Pandava brothers. I have found no scriptural basis for connecting this period of

Figure 4. Votaries circumambulating an effigy of Bhishma/Bhima on Tulsi Ghat

worship with Bhima, but the similarity of Bhima's and Bhisma's names—along with the fact that both are important characters in the Mahabharata narrative—suggests that it would be easy to mix them up. With respect to the Bhishmapancak, it appears that worshipers tend to conflate the two. This conflation is evident in the way that the revered bodies are made: boatmen (*mallās*) construct the images because, I was told, Bhishma is the Ganges' son, and boatmen are also the Ganges' relatives. Yet the right hand of at least some of the clay icons holds a mace (*gadā*), an implement that Bhima wields as a symbol of his supernormal physical strength. One informant suggested that Bhima's body is worshiped because of this strength, which manifests itself as power or *śakti*; worshipers attain a portion of this power by touching his body. Others described this power as attributable to Bhishma's celibacy and his nature as a great practitioner of austerities (*tapasvin*).[18] The practice of austerities is understood to imbue an ascetic practitioner with special power that permeates his physical form. It is not uncommon for householders to touch the body of a revered ascetic in hopes of accessing some of that power either in the form of general blessings or as energy that will help them attain a particular boon.

During each of the five days of the Bhishmapancak, votaries offer coins to the ritual specialists (*paṇḍa*) who work on the *ghāṭ*s, ideally beginning with one coin on the first day and working up to five coins on the last day. I heard a number of female Kartik votaries in Benares narrate a particular story associated with this practice, where Bhishma himself appears on the *ghāṭ*s to demand increasing amounts of money from Kartik bathers. Although each narrator recounted the story in her own way, the basic plot was similar in all versions. Like Bhishma, the ritual specialists who work on the *ghāṭ*s are called "*gangā-putra*," "Son of the Ganges," and in the story Bhishma appears to be himself a ritual specialist (*paṇḍa*). In a version of the story that I recorded in 1995, he is referred to as both "Bhishma" and "Bhimsen," a name for Bhima:

> There was an old lady who used to go and bathe every day. One day Grandfather Bhishma was standing on the *ghāṭ*, and he said, "Oh old lady, give me one rupee before you take a dip." She said, "I don't have any money today, Maharaj (Great King),[19] but I will pay you tomorrow." So the old lady bathed and went home. Then she decided, "I will not bathe on Assi Ghat any more. From now on I will bathe at Tulsi Ghat" (the next *ghāṭ* down). So the next day she went to Tulsi Ghat instead of Assi Ghat, but Bhimsen was standing there with his

stick, and he said, "Oh old lady, today give me two rupees before you bathe." She said, "I didn't bring any money today, Maharaj, but I will give it to you tomorrow." Once again she bathed and left. She thought, "I will not bathe at Tulsi Ghat any more. Now I will bathe at Janaki Ghat" (the next *ghāṭ* down). As soon she began to bathe there the next day, he came by and said, "Oh old lady, give me three rupees before you bathe." She said, "Oh Maharaj, I don't have it today. I will give it to you tomorrow." After bathing, the old lady went back home. On the fourth day she went to Kedar Ghat, but once again as soon as she began to bathe, he came by with his stick, and said, "Oh old lady, give me four rupees before you bathe." She said, "Oh Maharaj, I didn't bring it." After bathing, she went back home. She next went to Pancaganga Ghat, but the minute she began to bathe there, Bhishma took up his stick and said, "Oh old lady, give me five rupees before you bathe in the Ganges."

Now she went home and talked to her daughter-in-law. She said, "For the last four days, I have been bathing, and there is a fat man with a big stick who comes every day, and he says, 'Give me one rupee, two rupees, three rupees, four rupees.' I haven't paid him any of it. Today is the full moon, and today he is not going to leave me alone. Today he will definitely take money from me because it is the last day (for bathing). So what should I do?" The daughter-in law was very smart. She said, "Go and tell him, 'Come with me to my home. Instead of one rupee, we will give to you whatever you ask for, and we will feed you whatever you want to eat." On that day she went back to Pancaganga Ghat, and Bhishma again said, "Oh old lady, give me five rupees before you bathe in the Ganges." She said, "Maharaj, why are you asking for five rupees? Instead, my daughter-in-law has asked, 'Why don't you come to my home? We will give you whatever you want.' " So after the old lady bathed, he went with her.

The daughter-in-law of the old lady was poor, but she was very intelligent. So she made good food and offered it to him. She put out a stool and some water, and she gave these things to him. And then she asked, "Maharaj, I heard that you were fat and big. How did you become a small child when you came with the old lady?" (Apparently he has taken the form of a small child.) After eating everything, he became very happy and said, "If there is anything else to eat, please

> bring it to me." Since they were poor, they said, "Maharaj, we don't have anything else. We have only *litti* (small round bread)." So he said, "Bring that also." And he ate it. Then he said, "Is there anything else?" The old lady said, "Only the clay pots (*bhaṛehar*) that are filled up during Diwali with corns and sweets. There are some still left inside." So he said, "Bring that, too." And he ate that also. Then he asked for water and drank all the water they had stored in a clay water pot (*gagari*). Since he drank all the water, there was none left in their house.
>
> During the night, he said, "Oh old lady, now I need to go to the bathroom because you fed me a lot. Where should I go?" And she said, "Maharaj, go to any corner of the house and defecate there, and I will throw out the defecation tomorrow morning." So he defecated in all the four corners of the room. After that, he said, "Oh old lady, give me water so that I can wash myself." She said, "Maharaj, I don't have any water. Wipe yourself on my sari." So he wiped himself with her sari. The poor old lady began to think, "I brought this pundit to feed him here, and now he has defecated in all the four corners of the house. I should get up before sunrise and throw it out. Otherwise my daughter-in-law will get up, and she will be angry at me for this." So the old lady tried to gather up (the defecation) to throw it away, but it had all become gold. It was so heavy she couldn't lift it. She thought, "Why is it so heavy?" When it became light, she saw that it was shining, glittering gold. Then she saw that the sari that he had used to wipe himself had become a shining yellow garment (*pītāmbar*).[20] And the daughter-in-law got up and saw it as well. May Bhima give us what he gave them!

While much could be said about the various themes in this narrative,[21] its primary importance in this context has to do with the Bhima/ Bhishma's perceived power to grant boons—here in the form of wealth—in exchange for devotion. It also explains the practice of increasing the number of coins offered on each of the five days.

While undertaking Kartik bathing and worshipping Bhishma/ Bhima during these five days is said to benefit everyone, it is crucial for Kartik votaries who have been bathing in the Ganges daily throughout the month. Several informants insisted that regular Kartik votaries who do not continue their Kartik bathing during these five days lose all their merit to Bhishma/Bhima. Behind this belief, too, is a story I heard recounted in 1995 on two occasions in slightly different versions. In this story, Bhishma/Bhima functions as intermediary in a jealous competition between Radha, Krishna's beloved consort, and Rukmini, one of his many wives.

> Radha said to Krishna, "Oh Lord! Arrange for me to bathe in the Ganges for the whole month of Kartik, and stay with me for that whole month." Krishna said, "Ask Rukmini. I can only stay with you for the month of Kartik if Rukmini gives her permission." So Radha went to Rukmini and said, "Oh Sister!" Rukmini asked, "What?" Radha said, "Give me Krishna for one month." Rukmini said, "I will not be apart from Krishna for even one day! How is it that I should give him to you for one month?" So Krishna said, "Please stop fighting!" When he saw them both in that condition (angry and fighting), Krishna thought, "How shall I settle this dispute?" So he said, "Stop fighting, you two! Whoever feeds me early tomorrow morning, whether it be Radha or Rukmini, I will become hers."
>
> Krishna created an illusion (*māyā*) so that Rukmini remained asleep while Radha got up early in the morning, cooked, and fed all the cowherd boys[22] and Lord Krishna along with the cattle. After everyone was fed, when God (Krishna) was ready to leave, he went to Rukmini and he said, "Well, Rukmini, are you going to remain sleeping? It is time for me to take the cows out to graze." Now Rukmini woke up, and she said, "It is too bad that I remained sleeping and Radha did all the work! Now I have to give God to her." So Lord Krishna said, "Now are you are going to give me to Radha for one month or not?" (Then he went off to spend the month of Kartik with Radha.)
>
> Krishna would go from *ghāṭ* to *ghāṭ* with Radha to do his Kartik bathing, and he would joke around with the cowherdesses (*sakhīs*).[23] Half of the month passed in this way. One day while Rukmini was watching her sheep, the birds pecked at him, so she took a stick and chased them away. The birds said, "She is so proud of her sheep that she is chasing us away with a stick, but at Radha's place we peck pearls and jewels." This made Rukmini angry. She said, "If even birds have pearls and jewels to peck at Radha's place, why would Lord Krishna ever return from there?"
>
> The rest of the month passed, and when just five days were left—the five days of Bhishmapancak, when the Bhimsen is made—Rukmini called Bhimsen and told him, "Oh, Brother Bhimsen! Go and see if Krishna is having fun there or not."

> Bhimsen went there and from a distance he saw that Krishna was laughing, cracking jokes, swinging with some of the women (*sakhīs*) in a swing, and really enjoying himself. But Krishna saw Bhima coming from a distance, so he immediately took the form of a leper, very thin and sick. When Bhimsen saw him, he asked, "Oh Maharaj, what happened to you?" Krishna said, "What can I do? If Rukmini had not slept in that day, I would not have had to go with Radha. You can see what has happened to my body with Radha. I have to do her laundry, clean her saris, massage her, and do all kinds of service to her. You can see that because of this, my health has deteriorated to half of what it used to be." Bhimsen said, "You must be in great pain, Lord!" And Krishna said, "You see, I am just waiting for the month to pass somehow, and then I will go back."
>
> When Bhimsen returned, Rukmini asked, "How is everything there, Brother Bhimsen?" Bhimsen said, "What can I say? God has lost weight, he is very skinny, and he is in great pain." On the next day, the day of Ekadashi, she said, "Oh Brother, please go and see how God is." So when he went there on that day, he saw that God was having great fun doing a circle dance (*rāsa-līlā*) with the cowherdesses, laughing, and having a great time. Bhimsen suddenly appeared in the middle of this activity and said, "Oh Maharaj! The other day you were so skinny and in such bad shape! How did you become like this today?" So Krishna said, "Please don't tell any of this to Rukmini! Don't tell her, 'God is having fun there.' In return, for the five days from Ekadashi to Purnima, the merit of all people who ritually bathe during the month but not during those five days will go to you. And the rest of the month will be mine."[24]

In addition to explaining Bhishma/Bhima's connection to the five days of the Bhishmapancak, this story also highlights important connections that female Kartik votaries in Benares make between Krishna, Kartik, and the "circle dance," or *rāsa-līlā*, that Krishna is said to have danced with Radha and her cowherdess friends, the *sakhīs* ("female friends"). I will return to these important connections in subsequent chapters.

While the month of Kartik officially draws to a close on the day of the full moon, the final day of the Bhishmapancak, Benarsi tradition holds that those who have maintained the *vrat* of Kartik ritual bathing for the Bhishmapancak or for the entire month must continue this bathing for at least one more day, the first day of Margashirsh (also called Agahan), which is also popularly referred to as the second day of Kartik's full moon. On this day, Kartik votaries say that they bathe in honor of a demoness named Tirjata, or Trijata (*trijaṭā*) in Sanskrit, a minor character in the epic Ramayana. Trijata is a servant in the palace of the demon Ravana who befriends Sita and takes care of her during the time Sita is imprisoned there.[25] Popular belief in Benares maintains that, as a reward for Tirjata's loyalty, Ram granted her the boon that those Kartik votaries who do not bathe in her honor on the morning after Kartik's full moon will lose to Tirjata all the merit they have gained from the month-long *vrat*.

Kartik votaries gather at Dasashvamedh Ghat on this morning to honor Tirjata with thirty dips taken in her name, each dip representing the merit earned by one day of votive bathing during Kartik. Before dipping under the water, those who undertake this "Tirjata bath" place on their heads a small clay lamp along with eggplant, white radish, and sometimes sugar cane or Amla fruit. This produce represents new crops or foods that have been renounced for the month-long *vrat*, and it is customary for both types of foodstuffs to be offered

Figure 5. Votary bathing in Tirjata's name

to a deity or deities before one begins to consume them oneself after a period of not consuming them. After bathing in Tirjata's name, Kartik votaries consider it crucial also to visit two temples to avoid having her steal away their merit. The first is a small temple at Dasashvamedh Ghat dedicated to Shiva that opens only once a year, on this day. The second is a temple in Vishvanath Gali dedicated to Sakshi Vinayak, Ganesha in his form as a witness (*sākṣī*).

The main goal of Kartik votaries visiting the Shiva temple at Dasashvamedh Ghat is not the large Shiva icon, or *liṅga,* that sits imposingly in the middle of the temple but the small frieze of Kartikkeya, one of Shiva's sons, that is tucked away unobtrusively at the back of the temple. Along with customary offerings, such as flowers and incense, worshipers pile eggplant and white radish, the primary foods renounced for the month of Kartik, both on the *liṅga* and in front of Kartikkeya. One Kartik votary told me that icons of Karttikeya in a small temple on Pancaganga Ghat and in the Vishvanath Temple, Benares's main temple to Shiva, and are also visited on this day by Kartik bathers bearing vegetal offerings, but I was unable to confirm this.

I have noted that the month of Kartik derives its name from the Krittika asterism, which falls on or near Kartik's full moon. The Krittika asterism is named after a group of maidens, the Krittikas, who are said to have nursed and raised Karttikeya. Hence it makes sense that in Benares, as in other parts of India,[26] the full moon's conjunction with the Krittika asterism seems to be associated with Karttikeya and his worship. In Benares, however, worshipers referred to the deity they honor on this day in Shiva's temple not as "Karttikeya," nor by any of his other common epithets—Skanda, Kumara, and so forth—but by the name "Shyam Kartik." Furthermore, I encountered some disagreement among worshipers about who exactly Shyam Kartik is. Some informants explicitly equated Shyam Kartik with Karttikeya or at least ascribed to him many of the same traits that Karttikeya is widely believed to embody. But others described "Shyam Kartik" as the particular form of Krishna honored during this month or as Krishna in temporal form embodied as the month of Kartik. "Shyam," meaning "dark one," is a well-known epithet of Krishna, and "Kartik" is, of course, the name of the month.

The perspectives I encountered point to deeper affiliations between Krishna and Karttikeya. Both are worshiped in their child forms, both are vanquishers of demons, and both are associated with the peacock: Krishna wears a peacock feather, and Karttikeya rides on a peacock as his vehicle. Some textual sources even equate Karttikeya with Krishna, Vishnu, or a portion of Vishnu (see Rana 1995, 46–47,

54, 61). No matter how they describe him, however, female Kartik votaries that I spoke with in Benares tend to think of Shyam Kartik as a deity that one must specifically honor during the month of Kartik, and they warn that failing to worship him on the day following Kartik's full moon renders one's month-long observances fruitless.

After honoring Shyam Kartik, diligent Kartik votaries forge on to the Sakshi Vinayak temple, where they ask Ganesha (Vinayak) to bear witness to their month of observances, and offer eggplant and white radish to Tirjata to prevent her from stealing their merit. These offerings are piled up in front of an icon toward the rear of the Sakshi Vinayak temple that worshipers consistently identified to me as the demoness Tirjata. When I interviewed the priest of this temple and his son, however, both insisted to me that the icon that these worshipers honor is in fact not Tirjata at all but rather a form of Shiva called "Jata-Shiva." "*Jaṭa*" means "braid" or "knot of hair." Tirjata's name is derived from the fact that she wore her hair in three ("*tri-*") coiled braids, and the image of Shiva in the Sakshi Vinayak temple derives its name from the large, coiled knot of hair that Shiva here wears piled up on his head. A label on the wall above the icon affirms its identification as a form of Shiva. Those who work in the temple, however, did not seem to me to be particularly interested in discouraging popular understanding of this

Figure 6. Making offerings to Jata-Shiva/Tirjata

icon as that of the demoness Tirjata, perhaps because it brings a great deal of patronage to the temple on this day every year.

Most of the Kartik votaries in Benares that I spoke with conclude their Kartik bathing on this day. Some, however, continue their votive bathing for a few more days, until the fifth of Margashirsh's dark fortnight, when they perform *pūjā* to a Kadam tree. The Kadam tree is featured in a well-known story in which Krishna steals the clothes of a group of cowherdesses bathing in a nearby river. Krishna is said to have climbed up a Kadam tree with the clothes, forcing each of the women to prostrate before him in order to regain their garments. In Benares women offer small pieces of cloth to a Kadam tree in commemoration of this event and cry out for Radha to arrange a meeting between them and Krishna. The continuation of Kartik bathing until this day and some women's marking of the Kadam tree *pūjā* as the true end of the Kartik *vrat* point to larger connections between Kartik and Krishna, connections to which I have already alluded and about which much more remains to be said.

Chapter 2

Kartik's Religious Celebrations and the Churning of the Ocean of Milk

In addition to the month-long observances subsumed under the Kartik *vrat*, numerous shorter celebrations punctuate the month. There is a joke that in Benares nine festivals occur every eight days, and the saturated schedule of religious observance characteristic of the city does not exempt Kartik. Almost every day is a religiously important one for some Benarsi Hindu, and frequently two or more holidays coincide on the same date. Like the Kartik *vrat*, many of the calendrical celebrations that punctuate the month tend to exemplify auspiciousness, not only with respect to spiritual advancement, but also—and primarily, one could argue—with respect to worldly boons considered desirable from the perspective of everyday, householder life and embodied in the life-giving and sustaining powers of the goddess Shri-Lakshmi.

Categories that exemplify worldly auspiciousness include weddings, sexuality, and progeny; wetness and rains, abundance of food, and the well-being of crops; and health, medicines, and bodily well-being (Marglin 1985b, 175–81). Kingship and lordly power also embody auspiciousness, for the strength of a king manifests itself in the production of rain and good crops. The divine prototype of earthly kings is Vishnu, the deity worshiped most prominently during Kartik, and as Vishnu's consort Lakshmi embodies the life-giving powers that sustain the sovereignty of kings (cf. Marglin 1985a, 181–84). Vishnu is also paired with other goddesses, including the goddess Earth, Bhudevi, whom Vishnu protects from oppressive demons. In safeguarding Bhudevi, Vishnu also protects auspiciousness as it is manifest in the earth's fecundity and generativity, a role that flows from the sovereign power he embodies.

In her discussion of auspiciousness, Frederique Marglin highlights the well-known Hindu narrative of the churning of the ocean of milk by the gods and demons, which she argues is principally concerned with auspiciousness (1985a, 161, 209–14). This narrative appears first in the great Hindu epics, the Mahabharata and the Ramayana, and is then retold in different versions in a number of the Puranas. It recounts the establishment or reestablishment of order (*dharma*) and the gods' sovereignty in creation after a period of cosmic destruction. Puranic accounts of cosmogony describe the world as coming in and out of being in eternally recurring cosmic cycles of creation or emanation (*sṛṣṭi*), dissolution (*pralaya*), and recreation. At the end of a cycle of creation all the worlds are destroyed and immersed in a great cosmic ocean until the beginning of the next cycle of creation. Vishnu sleeps on the surface of this ocean, cradled on the coils of the serpent Ananta, until he awakens at the dawn of a new creation cycle. When it is time for the next cycle of creation to begin, the earth is fashioned anew, fresh and cleansed from the waters of dissolution. The churning narrative evokes cosmogonic imagery and functions essentially as a creation narrative. In most versions the churning is inspired by a desire for the nectar of immortality (*amṛta*)—the elixir of life—which the churning produces, but in some contexts Lakshmi becomes just as important, if not more important, than the coveted nectar. This is true, for example, in the version of the myth found in the Vishnu Purana (1.9), one of the more elaborate accounts.

The Vishnu Purana's account begins with a dispute between Indra, king of the gods, and the sage Durvasas, who offers Indra a garland of flowers, which Durvasas calls "the abode of Shri" (*śriyo dhāman*, 1.9.2). "Shri" is both an epithet of Lakshmi and a term (*śrī*) for the auspiciousness she embodies. Indra places the garland on the head of his elephant, who flings it to the ground. Angered by the show of disrespect, Durvasas pronounces a curse that in the three worlds Indra's own *śrī*, that is, his auspicious royal majesty, will be destroyed. As the curse comes to fruition, plants, herbs, and other flora begin to shrivel and die, and humans begin to act in immoral ways. Seeing their chance, the demons attack Indra and the other gods, forcing them to flee. Defeated and displaced by the demons, the gods approach Brahma for advice, and Brahma leads them to the ocean of milk to summon Vishnu and seek his help.

Vishnu instructs the gods to cast medicinal herbs into the ocean of milk and then to form an alliance with the demons, enlisting their help in churning the ocean to obtain the nectar of immortality, *amṛta*, from it. Vishnu promises the gods that only they will get the nectar. The serpent Ananta—the serpent on which Vishnu is said to sleep during the dissolution of the world between cycles of creation (*pralaya*)—acts as the churning rope, and Mount Mandara as the churning stick; Vishnu assumes the form of a tortoise and, taking the mountain on his back, acts as a pivot. The gods and demons grab opposite ends of Ananta and begin to churn.

A number of beings and entities emerge from the ocean as it is churned: Surabhi, the divine cow; the goddess Varuni, embodiment of spiritous liquor; the celestial Parijata tree; *apsarases*, celestial water nymphs; the moon; Dhanvantari, the physician of the gods and founder of Indian medicine (Ayurveda), holding the cup of nectar; and Shri-Lakshmi. Poison also comes forth, which in this version of the myth is seized by the snake gods (*nāgas*), although in other versions Shiva drinks the poison to inactivate it. The demons seize the nectar, but Vishnu assumes the form of a beautiful woman to distract the demons, who become beguiled and let down their guard. Vishnu snatches the nectar and gives it to the gods, who drink it. Outraged, the demons launch an attack, but the newly invigorated gods vanquish the demons and retake control of the three worlds, which then become prosperous once again. His sovereignty restored, Indra praises Shri (Lakshmi), to whom he attributes the reanimation of the worlds.

Like other versions of the narrative, that of the Vishnu Purana casts the churning primarily as a means to obtain the nectar of immortality. But the emergence of the nectar is dealt with only briefly; the text "does not tarry over the point, rushing ahead instead to extol the emergence of Śrī that immediately follows" (Hawley 1983, 304). The narrative both begins and ends with Shri: the flinging to the ground of the garland, here called Shri's abode, and the resulting disappearance of *śrī* from the worlds, resulting in their deterioration, is resolved in the end when *śrī*, having emerged from the ocean as Shri the goddess, returns to the world.

The return of divine sovereignty is abetted by the recovery of the nectar of immortality, which, like Shri, embodies auspiciousness. In the context of Hindu mythology, "immortality" refers to a long, prosperous, and healthy life, full of progeny and general well-being—in short, much of what is encompassed by worldly auspiciousness (Long 1976, n. 22, 181–82; Marglin 1985a, 212). Nectar, which Vishnu secures, fuels the gods' victory and restores Indra's sovereignty (his *śrī*), along with proper order, or *dharma*, to a world that has become barren and disordered. Dhanvantari is held to be a form of Vishnu, and the portrayal of him emerging from the ocean of milk holding the cup of nectar in his hands further emphasizes Vishnu's connection to auspicious nectar. Except for the poison, the other items that emerge from the milk ocean in this and other versions of the narrative also embody auspiciousness. Hence the narrative weaves together themes concerning Vishnu's sovereignty, nectar, the restoration of *śrī*/Shri, the victory of gods over demons, the return of proper cosmic order, and the attainment of auspiciousness.

The Padma Purana gives even greater emphasis to Shri's place in the narrative, explicitly portraying the ocean's churning as motivated not by hopes of attaining nectar but as an attempt to recover Shri-Lakshmi after she has disappeared from the world (4.8–10). A similar emphasis on Lakshmi's disappearance and ultimate restoration is also characteristic of versions found in the Brahmanda and Devi-Bhagavata Puranas.[1] Just as Shri is a primary focus of attention in many tellings of the narrative, so is Vishnu, especially with respect to his sovereign powers.[2] In the Padma Purana's version, Vishnu's sovereignty and ability to stabilize Shri-Lakshmi are of overriding importance and illustrate Vishnu's role as protector and maintainer of the earth.

The Padma Purana's account (Padma Purana 4.10.1–4) begins with the same dispute between Indra and Durvasas. Because of Durvasas's curse, the goddess Lakshmi—described here as the Mother of the Worlds (*jagatām mātā*)—disappears, causing the three worlds to disappear with her, along with all food and water. Rain ceases, rivers dry up, trees dry up, and all fruits and flowers disappear. Deprived of nourishment, thirsty and hungry, all the worlds' creatures approach Brahma and beg him to intervene. Brahma goes to the ocean of milk and calls upon Vishnu for assistance. Vishnu instructs him to have the gods and demons churn the ocean of milk, promising that Lakshmi will spring from it as a result and return to the worlds.

In this version the churning of the ocean acts more clearly as a process of disarticulation, separating that which is inauspicious from that which is auspicious. Inauspicious elements emerge first. Poison, which Shiva drinks to inactivate, is followed by Alakshmi, Lakshmi's elder sister. Alakshmi embodies inauspiciousness, and the gods instruct her to go forth and dwell in the homes of pernicious persons and bring them grief and poverty. A number of auspicious items also emerge, including Indra's elephant Airavata, Dhanvantari, the Parijata tree, Lakshmi, the nectar of immortality, and Tulsi, here described as Vishnu's wife and the "purifier of the world" (*loka-pāvanī*). This account does not mention some of the emergents cited in other versions of the myth, such as the divine cow Surabhi, jewels, or wine (*surā*).

The gods praise the newly emerged Lakshmi and ask Vishnu to marry her for the sake of the worlds. Lakshmi objects, however, arguing that her sister, Alakshmi, is elder to her and therefore must marry first. Vishnu therefore gives Alakshmi to the sage Uddalaka in marriage before he himself marries Lakshmi.[3] A fight ensues between the gods and the demons over the nectar. This version describes the battle only briefly, noting that the gods strike the demons and drink up the nectar, which Vishnu, having assumed a feminine form—presumably to delude the demons, as in other versions of the myth—distributes from a golden vessel.

Vishnu's dispatching of Alakshmi parallels the gods' dispatching of the demons, for both Alakshmi and the demons stand in the way of Lakshmi's restoration. Vishnu's marriage to Lakshmi not only unites him with auspiciousness, but helps restore it to the world as well. Marriage, with its connotations of sexuality and progeny, generally embodies auspicious values, but Vishnu and Lakshmi represent the ideal in this regard. As in many other contexts, here too the auspiciousness that Lakshmi embodies specifically includes Vishnu's sovereignty, the power of kingly prosperity that union with Lakshmi enables him to bestow on his realm (Marglin 1985a, 181–84; Hiltebeitel 1990, 143–91). The marital alliance forged between Vishnu and Lakshmi together with Vishnu's securing of the nectar stabilize auspiciousness on a cosmic level, encompassing both the divine and natural worlds.

The KMSP draws on elements present in the Vishnu Purana, Padma Purana, and other Puranic retellings of the churning myth to describe the birth of Tulsi, the basil plant singled out for special honor during Kartik, from the ocean of milk. The text alludes briefly to the conflict between Indra and Durvasas before describing the ocean's churning and the items that emerge from it.[4] Dhanvantari comes out of the ocean with the pot of nectar in his hands, gazes into it, and tears of joy fall from his eyes into the pot. These teardrops become Tulsi, and the gods give both Tulsi and Lakshmi to Vishnu (8.30–37). Tulsi's birth from nectar signals her life- and health-enhancing nature, and her status as co-wife to Vishnu suggests she is an allomorph of Lakshmi. Like nectar and Lakshmi, Tulsi, too, embodies auspiciousness.

Several informants in Benares insisted that the original churning took place long ago during the month of Kartik. I have not come across any textual affirmations of this assertion, but it is clearly present in the minds of many of individuals with whom I spoke, some of whom explicitly attributed Kartik's auspiciousness and religious importance to the historical relationship between Kartik and the churning event.

Referring to the items that emerged from the ocean as the fourteen jewels (*ratna*),[5] for example, one informant told me:

> When they churned the ocean of milk, fourteen jewels came out of the ocean. Nectar came out on Ashvin Purnima [the full moon that ushers in the month of Kartik]. Dhanvantari came out on the thirteenth day of Kartik's bright fortnight. From the sixth to the twelfth of Kartik's bright fortnight, the cow came out. Most of the jewels came out during the bright fortnight. That is why there are so many festivals during that fortnight. . . . All fourteen jewels came out in the month of Kartik. That is why Kartik is very pure (*pavitra*) and auspicious (*śubha*).

Like the narrative, many of the *vrats* and festivals that take place during the month of Kartik speak of the earth's renewal, the victory of gods over demonic forces, the (re)establishment of Vishnu's sovereignty, the restoration of order and auspiciousness, and the recovery and stabilization of auspiciousness through marriage to an auspicious bride. Nectar, Tulsi, and Lakshmi figure prominently throughout the month, and other milk-ocean emergents also come into play in important ways.

Connections between the myth and the month also persist in the churning narrative's resonance with climatic cycles in North India and Kartik's place in that cycle. In the churning narrative, a period of heat, drought, and hunger followed by a transitional period of oceanic churning ushers in Lakshmi's return to the world; the same essential process takes place every year when the hot, dry season in North India followed by the transitional period of the monsoon gives way to the restoration of the earth's abundance, completed by the stabilization of the earth's fecundity in the autumn, when Kartik falls. Furthermore, aspects of both the churning narrative and the month of Kartik resonate with larger Hindu imagery of cosmogenesis as established in the Puranas. Lakshmi's reemergence from the purifying milk ocean at the time of its churning is analogous to the process of cosmic recreation or emanation (*sṛṣṭi*) following a period of cosmic dissolution, which is embodied every year in the immersion and cleansing of the earth during the monsoon rains and the renewal of it's fecundity following the rainy period and culminating in the month of Kartik.

In ancient times the first day of Kartik's light fortnight—the time of Diwali, the grand celebration of Lakshmi—marked the New Year. In contemporary North India, the New Year is generally counted from the first day of the light fortnight of Chaitr, six months before Kartik, but Diwali is still recognized as the traditional New Year, and business castes continue to end their fiscal year on Diwali. A new year represents a kind of renewal of creation. Every year the ocean is, symbolically, churned again; and in Kartik, as time is renewed, so is auspiciousness.

Krishna and Kartik

Like Vishnu, Krishna, who is generally considered to be a form of Vishnu, is also worshiped in the month of Kartik, and various episodes of Krishna's life story are celebrated and commemorated throughout the month. The earliest Sanskrit scriptures that recount the stories of Krishna's life in some detail include such texts as Harivamsha, Vishnu Purana, and Bhagavata Purana. Krishna is said to be an incarnate form of Vishnu who appears on earth for the express purpose of slaying a demon, Kamsa, a task that he eventually accomplishes. He is born in the town of Mathura, which lies on the Gangetic plain just south of Delhi in a region known as Braj. His mother Devaki is Kamsa's sister, but Kamsa has been told that he will be killed by one of his sister's children, so he places Devaki in captivity in a dungeon. Through divine intervention, Krishna is whisked off at the time of his birth into the Braj countryside near Mathura, where, living among cowherds, he grows up on the banks of the Yamuna River.

Many stories of Krishna pertain to his life as Krishna Gopal, the cowherd Krishna. He proves to be a spirited and rambunctious youth. David Kinsley describes the child Krishna as a "divine player," a frolicking youth who delights in mischief and pranks, wreaking general havoc (1979, 60–70). He disobeys his mother and lies to her, untethers cows before milking time, and plays tricks on his neighbors, even urinating and defecating in their houses (Bhagavata Purana 10.8–9). Krishna is especially troublesome to the *gopīs*, the cowherdesses of Vrindavan. One of young Krishna's most characteristic traits is his passion for butter, and he constantly steals the beloved substance from the *gopīs*. They complain endlessly to Yashoda, Krishna's foster mother, about her son's many antics, but the *gopīs* also find Krishna to be irresistibly adorable, and they take great delight in his boyish charm.

The youthful Krishna also slays demons, an activity that Kinsley portrays as part of his youthful play (1979, 70–74). Krishna's uncle Kamsa dispatches many of these demons. Fearful of the child snatched away from his sister's dungeon, and suspicious that Krishna the cowherd boy is in fact his sister's child, Kamsa sends demon after demon to kill him. Krishna manages to destroy them all, however, and he disposes of them "as if it were all a game" (70). He protects the people of Braj too, from demons and other dangers, but he uses his supernormal powers to perpetuate their ignorance regarding his divine status.

As an irresistible young man, Krishna becomes a great lover of women, and the *gopīs* whom he torments in childhood later fall into Krishna's arms in the bowers of Vrindavan, a forest north of Mathura, eager to enjoy his passionate embrace. In this role Krishna is the Divine Lover who "expresses in its every facet the playful nature of love and love-making" (Kinsley 1979, 78). One of the most famous images of Krishna situates him in the *rāsa-līlā,* the famous "circle dance," where Krishna, surrounded by a circle of *gopīs* in the forest, not only dances with them, but also multiplies himself many times over so that he can make love to each and every one of them. While earlier texts focus on Krishna's daliance only with the *gopīs*, subsequent traditions pair Krishna with one consort, Radha, and later texts, such as the Brahmavaivarta Purana, portray Radha as the chief of the *gopīs* and Krishna's primary partner. In such contexts, the *gopīs* are depicted as Radha's attendants and companions and are referred to as her *sakhīs*, meaning "female friends." Such an understanding of Radha as the leader of the *gopīs*/*sakhīs* dominates popular understandings of the Krishna story that I encountered in Benares. The episode of the *rāsa-līlā* is often taken to convey the intimacy of the bond between God and His devotees: God's distance is overcome in devotion, where God's relationship with every soul becomes intimate, personal, and unique. It is also said to continue eternally in Krishna's heaven, Goloka, where souls enjoy eternal, blissful communion with Krishna.

Eventually Krishna kills Kamsa, and in his later life he leaves Vrindavan to take up residence in Dvaraka, where he acquires a vast number of wives and assumes the rulership of the Yadava clan. When he leaves Vrindavan for Dvaraka, the *gopīs* are said to pine away for him, longing to bask in his presence once again. The emotions that the *gopīs* experience in yearning for their absent beloved are captured in the word *viraha,* or "separation," which has acquired religious connotations as the soul's yearning for God. In due course Krishna perishes, abandoning his human body and returning to the heavenly realms whence he came.

In Benares, the main events of Krishna's life are reenacted every Kartik in a series of performances known as the Krishna Lila. The term *līlā* means "play," both in the sense of carefree enjoyment and in the sense of performance. Hence "Krishna Lila" refers both to Krishna's playful actions as a mischievous youth, demon slayer, and divine lover, and to the nightly, staged performances that take place on Tulsi Ghat, reenacting the major events in Krishna's life story.[6] The main sponsor of the Krishna Lila is Professor Vir Bhadra Mishra, *mahant* (abbot) of the Sankat Mochan temple in Benares and professor of Civil Engineering at Benares Hindu University. The Krishna Lila takes place outside his home on Tulsi Ghat every evening for approximately three weeks, from the twelfth day (*tithi*) of Kartik's first fortnight (the day of Govatsa Dvadashi, discussed below) until the day after Kartik ends.

The fact that the Krishna Lila takes place in Benares during the month of Kartik is significant. Krishna is, after all, a form of Vishnu, and this is a month dedicated to Vishnu's worship. Krishna's role as slayer of demons and protector of the people of Braj is celebrated in a number of Kartik's holidays; cattle, which figure prominently in Krishna's early life as a cowherd, are also honored at a number of points throughout the month. The episode of the *rāsa-līlā* plays an important role in Kartik in a number of ways as well.

In his work on performances of Krishna *līlā* in Braj, John S. Hawley proposes that Krishna's *līlā,* especially with respect to Krishna's role as a thief of butter, is symbolically a return to the point in time before the ocean of milk was churned and auspiciousness, Lakshmi, became concentrated in Vishnu's domain; Krishna's play disperses auspiciousness in all directions (1983, 301–307). Hawley contrasts Vrindavan, the realm of dispersed auspiciousness, with Vaikunth, which he describes as the realm of stable auspiciousness, where *śrī* and nectar (*amṛta*) are "forged into a stable and systematic whole" (305). Focusing on the image of Krishna's *rāsa-līlā* dance with the *gopīs,* Marglin portrays Krishna's play as analogous to the unchurned milk ocean, both of which she describes as transcending the ordinary flow of time: auspiciousness always becomes inauspiciousness with the passage of time, but the eternally lush, forested bowers of Krishna's Vrindavan represent a transcendent type of auspiciousness that never wanes. Marglin contrasts the playful realm of the young Krishna of Vrindavan, characterized by sweetness, with the later, princely realm of Krishna's Dvaraka, characterized by sovereignty; whereas sweetness transcends temporally bounded auspiciousness, sovereignty cannot escape it, since auspiciousness is one of sovereignty's chief concerns (1985a, 195–216).

The month of Kartik embraces the realm of Vrindavan as well as that of Vaikunth. The churning of the ocean that restores and stabilizes auspiciousness rejuvenates the world, reviving its opulence and vitality; this fresh, vibrant, and fecund world becomes the appropriate stage for Krishna's sweet, rambunctious play. Sovereignty and sweetness, Vishnu's lordship and Krishna's youthful exuberance, time-bound auspiciousness and transcendent auspiciousness all come together in the enticing, nourishing lushness of Kartik.

In the rest of this chapter, I discuss some of the most important individual celebrations that occur throughout the month of Kartik. These celebrations exemplify auspiciousness-related images and themes found in the churning narrative and the accounts of Krishna's youthful play, and I highlight these images and themes in my discussion. I will not attempt anything like an exhaustive description of each and every religious observance that takes place in Benares during Kartik, which would be a book in itself, but will instead focus on major *vrats* and festivals that are part of the annual cycle and are celebrated widely in the city. In the chapters that follow, I hope to show how women engage Kartik's themes of auspiciousness selectively in their practice of Kartik *pūjā*, appropriating elements that figure most prominently and meaningfully in their own lives. Martial victory over demonic forces, for example, is a theme that permeates Kartik, but it does not come to the fore at all in women's Kartik traditions, perhaps because matters pertaining to military conquest tend to be more important to men than to women. But themes of spiritual renewal, fecundity, sexuality, and marriage, among others, figure prominently in women's Kartik traditions, where they play out in ways that are informed by the concrete, embodied experiences that tend to shape the contours of women's lives.

Table 1. Selected religious celebrations during the month of Kartik

Kartik's first fortnight ("dark fortnight")

Sharat Purnima (the last night of Ashvin)	1.	2.	3.	4. Karva Cauth
5.	6.	7.	8.	9.
10.	11.	12. Govatsa Dvadashi; Krishna Lila begins	13. Yamatrayodashi, Dhanteras	14. Narak Caturdashi
15. Diwali				

Kartik's second fortnight ("light fortnight")

1. Govardhan worship, Annakut	2. Bhaiya Duj, Yamdvitiya	3.	4. Nag Nathaiya	5.
6. Dala Chat	7.	8. Gopashtami	9. Akshaya Navami	10.
11. Prabodhani Ekadashi, Tulsi Vivaha	12.	13.	14. Vaikunth Caturdashi	15. Kartik Purnima ("full moon")

Sharat Purnima (Autumn Full Moon)

Kartik begins on the full-moon night of Ashvin. The clearing of the sky that marks the arrival of autumn is dramatically apparent on this night, when the full moon shines bright and crisp against a cloud-free sky. This night is called Sharat Purnima, "Autumn Full Moon," comparable to what is commonly known in the West as the Harvest Moon. On Ashvin Purnima, nectar (*amṛta*) is said to rain down from the moon and reach the earth in great abundance. The nectar that falls from the moon during Kartik is considered to be a lunar version of the original, divine nectar that the gods pulled from the ocean of milk in ancient times. A few informants even claimed that the original nectar emerged long ago on this very day. At nighttime, many people in Benares, as in other parts of India, place out on their rooftops white foods—especially *khīr*, a sweet pudding made with rice and milk—although in Benares, as in other parts of India, it seems to be primarily Vaishnavas who do this. White is the color of the moon, and on this night the moon's nectar is thought to fall into these foods, which are then eaten the next day as food that has been imbued with divine grace (*prasād*).

One informant described the potency of the nectar that falls to earth at this time as due to both the perceived close proximity of the moon to the earth on this night and the favorable climatic conditions that prevail at this time. Nectar is thought to fall from every full moon but without reaching the earth with the same intensity. During the rainy season, clouds and rain obstruct the fall of the moon's nectar and prevent it from reaching the earth; during the summer months the hot rays of the sun increase the temperature between the moon and the earth and dry up the nectar. At the time of the full moon of Ashvin, however, the sky is free of clouds, and the temperature is moderate, so the moon's nectar is thought to reach the earth more easily. The potency of the nectar that falls on this night may also be attributable to the perceived impact of the Ashvini asterism, with which the moon comes into conjunction on Ashvin Purnima. Each asterism has a ruling deity, and the twin deities known as the Ashvins rule Ashvini. The Ashvins are healing deities, and some Benarsis view the effect of this month's full moon and the quality of the nectar that falls to earth at this time as embodying healing qualities.

Some consider the rain of lunar nectar to be just as potent on the next full moon, Kartik Purnima, and some told me they place white foods out on their rooftops again on that night, hoping to catch and consume one last bit of the season's moon nectar. Moreover, while Benarsis tend to apply the term "Sharat Purnima" to Ashvin's full moon, some call the night of Kartik Purnima by this name as well. A few of those with whom I spoke described the whole month, from Ashvin Purnima to Kartik Purnima, as a time of life-giving moon nectar, with the two full-moon nights that bound the month being the most potent dates. One medical doctor who is also a professor of Ayurveda (Indian medicine) at Benares Hindu University told me that the entire month of Kartik is particularly auspicious for collecting medicinal herbs from Indian hills and forests because the moon's healing nectar falls directly into plants during this time. This doctor described nectar, too, as embodied in all elements of lifestyle, diet, and medicine that are conducive to health and long life, claiming that the ritual injunctions, food regulations, and medicinal fruits and herbs associated with Kartik, its *vrat*, and some of its individual festivals were particularly conducive to bodily well-being and hence exemplary forms of nectar.

Both nectar and the moon, of course, are among the auspicious items that emerge from the milk ocean. But the connection between them is deeper. One of the terms for "moon" in Sanskrit is *soma*. The term "*soma*" also refers to the intoxicating Vedic libation consumed by the gods. Hawley notes that *soma* is also an allomorph of nectar (1983, 303–304). In the Puranas *soma* is described as the essence or source of medicinal herbs and plants (e.g., Brahma Purana 7.10, Varaha Purana 35.4). The medicinal nature of the nectar that the moon pours out during Kartik reminds us that in many versions of the churning myth Dhanvanteri, the physician of the gods, emerges from the ocean of milk with the nectar in his hands. This event is held to have occurred during Kartik and is commemorated on the thirteenth of Kartik's dark fortnight.

Like nectar, Lakshmi also emerged from the ocean's depths at the time of its churning, and the night of Ashvin Purnima is also a festival dedicated to this auspicious goddess. This celebration is known as Kojagari, and devotees perform a special form of worship to Lakshmi, along with Indra and his elephant Airavata (another milk-ocean emergent), and ask for her blessings.[7] The festivities include playing dice, consuming certain white-colored food or drink, such as coconut milk or *khīr*, and remaining awake all night (*jāgaraṇa*). Lakshmi is said to roam on this night asking, "*Ko jāgarti*?" which means, "Who is awake?" in Sanskrit, and those who remain awake are more likely to win her blessings. Devotees place a light outside of their houses on this night as an invitation to Lakshmi to pause and bless the inhabitants (Underhill 1921, 58). This night also marks the beginning of the month-long rite of lighting sky lamps along the *ghaṭs* in Benares.

Some textual sources cite the night of Sharat Purnima as the night that the *rāsa-līlā* of Krishna and the *gopi*s took place. Other sources, however, locate it during Kartik Purnima, the full moon with which Kartik ends, or the last five days of the month (e.g., Underhill 1921, 83; Mukherjee 1989, 210ff., Raghavan 1979, 172). The fact that the *rāsa-līlā* is said to have taken place on both of the full moons that bound Kartik is significant, and I will return to this point at the end of this chapter.

Hawley notes that the churning of the ocean of milk sometimes provides the mythological backdrop for scenes depicting the child Krishna with a pot of butter, and he draws a connection between the milk ocean's churning and Krishna's attraction to butter (1983, 302–306). The churning of ordinary milk, after all, usually results in butter, not nectar. In some versions of the myth—in the Mahabharata, for example—the churning does produce butter (in the form of clarified butter, or *ghī*), among other substances (1.18.28). Like butter, the nectar that falls on Sharat Purnima comes from milk, in this case the ocean of milk. The Devi-Bhagavata Purana recounts that one day, while walking with Radha in Goloka, Krishna is seized with a sudden desire to drink milk; he creates from his left side Surabhi, the divine cow that many versions of the churning narrative describe as emerging from the milk ocean, and her calf. She, the cow who arises from milk, is now herself milked: her milk is described as superior to nectar (*sudhā*) and, like nectar, is said to be a drink that bestows immortality. Krishna drinks the milk, and whatever is left over falls from the jar and spreads forth to create a "lake of milk" (*kṣīra-sarovar*), a heavenly embodiment of Vishnu's cosmic ocean of milk, and Radha and the *gopīs* play in it (9.49.2–10). The Narada Purana (3.82.213) describes Krishna as perpetually playing with Radha in an ocean of nectar.

Like the ocean of milk, the rain of nectar that falls on Sharat Purnima forms a backdrop to Krishna's divine *līlā*. Both butter and nectar are auspicious foods that emerge from churned milk and in that sense are comparable. Yet while nectar embodies the promise of immortality—spiritual auspiciousness—or a long, healthy, abundant life—worldly auspiciousness—Hawley argues convincingly that in the image of Krishna as a thief of butter, butter embodies love (1983, 10, 266–67, 285–86). It is then perhaps no wonder that most of my informants referred to Kartik as both an auspicious month and a month dedicated to religious devotion, *bhakti*, which embodies a devotee's love of God.

Karva Cauth

The fourth (*cauth*) of Kartik's dark fortnight marks one of the most important *vrat*s of the year for married Hindu women in Benares, who observe this *vrat*, called Karva Cauth, for the long lives and good health of their husbands. The *vrat* entails total abstention from food and water for a full day until after moonrise, when votaries worship the goddess Parvati and then the moon before breaking the fast. The name of the *vrat* is derived from a special type of earthen pot with a spout (*karvā*) that is used during the evening worship.

The moon figures prominently in one important Karva Cauth narrative, too. While many different Karva Cauth stories exist, the one that seems to be most popular among votaries in Benares has to do with a woman who inadvertently breaks the fast before the appropriate time. In the narrative, the woman's brothers are worried about her well-being and don't want her to postpone eating any longer, so they deceive her into thinking that the moon has risen when, in fact, it has not yet done so. The woman's husband dies, but, following advice given to her, she preserves her husband's body for a full year, and on the next Karva Cauth, she maintains the fast correctly, breaking it only after the moon has risen and she has performed her worship. As a result, her husband is brought back to life.

Falling just days after the celebration of Sharat Purnima, the worship of the moon during the Karva Cauth *vrat* in order to enhance the length and vigor of one's husband's life clearly seems related to traditions regarding the moon's nectar-rich state at this time, and women's performance of the Karva Cauth *vrat* appears to be a way of securing the life-giving powers of the moon's nectar-rich rays on behalf of their husbands. Hence the life- and health-enhancing effects of the moon's nectar come to be harnessed to women's larger goal of *suhāg* (Sskt. *saubhāgya*), the auspicious state of being a married woman, of which the husband's long and healthy life is the most essential component.

Govatsa Dvadashi

The twelfth of Kartik's dark fortnight marks the *vrat* of Govatsa Dvadashi, "Calf's Twelfth." On this day cows and calves are worshiped and adorned with sandalwood paste, flower garlands, and the like. The KMSP refers to a cowherdess named Ekangi, who performed this *vrat* and within three years obtained wealth and foodgrains, connecting this *vrat* to the attainment of auspicious householder boons (9.14). It is widely known that in the Hindu tradition cows are considered sacred, so it is not particularly surprising that certain days are set aside for cow worship. But the cow is also one of the items produced from the ocean of milk. The Nirnayasindhu and Dharmasindhu advocate that at the time of worship on Govatsa Dvadashi, one recite a mantra praising the cow as the Divine Mother, "who arose from the ocean of milk" (NS 294, DS 211). Krishna, the divine cowherd, also has a special relationship with cows, and in Benares Govatsa Dvadashi marks the beginning of Krishna Lila on Tulsi Ghat.

Yamatrayodashi and Dhanteras

The thirteenth of Kartik's dark fortnight, the day after Govatsa Dvadashi, marks the beginning of the five-day period around the celebration of Diwali, the festival of lights. On this night the lights set out every night during Kartik both in the sky lamps and as offerings at the base of a Tulsi plant are joined by more lights, which are placed in front of the doorways of homes. This light is an offering to Yama, the Host of Death, to avert untimely death during the time of the Diwali festival.[8] This day is also Dhanteras, "Wealth Thirteenth," a celebration aimed at increasing wealth and prosperity.

Dhanteras engages themes of cleansing, renewal, and the securing of auspiciousness in the form of Lakshmi. In Benares, as in other parts of India, houses that have not yet been cleaned in preparation for Diwali are thoroughly cleansed and whitewashed, and Lakshmi, the goddess of wealth, is worshiped in the evening. It is requisite to purchase at least one new cooking or eating utensil on this day, such as a pot, plate, glass, or silverware. In the evening temporary stalls selling kitchen items spring up along the streets of the city, and crowds suddenly appear to examine the merchandise and make their purchases. Some sources also connect the "*dhan*" in the name "Dhanteras" not just to wealth (which is one meaning of *dhan*), but also to Dhanvanteri. Dhanvantari is said to have arisen from the ocean of milk with the pitcher of nectar in his hand on this very day, and Ayurvedic practitioners honor Dhanvantari with a special *pūjā*. At Benares Hindu University, professors in the medical departments perform a fire ritual (*havan*) to Dhanvantari, in which healing herbs are placed in a ritual fire as offerings to the deity. On this day, too, new medical students are initiated into their departments in honor of Dhanvantari's birthday. Hence this day involves the securing of wealth, food, and prosperity, as well as health, healing, and "immortality," here understood as the avoidance of death—all themes that figure prominently in the narrative of the milk ocean's churning.

Narak Caturdashi

The day before Diwali is Narak Caturdashi, "Hell Fourteenth," another day that involves the lighting of special lights. In Benares, people place small clay lamps in front of their homes and on piles of garbage. There are a variety of interpretations regarding the meaning of this day. Popular belief in Benares holds that it is inauspicious to die on this day, for if you do, you go straight to hell. But both textual sources and informants assert that lights offered on this day can destroy past sins or liberate souls from hellish realms, goals illustrative of spiritual auspiciousness.[9] The KMSP prescribes that on this night and the following night, men should take up firebrands in their hands to light a path for their ancestors (*pitṛ*), so that dead men and ghosts who are in hell can see the way out (9.65–66; cf. Kane 5/1, 198). Informants in Benares also described this day as one of ancestral worship, claiming that the gates to hell are thrown open so ancestral souls that have completed their period in hell can leave, with the lights illuminating the way. The lights also serve the interests of ancestral souls who may already be on the way to heaven but risk losing their way; they will see the gates to hell and avoid entering.

Other sources describe this day as a celebration of Krishna's victory over the demon Naraka.[10] The Bhagavata Purana (10.59) recounts that Krishna vanquished Naraka and entered his abode, finding there sixteen thousand princesses whom Naraka captured when he conquered their fathers. The princesses, described as portions (*aṁśa*) of Lakshmi, instantly fall in love with Krishna, who later assumes sixteen thousand forms and with each form marries and makes love to each princess. This episode obviously bears resemblance to the *rāsa-līlā*, which also entails that Krishna multiply himself and present a unique form to each female participant.

The Bhagavata Purana also interjects into the narrative of Krishna's victory an abbreviated version of a story that appears in the KMPP (chap. 1). According to the KMPP, in distributing flowers among his sixteen thousand wives, Krishna accidentally leaves out his wife Satyabhama, and she becomes very angry with him. To appease her, Krishna fights Indra to obtain the heavenly wish-fulfilling tree dwelling in Indra's heaven. Krishna wins the tree and gives it to Satyabhama, who plants it in her courtyard. The Bhagavata Purana summarizes the story briefly and names this tree as the Parijata tree, which is among the objects that emerge from the ocean of milk. The Parijata tree is of special importance during Kartik, and Parijata flowers are used daily in Krishna worship only during this month.[11]

Occurring the day before Diwali proper, this day is also known as "little Diwali" and ushers in a period of devotion to Lakshmi, who is at the center of Diwali worship.[12]

Diwali

In practice the Diwali season lasts from around Dhanteras until the second day of Kartik's light fortnight, but the KMSP cites Naraka Caturdashi as the real beginning of Diwali, which it describes as lasting for three days (9.48–49). Falling in the middle of the month on Kartik's new moon (*amāvasya*), the last day of Kartik's dark fortnight, is the main celebration of Diwali, the famous Hindu festival of lights. Many of the festivities that take place on this holiday, however, continue on through the night and into the next day.

Diwali is primarily a celebration of Lakshmi, who is worshiped and welcomed into people's homes on the evening of Kartik's new moon with an abundance of lights. The celebration is most important for business castes, which end their fiscal year on Diwali and worship Lakshmi in hopes of a prosperous forthcoming year. But Hindus from across the caste spectrum participate in holiday festivities. In Benares celebrants don new clothes, worship Lakshmi in the evening, and illuminate their homes with copious numbers of traditional clay lamps (*dīpas*) or electric lights, while the crackle of firecrackers and fireworks fills the city all night long. In anticipation of this holiday, Hindu householders thoroughly cleanse their houses, often whitewashing or painting them as well so that they will be ready for the goddess, who roams the earth at night. It is said that she will only enter houses that are clean and well lit, and homes that she enters this night will secure her presence for the entire year. The cleaning and purification that take place for Diwali ritually reenact the cleansing, purifying action of the monsoon rains, which restore the earth's fertility, just as the churning of the ocean of milk restores to the world Lakshmi and all that she represents.

There is a clear symmetry between the celebration of Lakshmi and light that takes place on Kojagari, the Lakshmi festival with which the month begins, and the celebration of Lakshmi and light that recurs on Diwali, even though the first celebration occurs under a full moon while the latter takes place at the time of the new moon. Textual sources equate both celebrations with the Kaumudi festival, the ancient celebration of moonlight.[13] Some sources even place the Kaumudi festival on the night of Kartik Purnima, the full moon night with which the month ends, which is also a night of lights and festive celebration

Figure 7. Diwali *pūjā* altar in a Benares home

(e.g., Sharma 1978, 32). Hence the three main turning points of the month—beginning, middle, and end—are marked as especially potent, auspicious times that are celebrated with light and festivity.

Kingship and divine victory over demonic forces are important Diwali themes. The deity Ram is said to have returned to his kingdom in Ayodhya on Diwali after fourteen years in exile, having conquered the demon Ravana. Some contemporary sources cite Diwali as the day of Ram's coronation.[14] Vishnu's victory over Bali, king of the demons, is also said to have occurred on Diwali. Bali is said to have become very powerful and to have taken over the worlds, which Vishnu won back from him. Assuming the form of a dwarf, Vishnu approached Bali and asked for land equal to what he could cover in three steps. Bali granted the wish, and Vishnu, assuming a giant form, covered heaven and earth in two steps. With the third step he placed his foot on Bali's head and thrust the demon into the netherworld, installing Bali as king of one of the seven regions of hell (*pātāla*).[15] In exchange for the gods' restored dominion, Vishnu granted that every year, Bali, who is transformed from adversary to devotee, would rule the earth again for three days during the Diwali season, from Narak Caturdashi to the first day of Kartik's bright fortnight (KMSP, 9.49–57). As in the past, Bali's temporarily restored dominion in the present ends in his banishment to the netherworld after Diwali.

Diwali's association with both Bali and Lakshmi also provides a link between the holiday and the narrative of the churning of the ocean of milk. Vishnu's recovery of dominion over the worlds after a period of demonic "takeover," a pattern that characterizes the Bali narrative, echoes the pattern that we see in the narrative of the milk ocean's churning, where the same type of victory occurs. Furthermore, the KMSP recounts that at the time of Kartik's new moon, Lakshmi and the other gods and goddesses were released from Bali's prison, and all the deities accompanied Lakshmi to the ocean of milk, where they all lay down and fell asleep.[16] Some popular contemporary sources also cite Diwali as the day Lakshmi emerged from the ocean of milk at the time of its churning and chose Vishnu as her husband.[17] The KMSP advocates that after midnight on Diwali, women should take up winnowing baskets and play small drums to chase Alakshmi away from their homes (KMSP 9.100). My research associate, Sunita Singh, confirmed that many Benarsi women do indeed perform this noise-making ritual to chase away the goddess of ill fortune, who in Benares tends to be known by the name Daridr or Dalidr, "Poverty-Stricken One." As in the Padma Purana's account of the churning of the ocean of milk, Alakshmi is driven away while Lakshmi is welcomed back and her restored presence on earth is celebrated.

Like the day that precedes it, Diwali is a day for performing ancestral mortuary rituals. Worship of Yama, both the god of death and the world of the dead, is important during the Diwali season, as is concern with one's departed ancestors. A month before Diwali is a fortnight dedicated to ancestral worship (*mahālaya*), when one invites one's ancestors to abide among the living and receive their attention. On Diwali, the ancestors are shown the way to leave, with firecrackers and lights illuminating their path (Raghavan 1979, 165–66). But the leaving is also potentially a leaving from undesirable, hellish worlds, as during Narak Caturdashi, to journey onward to more desirable realms. Hence Diwali is a celebration of the spiritual advancement of one's ancestors, not simply their return to worlds from which they came.

Kartik Shukla Pratipada/Govardhan Worship/Annakut

The Diwali season continues into the first day of Kartik's bright fortnight (*śukla pratipadā*), the traditional beginning of the new year. This is the final day of Bali's annual three-day dominion and the anniversary of his defeat, so worship of Bali is advocated. One is also supposed to gamble or play dice. The KMSP traces this practice back to the deity Shiva, who is said to have created the game of dice (*dyūta*) on this very day (10.2). Shiva played with Parvati, who won his clothing and adornments from him. Shiva was made to wander naked and miserable (10.20).

The KMSP cites the story of Shiva gambling with Parvati to explain why gambling is compulsory on this day: humans do as the gods did in previous times, and those who are victorious will have a prosperous year (KMSP 10.21).[18] But Don Handelman and David Shulman (1997) describe Shiva and Parvati's dice game in relation to cosmic processes of emanation and dissolution of creation. They cite a passage from the Skanda Purana (4.2.88.5–8):

> God of gods, the entire universe is your game. The twelve months are the squares on the board. The playing pieces are the thirty lunar days, both light and dark. The two dice are the summer and winter paths of the sun [*uttarāyana/dakṣināyana*]. The stakes are victory and defeat, called emanation (*sṛṣṭi*) and dissolution (*pralaya*). If the goddess wins, that means emanation; if Shiva wins, that means non-emanation (*asṛṣṭi*).[19]

The story of Parvati's victory over Shiva at dice is more than simply a justification for gambling during Diwali. Let us not forget that Parvati won the game she played long ago on this New Year's Day, a victory that the Skanda Purana names "emanation" (*sṛṣṭi*). *Sṛṣṭi* refers to the process of cosmogenesis; *pralaya* refers to the dissolution of the world at the end of a cycle of creation, when all the worlds are immersed in a great ocean of water. Creation itself is at stake in this game, along with the year—the twelve months, thirty lunar days, and so forth that the game pieces represent. With the threat of cosmic dissolution looming large, the goddess's victory represents a victory for the emanated world and the year. The thwarting of cosmic destruction in this narrative echoes that which occurs at the churning of the ocean of milk; the return of Lakshmi at Diwali, Parvati's triumph over Shiva, and Vishnu's triumph over Bali all parallel the gods' victory over the demons in the churning narrative. The forces of dissolution and cosmic destruction are vanquished once again.

The first day of Kartik's light fortnight is also the day of Govardhan *pūjā,* worship of the lord of Mount Govardhan ("Cow-Dung Wealth"), a mountain located in Braj. The narrative of Govardhan also speaks of divine thwarting of cosmic destruction. While there are several versions of the story, renditions recounted in the Vishnu and Bhagavata Puranas narrate that Krishna convinces the cowherds of

Braj to stop giving harvest offerings to the god Indra and to give them instead to the god of Govardhan mountain (Govardhannath). Infuriated, Indra summons the destructive clouds of cosmic dissolution (*sāṁvartaka*) and convinces them to harass the people of Braj with torrential rains. As the water rises, the people of Braj become increasingly fearful, and they approach Krishna for help. Krishna lifts up the Govardhan Mountain and invites the people and their cows to take shelter in the cavity below the mountain, while he holds it above their heads, like an umbrella. After seven days, Indra withdraws the clouds; Krishna coaxes the people out of the mountain's cavity and restores Mount Govardhan to its rightful place (Vishnu Purana 5.10–11; Bhagavata Purana 10.24–25). Hence in this narrative the threat of large-scale destruction from Indra's torrential rains, like the threat of cosmic dissolution in Shiva and Parvati's game of dice, is averted.[20]

Govardhan *pūjā* honors the Lord of Mount Govardhan, Govardhannath. In Vaishnava homes in Benares, as elsewhere, women perform *pūjā* and offer food to images of Govardhannath that they have made out of cow dung. Rice, milk, and milk-based sweets are popular food offerings on this day, and one is supposed to worship cows, as well as calves and bulls.[21] In the evening, celebrants place the image at their front gate so that Govardhannath will safeguard the home for the upcoming year. One major theme of this celebration, therefore, is divine protection: Krishna's protection of the people of

Figure 8. Women performing Govardhan *pūjā*

Braj, and Govardhannath's protection of those who worship him. Abundance of food is another major theme, and Govardhan *pūjā* is allied with the celebration of Annakut, "mountain of food." In Braj, Mount Govardhan is worshiped with a mountain of food (*annakuṭa*), which is placed on display (Toomey 1986, 1990, 1994). At the Gopala temple in Benares, a Krishna temple, a similar celebration and feast occur, although the center of feasting activity is in Vishvanath Gali at the Vishvanath and Annapurna temples (Eck 1982, 271).[22] In her interpretation of the Govardhan story, Charlotte Vaudeville equates Indra and his clouds with the monsoon season and notes, "Every year, when the autumnal session (*sic*) sets in, Indra and his blue clouds depart, leaving behind an abundant food crop. This is interpreted as a 'victory' " (1991, 107). As the new year is ushered in, the protection that householders seek includes the successful "defeat" of both natural and supernatural destructive forces, safeguarding the victory of abundance for the upcoming year.[23] This is the same auspiciousness sought from Lakshmi during Diwali. Abundance of cows and food represents wealth; the Govardhan Mountain is regarded as a source not only of food, but wealth as well (Toomey 1994, 108). Wealth is, of course, Lakshmi incarnate.

Yamdvitiya or Bhaiya Duj

As the Diwali season winds down, women all over North India prepare to honor their brothers on the second day of Kartik's bright fortnight, known as "Yama's Second" (*yam-dvitiyā*) or "Brother's Second" (*bhaiyā-dūj*). Married women may return to their natal homes, or their brothers may travel to their sister's conjugal homes. Sisters are supposed to feed their brothers, recite mantras for their welfare, and place auspicious marks (*tilak*) on their foreheads, while brothers may present their sisters with gifts. The KMSP asserts that both sister and brother benefit by observing the rite of Bhaiya Duj: a man attains wealth, strength, longevity, and other auspicious worldly boons, and a woman avoids widowhood, thus maintaining her status as an auspiciously married woman (*suhāgin*) (KMSP, 11.26, 34–39, 69–70).

In Benares, women and girls gather together in groups to perform an elaborate collective *pūjā* on their brothers' behalf. They also sing songs and narrate stories specific to this holiday. Stories commonly told both in Benares and elsewhere tell of a woman who saves her brother's life from adversaries, who are usually represented by figures drawn on the ground or fashioned in cow dung and smashed

Figure 9. Women and girls performing a Bhaiya Duj *pūjā* in Benares

with a rice pestle at the end of the story.[24] In some versions, a woman saves her brother from a variety of enemies as he journeys from her home, where he has been welcomed and fed, back to his own home (e.g., Tiwari 1991, 77–79). A Bhaiya Duj story that I heard narrated in Benares and that is summarized below tells of a sister who saves her brother from death at the time of his marriage.

> A king had a son and a daughter who had never known abuse. At the time of the boy's wedding, when the marriage preparations were under way, the messengers of Yama (*yamdhūt*) arrived and said, "The boy has never been subject to any abuse. This is no good: we must do something. We will take his life at the time of his marriage, as he puts *sindūr* in the bride's hair-part." The girl heard this, so when her brother's marriage procession (*barāt*) began to leave she insisted, "I will go, too!" Everyone said, "She must be crazy to demand this! But if she is so insistent, let her go." So she went along.
>
> For the whole journey of the marriage procession, she kept yelling abuses at her brother, saying, "I am going to eat my brother; I am going to chomp on my brother." When the marriage procession arrived at the bride's house, the boy locked his sister in a room to keep her out of the way. She kept

> yelling over and over, "I am going to eat my brother; I am going to chomp on my brother." The marriage started. When the boy went to put *sindūr* in the hair-part of the bride, the sister began to scream loud verbal abuses (*gālī*) at him. At this moment the messengers of Yama arrived and said, "This boy has already been subject to so much abuse! Let's leave him alone." So they left.
>
> The next morning, people asked the girl, "Why did you do what you did?" She said, "If I had not done this, my brother would have died. Since he grew up in such love and affection, and since my mother never abused nor cursed him, the messengers of Yama were jealous and said, 'We should take him.' My abuses saved his life." May God give to everyone's brother what He gave to her brother![25]

This story emphasizes the boy's escape from the clutches of Yama, the lord of death and the underworld, through his sister's intervention. Averting untimely death, embodied by Yama, is, in fact, an important Bhaiya Duj theme and is emphasized by the KMSP (e.g., 11.2, 26, 70). Yama is the son of Surya, the sun god, and his sister is Yamuna, both a goddess and a river that runs through Mathura. According to a well-known Bhaiya Dhuj story, Yama goes to visit his sister Yamuna on the day of Bhaiya Duj, and she bathes and feeds him. Pleased with his sister's attentions, Yama insists that she ask him for a boon:

> Yamuna said, "If you insist on giving, then give the boon that whoever bathes in my waters will not have to go to hell." Hearing this, Yama became worried and said, "Sister! What have you asked? If this happens, Hell will become empty." Yamuna realised her mistake. She modified her demand and said, "Do at least this much, that those brothers and sisters who bathe at Vishram Ghat (in Mathura) while holding hands will not have to go to hell." Yama accepted this. From that day onward, Yam Dvitiya became so important that numerous men and women began to bathe at Vishram Ghat, and brothers began to accept a *tilak* from their sisters, offer them gifts of saris, ornaments, and money, and eat at their place. Thus, those brothers and sisters who bathe lovingly on this day at Vishram Ghat do not go to hell at the end of their lives but acquire a divine body and go to heaven. (Gautam, 181–82)

Bathing in the Yamuna River at Vishram Ghat in Mathura on this day continues to be popular among sister-brother pairs. Several informants mentioned this as an important goal, although only a handful had ever achieved it.

A version of the Yama-Yamuna story is also recounted in the KMSP (11.42–66). This narrative, however, stresses the need for a man to offer libations to both ancestors and gods on this day and to worship Yama before taking food from his sister and presenting gifts to her. In this version of the story, Yama promises Yamuna that those who undertake these ritual observances shall never enter hell. This version of the narrative also describes Bhaiya Duj as a day when Yama releases sinners from the hells. Hence the concern not only for worldly auspiciousness, but also for spiritual advancement—especially of one's ancestors—that permeates the Diwali season beginning with Narak Caturdashi continues to be a theme on this holiday.

Nag Nathaiya

On the fourth *tithi* of Kartik's light fortnight, thousands of people gather at Tulsi Ghat to witness an episode of the Krishna Lila known as Nag Nathaiya. While other performances of Krishna Lila take place at night, this one occurs in the late afternoon, well before darkness falls, and is witnessed by a far greater number of spectators than any of the other episodes. This *līlā* celebrates Krishna's conquest of the serpent Kaliya. The Bhagavata Purana (10.16–17), which recounts the story, describes Kaliya as a deadly snake who resides in the Yamuna River, poisoning the waters with his lethal venom and killing all the plants, birds, and animals in the vicinity. Krishna decides to purify Yamuna's waters by ridding them of Kaliya. He jumps into the water and fights Kaliya until he conquers the serpent and begins to dance on its bruised and bloodied hood. Krishna spares Kaliya's life but banishes him and his wives from the Yamuna, sending them to live out their days far from the lush pastures of Vrindavan. With Kaliya's departure, all the vegetation that had withered from the poison's effects returns to life.

When Krishna's victory over Kaliya is reenacted at Tulsi Ghat, a large branch of a Kadam tree is planted at the edge of the river, and the young boy acting as Krishna—who functions in this context not as a mere actor, but as the embodied form (*svarūp*) of Krishna—jumps from the tree branch into the river, where an effigy of Kaliya lies in wait.[26] The child embodying Krishna climbs onto the effigy's head and strikes a flute-playing pose. Propelled by human assistants, the serpent effigy along with the boy Krishna on its head make a circular sweep in the water, parading in front of thousands of spectators, who

Figure 10. Nag Nathaiya

watch the display from the river bank or from boats floating on the Ganges' waters. The image of Krishna dancing on Kaliya's serpent hood calls to mind the image of Vishnu pushing the demon Bali into the underworld with his foot, an event that is commemorated just days before the Nag Nathaiya is reenacted on Tulsi Ghat. In both cases, Vishnu/Krishna vanquishes his demonic opponent by placing his feet (or foot) on the head of his adversary, who is not killed but banished to a distant place; and in both cases, the demonic opponent is transformed from adversary to devotee.

The Bhagavata Purana declares that Kaliya's departure from the Yamuna River through Krishna's intervention renders Yamuna's waters free of poison (*nirviṣa*) and "possessing nectar" or "nectar-like" (*sāmṛta-jala*) (10.16.67). Like the churning executed by the gods and demons, Krishna's victory over Kaliya results in the extraction of poison from originally undifferentiated liquid and its ultimate elimination, along with the emergence of nectar, or in this case, nectarlike water. Both events also mark the victory of divine forces over adversarial ones and induce the transformation of a barren, withering landscape to one that is lush and vibrantly alive. Such a victory is consonant with the "victory" of abundance celebrated during Annakut and embodied in the lush vegetation and ripening harvest of the postmonsoon season.

Dala Chath or Surya Chath

Beginning on the evening of the fifth *tithi* of Kartik's light fortnight is an arduous *vrat* that is celebrated exclusively by married women. While the *vrat* is observed most fervently in Bihar, it has become increasingly popular in Benares as more and more Biharis have come to live there. Although the *vrat* is spread out over several days, it is named after the sixth of Kartik's light fortnight and is called Surya Chath, "Sun Sixth," or Dala Chath, "Basket Sixth," after the baskets used for holding and making offerings during the *vrat*. Performing this *vrat* is said to bring fulfillment of a variety of worldly desires, but it is observed in particular to attain male children and secure well-being and longevity.

This *vrat* entails rigorous fasting, culminating in a *pūjā* that is performed at the Ganges' banks at sunset on the last full day of the *vrat*. Crowds of female votaries, many of whom are accompanied by their husbands and/or children, gather at the river's edge in the

Figure 11. Dala Chath votaries immersing themselves in the Ganges River

evening with stalks of sugar cane and baskets filled with food offerings. Votaries enter the water and root the sugar cane in the mud of the river bottom, with stalks rising above the water's surface. Standing in the water, they pay homage to the setting sun-god Surya, who figures prominently in this *vrat*, with prayers and water libations (*argh*), departing home only after sunset. They then return to the riverbank early the next morning before the sun has risen, preferably having stayed awake for the whole night, and remain there through sunrise, taking *darśan* of the sun and making offerings before returning home.

There are several stories told in conjunction with this *vrat*, but one well-known narrative has to do with the death of a young boy. An informant and long-term observer of this *vrat* who recounted the story to me explained that the boy's mother takes her dead child into her lap and goes to stand in the river and pray to Surya. She begins praying in the evening before sunset, and when it becomes dark she chooses to remain in the water all night long in order to continue her prayers as soon as the sun rises again. In the morning, Surya sees that she is still in the river and, realizing she has spent the whole night in the water, takes pity on her and restores her son to life. The woman who recounted this version of the story to me also told me that in Bihar, her home state, some women continue to observe the *vrat* by remaining immersed in a river or pond for the entire night. Other informants told me the same thing, although I myself did not ever witness such a method of observing the *vrat*.

Dala Chath appears to embrace many of the same themes of auspiciousness that recur throughout the month. The sugar-cane stalks used in this *vrat*, for example, represent the new harvest, and as such they embody themes of fecundity and the renewal of the earth's fertility. The Dala Chath narrative recounted above also speaks of the renewal of life. Surya's centrality in this narrative is also telling, considering the important role played by light throughout the month. Other *vrats*, including those that occur on "sixths," are dedicated to Surya, but the calendrical context in which this *vrat* occurs suggests resonance with light-related motifs characteristic of numerous other practices and celebrations that occur during the month and have to do with both worldly and spiritual auspiciousness. The role played by the river in this *vrat* also seems significant: the immersion of the mother and her dead son in the river throughout the night, the son's revivification, and their victorious reemergence parallels the revivification of the earth that follows Lakshmi's emergence from the ocean of milk in the churning myth.

Gopashtami

The eighth of Kartik's light fortnight, Gopashtami or "Cowherd Eighth," marks the last of the three Kartik celebrations devoted to cows and their worship (the other two being Govatsa Dvadashi and Govardhan *pūjā*). Some popular sources name this as the day that Krishna began not only to graze cattle in the forest, but also to slay demons (Bharatīyā and Raṇvīr 1974, 161; Gautam 1982, 185). Kartik's connection to Krishna and Vishnu/Krishna's vanquishing of demons is affirmed once again, along with the connection to cows, milk, and all they represent. Honoring cows on this day is said to help one attain both worldly and spiritual goals (e.g., Vālā, 166). In Benares people do *pūjā* to cows and adorn them with garlands.

Akshaya Navami

The ninth day (*navamī*) of Kartik's light fortnight is Akshaya Navami, "Indestructible Ninth." The KMSP calls this day Kushmanda Navami and declares it to be the day that Vishnu vanquished the demon Kushmanda, "pumpkin-gourd," so named from the pumpkin-gourd creepers that grew from his head (31.2). It is also said to be the day on which began Dvapara Yuga, the third of four "ages" recognized in traditional Hindu texts (31.1). Hence this day celebrates both Vishnu's victory over demons and renewed beginnings, themes that we have seen recurring throughout the month. The name of the day most commonly used in Benares, however, "Akshaya Navami," has to do with the belief that all pious acts performed on this day bring one spiritual merit that is indestructible.

In Benares women observe the day as a *vrat* day, marking it with a special *pūjā* that they perform in the morning at the *ghāṭ*s. Facing the river and the newly risen sun, they draw on the ground a ritual diagram consisting of thirty squares. The diagram is made with turmeric, a substance commonly used to draw *vrat*-related images, and a variety of offerings are placed in the squares, including rice, dried fruits, peanuts, fruit, sugar puffs (*lychidānā*), flowers, sweets, or small clay lamps. A pundit is called over to recite the declaration of intention that votaries make in conjunction with *vrats*, and observers of the *vrat* offer the pundit a donation of money, silver or gold, and so forth, that is hidden, usually wrapped inside a cloth (*gupta-dāna*).[27] A number of popular sources also advocate donating on this day cows, gold, land, and other gifts in order to secure great merit.

Figure 12. Akshaya Navami *pūjā*

The squares that comprise the ritual diagram used for the *pūjā* are called *koṭhā*, which means "square." As one votary explained to me, observers of the *vrat* symbolically fill up the *koṭhā* or squares with spiritual merit. But "*koṭhā*" is also is the term for a granary or storage area for grains and other foodstuffs. Given that the different squares are filled with rice grains and other food items, it seems reasonable to see the *pūjā* as evoking symbolism regarding concern for an abundance of food and hopes that one's cupboards remain eternally full.[28]

This day is also known as the ninth day of Amla, a type of fruit. On this day observant Hindus, especially women, perform *pūjā* to an Amla tree and eat a meal beneath it. Potatoes, puffed bread (*pūri*), and a type of sweet called *halvā* are among the foods most commonly consumed at this picnic. While Akshaya Navami and Amla worship may well have different origins, Benarsis tend to see them as different dimensions of the same *vrat*. Many of the women whom I witnessed performing the Akshaya Navami *pūjā* at the *ghāṭ*s in Benares told me they also perform Amla *pūjā* on that day, and I was able to join groups of women for their Amla *pūjā* and picnic every year that I was in Benares doing research for this project.

The KMSP attributes great importance to Amla, dedicating an entire chapter (chapter 12) to the fruit. It claims that while the sun is

Figure 13. Votaries performing Amla *pūjā* and having a picnic under an Amla tree

stationed in Libra—that is, during the month of Kartik—all pilgrimage places (*tīrthas*), sages, gods, and sacrifices come to dwell in Amla, and the worship of Amla can destroy sins and help one attain all desired objects. The text advocates having an outdoor picnic (*vanabhojana*) in a forest or park in which Amla and other trees reside. Before eating, one is enjoined to perform a fire sacrifice (*homa*) at the base of an Amla tree and to solicit blessings for intelligent sons, good fortune, wealth, and so forth.

Amla is an autumn fruit, and in keeping with harvest and food-abundance themes characteristic of Kartik, on at least one level Amla *pūjā* seems to be a type of "first fruits" celebration. But Amla has larger importance as well. The KMSP describes Amla as a goddess, equating her with Lakshmi and other Vaishnava goddesses (12.99–101). Hence the worship of Amla is another form of honoring and promoting auspiciousness, Lakshmi. Amla is also called Dhatri (*dhātrī*), which means "supporter" or "sustainer." "Dhatri" is an epithet of the goddess Earth, Bhudevi, who, like Lakshmi and Tulsi, is a consort of Vishnu. Amla's fecundity, like that of the Earth, is also restored in the autumn during or around the time of Kartik, when its fruit comes into season. Hence the celebration of Amla during Kartik is analogous to the celebration of the earth's renewed fruitfulness. Another meaning of "dhatri" is "nurse," and in Ayurveda the Amla fruit is said to have healing qualities. In contemporary India, Amla continues to be an important ingredient in Ayurvedic preparations, tonics, and cosmetics.

The KMSP describes Amla as originating at the very begining of the time cycle, when a vast ocean had flooded the worlds. Brahma was performing silent repetition (*japa*) of the names of God (Mahā-Brahman) when tears of love rose in his eyes and fell to the ground; the Amla tree grew from those drops and sprung up laden with fruits (12.10–14). This description of the Amla tree's origin from Brahma's fallen tears echoes the same text's description of the Tulsi's origin from Dhanvantari's tears falling into his pot of nectar. Like Tulsi, Amla also is said to be especially dear to Vishnu, and the text attributes similar merits to the worship of both.

Some sources describe the tenth of Kartik's light fortnight, the day following Navami, as the day that Krishna slew Kamsa, an event commemorated in Mathura with great enthusiasm (Sharma 1978, 116; Gautam 1982, 187). While such a link to sacred history certainly resonates with themes that permeate Kartik, there is no such celebration in Benares. Krishna's victory over Kamsa is, however, reenacted in the Krishna Lila of Tulsi Ghat on the full moon night that marks the end of the month.

Prabodhani Ekadashi and the Tulsi *Vivaha*

The eleventh of Kartik's light fortnight coincides with the beginning of the five-day Bhishmapancak *vrat* and marks a special day of Vishnu worship. Vishnu is the patron deity of every eleventh *tithi*, but the eleventh of Kartik's bright fortnight is especially important, for it marks the last day of Vishnu's slumber during the inauspicious four-month period, or *caturmāsa*, that corresponds roughly to the period of the monsoon rains. The *caturmāsa* begins right after the eleventh of the bright fortnight of Ashadh, a day known as Shayani Ekadashi, "sleeping eleventh." It is believed that on this day Vishnu retires to sleep, floating in a vast ocean on the back of his serpent Ananta. For the duration of his slumber, which lasts for four months, some individuals observe a special *vrat* and abstain from various foods that are prohibited during this time. Vishnu finally awakens from his slumber on the eleventh of Kartik's bright fortnight, Prabodhani Ekadashi or "waking eleventh."[29]

A story narrated in both versions of the Kartik Mahatmya grounds Prabodhani Ekadashi in sacred history as the day of Vishnu's awakening. Once, during the month of Kartik, a demon named Shankha, who is a son of the Ocean, tried to conquer the gods by snatching from them the Vedas, the core scriptures of the Hindu tradition. Fearful, the Vedas ran away and tried to hide in the ocean, but Shankha followed them. The gods approached Vishnu for help; seeing that Vishnu was asleep, they woke him up by singing and playing musical instruments. Vishnu intervened, eventually helping to restore the Vedas to the gods. To commemorate that victory, Vishnu promised that the Vedas would continue to reside in water every year during the month of Kartik (KMPP 3.23; KMSP 13.24ff.). The day on which the gods are said to have woken Vishnu to ask for his help is the day of Prabodhani Ekadashi. This account also reinforces the spiritually meritorious nature of daily bathing during the month, for Kartik bathers receive special benefit from the sanctifying presence of the Vedas residing in the water with which they bathe. This narrative establishes, too, the injunction to worship Vishnu throughout the month of Kartik. Vishnu is said to be pleased with the propitious way in which the gods awoke and therefore decrees that for one month, people should honor him daily with auspicious acts like singing, playing on musical instruments, and the like (KMPP 3.19).[30]

Prabodhani Ekadashi is a special *vrat* day within the larger Kartik *vrat*. On this day, some families in Benares perform a special *pūjā* to celebrate Vishnu's awakening. The notion of divine slumber has come to be extended to other deities as well, especially Shiva, and some Shaiva families in Benares also honor Shiva's awakening on Prabodhani Ekadashi with a special Shaiva *pūjā*. The KMSP proclaims that a fast performed on this day is capable of destroying the accumulated negative effects of one's sins and bringing one prosperity, progeny, knowledge, happiness, and wealth (33.1–8). In addition to fasting, one is also enjoined to remain awake throughout the night, singing and playing instrumental music, reading from the Puranas, making different types of offerings, and showing one's devotion to Vishnu in a variety of ways (33.9ff). In Benares, worshipers gather in Vaishnava temples around the city to spend the night singing devotional songs and engaging in worship.

The awakening of the gods represents a return of auspiciousness after the inauspicious *caturmāsa*. In Benares, as in other parts of North India, Hindus suspend all auspicious life-cycle rituals, such as marriages or religious initiations, during the *caturmāsa*, resuming them only after Prabodhani Ekadashi. The image of Vishnu's awakening from an ocean-borne slumber also suggests renewal and rejuvenation on a cosmic scale. Vishnu sleeps on a vast ocean during the period of dissolution between cycles of creation, too, an image that clearly is evoked in this context. When Vishnu awakens from his cosmic sleep, he ushers in a new cycle of creation. The divine awakening that occurs at the end of the *caturmāsa* partakes of the same symbolism and suggests the rejuvenation of the world. Vishnu's generative ocean-bed also evokes the image of the milk ocean churned by the gods and demons, and the KMSP states explicitly that Vishnu sleeps in the ocean of milk during his four-month slumber (33.28). On the popular level, in fact, no distinction is made between the ocean of milk churned by the gods and demons, the cosmic ocean into which creation continually dissolves and reemerges, and the ocean on which Vishnu sleeps during the *caturmāsa*.

While the gods' awakening gives this day its name, the marriage of Tulsi that takes place on this day is equally, if not more, important. Tulsi, the basil plant honored daily during Kartik, is considered to be a goddess as well as a plant, and in this month she comes to be elevated to the status of God's bride. On the day of Prabodhani Ekadashi, devotees stage a wedding celebration known as Tulsi *vivāha*, "Tulsi's wedding." The KMPP says nothing about Tulsi's wedding, but the KMSP devotes a full chapter to it (chapter 31). Many women perform Tulsi's marriage in their homes, constructing a marriage pavilion in the house or courtyard and decorating it with flowers and stalks of sugar cane, symbolic of the earth's fecundity. The bride and groom are then adorned and placed in the middle of the marriage pavilion. Popular *vrat* manuals suggest that one use a Shaligram stone, a type of stone that is considered a natural form of Vishnu, for the groom, but in Benares women tend to use a small brass image of either Vishnu or Krishna. The pairing of Vishnu and Tulsi, like that of Vishnu and the goddess Earth, Bhudevi, represents an alternative tradition to the standard pairing of Vishnu and Lakshmi and probably has different historical origins. Symbolically, however, Lakshmi, Bhudevi, and Tulsi act in many ways as multiforms of one another. All three embody female powers of fecundity and life-bearing potential. Bhudevi, the goddess Earth, embodies the fertile potential of nature and the gift of abundance. As a plant, Tulsi embodies the manifestation of that potential in vegetation. Predominant interpretations of Tulsi, however, are more expansive, suggesting that Tulsi's powers, like Lakshmi's, promote broad worldly and spiritual auspiciousness.

Figure 14. Preparing Tulsi's wedding in the courtyard of a Benares home

Commingling of traditions pertaining to Vishnu's three wives is apparent in a story that appears in almost identical form in both versions of the Kartik Mahatmya. This narrative tells of battles that take place between the gods and the demon Jalandhara. This story essentially forms a sequel to the battle that took place in conjunction with the churning of the ocean of milk and shares with the churning narrative many underlying themes. Jalandhara is born when Shiva throws into the ocean a flame of fire that emerges from Shiva's third eye when Shiva becomes angry. Brahma performs the necessary birth rituals for the child, names him, and proclaims that he will be invincible to all living beings except Shiva. When Jalandhara grows up, he attains as his bride Vrinda, daughter of the demon Kalanemi, and attains sovereignty over the gods. The demons—who, we are reminded, had been defeated by the gods at the time of the milk ocean's churning—now become emboldened and come to the earth to serve their new ruler.

Jalandhara comes to learn about the churning of the milk ocean and the gods' seizure of the jewels and other items of value that emerged from it. The ocean of milk is identified as Jalandhara's oceanic father, and upon hearing of the churning, Jalandhara becomes angry and demands that all things of value taken from his father by the gods be returned immediately. When the gods do not comply, Jalandhara declares war on them. Vishnu fights on behalf of the gods, but Vishnu's wife, Lakshmi, extracts from him a promise that he will not kill Jalandhara. Lakshmi, who was born from the ocean of milk at the time of its churning, considers Jalandhara to be her brother, and she recoils at the thought of her husband killing her brother. Vishnu, furthermore, does not want to dishonor Shiva, from whose part Jalandhara was born, by killing him. So Jalandhara vanquishes the gods and begins to rule over the three worlds.

Jalandhara, however, comes to desire Shiva's wife, Parvati, and he wages a new war on Shiva to attain her. The fight drags on, and Vishnu comes to realize that Jalandhara cannot be killed because of the virtue of his wife Vrinda. Vrinda is a *pativratā*, a devoted and chaste wife, and the spiritual powers attained by a *pativratā* are capable of increasing her husband's lifespan. As long as Vrinda remains chaste, Jalandhara will remain unvanquished, so Vishnu tricks Vrinda by coming to her in the form of Jalandhara and making love with her. Once this happens, Jalandhara becomes vulnerable, and Shiva is able to kill him. Here, as in the narrative of the milk ocean's churning, the demons are vanquished through Vishnu's intervention, manifest in both cases in Vishnu's power to perpetuate illusion.

When Vrinda learns of Vishnu's deception, she curses Vishnu and performs self-immolation (*satī*) by entering fire. Vishnu has become infatuated with Vrinda and is devastated by her death; he covers himself with her ashes and refuses to move. The gods appeal to the Great Goddess to wield her nature as illusion (*māyā*) to dispel Vishnu's grief. She produces three seeds that represent the three qualities (*guṇa*s) she embodies as Mulaprakriti, "Primordial Matter": purity (*sattva*), activity (*rajas*), and lethargy (*tamas*).[31] Jasmine (Malati), Tulsi, and Amla are born from the three seeds. Tulsi is widely regarded as a form of Vrinda and a goddess who embodies Vrinda's qualities of wifely devotion.

A different version of this narrative occurs in Padma Purana 6.3–19, where the ocean of milk plays a larger role. During the battle between gods and demons, the deity Brihaspati continually restores to life gods killed in battle with herbs taken from Drona Mountain, which this version of the narrative explicitly locates in the ocean of milk. Jalandhara appeals to the milk ocean to drown Brihaspati, but his appeal is unheeded. Hence Jalandhara resorts to kicking Drona Mountain, which retreats to the netherworld, pledging to return only when Jalandhara has vanquished his enemies (6.8). The life-restoring herbs of the Drona Mountain bear obvious resemblance to the nectar borne in narratives of the milk ocean's churning by Dhanvantari, who, like Brihaspati, has healing powers. As in the churning narrative, too, the gods are unable to defeat their adversaries without the life-promoting substance hidden within the ocean of milk, so Jalandhara takes over the worlds. Vishnu goes to live in the ocean of milk, where he resumes his reclining position (6.7.84–86, 6.10.23).

Jalandhara wages a second battle against Shiva and tries to steal Parvati by disguising himself as Shiva. Vishnu is roused from his oceanic rest by an intuition that something is amiss, and he dispatches Garuda to find out what is happening on the battlefield. When Garuda discovers Jalandhara trying to seduce Parvati, he implores Vishnu to steal away Jalandhara's wife Vrinda. Using his power of illusion (*yogamāyā*), Vishnu leaves Lakshmi lying on their oceanic bed and takes up another form to find Vrinda and sleep with her. As in accounts of the churning of the milk ocean, here too Vishnu abandons his oceanic rest when demonic forces threaten divine rule, entering into the fray in order to help restore divine dominion. Here, however, the end of Vishnu's rest on the milk ocean is followed closely by his sexual union with Vrinda, said to be another form of Tulsi—a sequence of events strikingly similar to Vishnu's awakening and then marriage to Tulsi celebrated on Prabodhani Ekadashi.[32]

Like the time of the milk ocean's churning, the *caturmāsa* period of the monsoon is transitional and ambiguous; while gods and demons join together as partners or battle as enemies, or while deities sleep, Vishnu's dominion and his securing of Lakshmi—embodied in rain and the earth's fecundity—are not assured. The divine marriage that takes place on Prabodhani Ekadashi, like the ultimate union of Vishnu and Lakshmi in marriage recounted in many versions of the churning narrative, suggests the (re)establishment of both auspiciousness and Vishnu's sovereignty in his realm, the three worlds, following the dangerous and inauspicious monsoon period.

The Devi-Bhagavata Purana (9.17–25) recounts a version of Jalandhara narrative that gives the story a Krishnaite twist. The text describes Tulsi as an incarnation of Lakshmi, born in a fully mature form on the night of Kartik's full moon. Tulsi marries the king of the demons, here named Shankhacuda and identified as the incarnation of Krishna's dearest childhood friend, Sudama. It is said that both Tulsi and Sudama had in their former lives dwelled in Krishna's heaven, Goloka, but through Radha's curse had been compelled to take human births. Brahma promises Tulsi that after her marriage to Shankhacuda she will attain Krishna as her husband, which is Tulsi's ultimate goal.

Like Jalandhara, Shankhacuda attains dominion over the gods and other beings. And as in the other versions of the narrative, the demon's ascendancy leads to a battle between divine and demonic forces that results in the gods' victory only after Vishnu deceives Tulsi, taking the form of her husband and making love with her. Upon his death, Shankhacuda is instantly reborn in Krishna's heaven as the loyal Sudama, with his bones becoming conch shells (*śaṅkha*). Conch shells are broadly used in Vaishnava worship. Tulsi curses Vishnu to become a stone, which results in his manifestation as the Shaligram, the stone considered to be a natural form of Vishnu and which is said to be found only in the Gandaki River. Vishnu invites Tulsi to become his wife, proclaiming that her body will become the Gandaki River itself, with her hair becoming sacred trees. Enumerating the auspicious and purifying qualities of Tulsi leaves and plants, Vishnu proclaims that she will remain in Goloka, Krishna's heaven, as his wife and presiding deity but will remain on earth in the form of the Tulsi plant. She finally leaves her mortal form and, assuming a divine form, takes residence in Vishu's breast along with Lakshmi.

While Tulsi weilds powers of healing and purification, in these narratives it is clearly her status as bride and wife that comes to the fore. In the Devi-Bhagavata Purana, it is distinctly Krishna, not Vishnu, whom Tulsi seeks as her husband, declaring Krishna to be more pleasing to her than Vishnu. In Benares, perspectives on Tulsi's identity include both the view that Tulsi weds Vishnu and the view that Tulsi is one of the many wives that Krishna attains after taking up his princely life in Dvaraka.

Vaikunth Caturdashi

The fourteenth of Kartik's light fortnight is known as Vaikunth Caturdashi, "Heaven Fourteenth." Vaikunth is Vishnu's heavenly realm, and popular belief holds that the doors to Vaikunth are thrown open on this day to allow free passage inside to the souls of all those who maintain a *vrat* on this day. Two weeks earlier, on Narak

Caturdashi, the doors of hell are opened to allow souls safe passage out of the netherworld, and the opening of heaven's doors on the fourteenth of Kartik's light fortnight marks symmetry between Kartik's two "fourteenths" (*cāturdaśī*). One informant highlighted the relationship between the two, remarking that the souls who had left hell two weeks earlier could now be welcomed into heaven.

A story in the KMSP (chap. 35) that several informants also narrated to me, albeit in varying forms, recounts that Vishnu once came to Benares on the day of Vaikunth Caturdashi to worship Shiva. During the period just before sunrise (*brahma-muhūrta*), he bathed at Manikarnika Ghat, a *ghāṭ* in Benares located a short distance away from Pancaganga Ghat that is dedicated to the burning of corpses. He then went to the Vishvanath Temple to worship Shiva, taking along a thousand golden lotuses to use in his worship. Wishing to test Vishnu's devotion, Shiva secretly stole away one of the lotuses. When Vishnu discovered the missing flower, rather than interrupt his worship, he plucked out one of his own lotuslike eyes to replace it. Pleased with Vishnu's devotion, Shiva gave him the discus Sudarshana to use as a weapon against unruly demons and declared that on this day, Vishnu should be worshiped before Shiva.[33]

In Benares, both the thirteenth and fourteenth of Kartik's bright fortnight are considered particularly important days to do *pūjā* at the Bindu Madhava temple at Pancaganga Ghat. Outside the temple, merchants sell cream, flowers, fruit, and other delicacies suitable for offering to the deity, while inside, thousands of votaries fight their way through the densely packed temple to worship Bindu Madhava and get his *darśan*. On the mornings of both days, too, crowds of votaries gather at the edge of Pancaganga Ghat to burn ghee lamps and offer Tulsi leaves into the Ganges River while chanting the thousand names of Vishnu or the mantra "*Oṁ viṣṇāve namaḥ*" ("Om, reverence to Vishnu"). On the fourteenth, they then proceed to the Vishvanath temple to worship Shiva with Bel or Tulsi leaves.

Kartik Purnima

While celebration of light persists throughout the whole month of Kartik, it is especially prominent on this final night of the month, Kartik's full-moon night, as it is during Kojagari *pūjā*, which falls at the beginning of the month, and Diwali, which falls in the month's middle. Kartik Purnima is also known in Benares as "Diwali of the Gods" (Dev-Diwali), and it is celebrated in grand style. As the full moon rises over the Ganges, hundreds of thousands of lamps light up the *ghāṭ*s up and

Figure 15. Crowd of votaries at Pancaganga Ghat

down the river along the edge of the city, and boatloads of spectators float along the Ganges' waters to enjoy the remarkable sight. Kartik Purnima is also the single most popular day of the year for bathing in the Ganges, especially at Pancaganga Ghat, since ritual bathing on this day is thought to be extraordinarily meritorious, as are gifting (especially of cows), feeding brahmins, fasting, and other religious activities.

The KMSP and other sources explain the lighting of lamps on this night in relation to Shiva's victory over the Tripuras, three demons set on destroying the three worlds (KMSP 35.33–42). The Bhagavata Purana recounts that Shiva attacks the demon armies of the Tripuras, killing many of them, but the master craftsman Maya revives the demons by placing their bodies in a pond of nectar (*amṛta*), an image that clearly evokes the story of the milk ocean's churning. The role played by the immortality-granting nectar in this story is analogous to that played by the life-giving herbs supplied to the gods in the Jalandhara narrative. Learning of Maya's trick, Vishnu and Brahma take the form of a cow and calf and, going to the demons' domain, they drink up all the nectar. Deprived of the life-giving liquid, the demons become powerless against the gods, and Shiva completely destroys their abodes (Bhagavata Purana 7.10.53–70). The lighting of lamps on this day is said to commemorate lamp offerings that the gods made to Shiva as a way of celebrating his victory (KSMP 35.38). In particular, it is advised that one offer a lamp of 720 wicks, which *Ramanand Prakash*, the booklet published at the Shri Math on Pancaganga Ghat, describes as representing the 360 days and nights of the year, recalling the New Year symbolism surrounding Diwali. Like the account of the milk ocean's churning, the story of Shiva's victory is one of divine securing of nectar, defeat of demonic forces, and cosmic renewal.

Vishnu also figures prominently on this holiday. According to both Kartik Mahatmyas, Vishnu assumed his fish incarnation (*matsya avatāra*) on this day (KMPP 8.17, KMSP 34.28).[34] The Devi-Bhagavata Purana describes this as the night when Krishna's *rāsa-līlā* took place, an assertion that persists in some contemporary sources, and claims that the Ganges herself first appeared in Krishna's dance circle, the *rāsa-maṇḍala*, on the night of Kartik Purnima. The text claims that while Krishna worshiped Radha on this night, Sarasvati and Shiva began to sing, and all the gods became enchanted by the singing. When they came to their senses, they saw that everything had become deluged with water, for Radha and Krishna had taken on the form of liquid and had become the Ganges. They are transformed into the Ganges, we are told, for the sake of humans—presumably so that humans may bathe in the Ganges to be cleansed of their sins and to attain liberation. Krishna and Radha ultimately return to their anthropomorphic forms and continue their *rāsa* dance, but the goddess Ganges is said to remain in the *rāsa* circle on Kartik's full-moon night (Devi-Bhagavata Purana 9.12). She is described here as one of Vishnu's wives, along with Lakshmi, Tulsi, and Sarasvati.[35]

The month ends where it begins, with light, the full moon, and the *rāsa-līlā*, bringing us in a full circle back to erotic dance and liquid flow. Indeed, the term *rāsa-līlā* is probably derived from the term *rasa* (Hawley 1981, 162–63), whose meanings include """juice,""sap," or "liquid." *Rasa* is stuff that flows, and on this night the gods flow, nectar flows, Radha-Krishna flow, and the Ganges flows in the *rāsa maṇḍala*. *Rasa* is also a term for nectar, which is often called *rasāmṛta*, "the juice of *amṛta*." *Rasa* can also refer to intoxicating drink; in this sense it is analogous to *soma*, the intoxicating Vedic libation that is also an allomorph of nectar.

The image of Radha and Krishna becoming rivers and flowing into one another on the night of Kartik Purnima has obvious sexual connotations, for it suggests a commingling of male and female bodies. The liquidy flow of their divine bodies echoes the flow of nectar that starts on Sharat Purnima, the full-moon night with which the month begins, and the flowing of generative fluids that emerge from human male and female bodies. Wendy Doniger O'Flaherty has noted deep connections in Vedic texts of *rasa* and *soma*—both of which are forms of nectar (*amṛta*)—with semen and milk, which in turn are allomorphs of one another (O'Flaherty 1980, 17-28). Like semen, milk is considered a generative fluid and in some contexts is directly analogous to male seed (43). The narrative of the churning of the ocean of milk is suggestive of milk's generative capacities, which in this narrative take on a cosmic dimension. All these flowing liquids suggest the auspicious power that Kartik as a whole embodies.

Butter, Krishna's favorite food, is also symbolic of auspicious and generative sexual fluids. Butter comes from milk, of course, but butter connotes semen as well. The image of churning—which in the narrative of the milk ocean produces nectar, Lakshmi, and the other precious "jewels"—is also used to describe the production of semen (O'Flaherty 1980, 27–30; Hawley 1983, 292–93). In Krishna devotion, butter also embodies the feelings of love characteristic of devotional experience and embodied by Krishna himself. Devotional love in turn is strongly associated with *rasa*. Sanskrit poetics identifies several basic moods, called *bhāvas*, that poetry or art may evoke; the spectator or listener experiences these as subjectively felt aesthetic emotions, called *rasas*. The *rasa*s are reconfigured in Krishna devotional traditions to embody and express devotional emotions experienced by devotees. In Krishna devotion, the term *bhāva* comes to refer to the devotee's worshipful attitude, while *rasa* refers to the joyful experience of the love relationship between a human being and Krishna (Toomey 1990, 161).

Krishna devotion selects from aesthetic theory emotions that are patterned after identifiable human relationships. The devotional appropriation of aesthetic conceptions of the *bhāva*s and *rasa*s is codified in Bengali Vaishnavism, most especially in the works of the theologian Rupa Goswami. Five *bhāva*s, with their accompanying *rasa*s, come to the fore: the peaceful (*sānta*) *bhāva*, which emphasizes the experience of Krishna as Supreme Being; the *bhāva* of servitude (*dāsya*), where one experiences him as a master to be served; the *bhāva* of friendship (*sakhya*), where he is approached and loved as one's coequal friend; the *bhāva* of parental affection (*vātsalya*), where one assumes the role of a loving and nurturing elder caring for Krishna as a child; and the amourous (*mādhurya*, *śṛṅgāra*) *bhāva*, in which one envisions Krishna as an erotically appealing male lover (Toomey 1990, 161; Haberman 1988, 52–57). These last two *bhāva*s and their attendant *rasa*s are the ones that come to the fore in the women's devotions to Krishna that take place throughout the month.

Like the lunar nectar that flows on Kartik's full moons and throughout the month, *rasa* also flows: in the silent, gentle rain of moon nectar, the fluid bodies of Radha and Krishna commingling in liquid form, and the devotional love for Krishna that flows in the hearts of devotees. Like *rasa,* the Ganges flows as well—not only on the night of Kartik Purnima, in the circle of the *rāsa-maṇḍala,* but daily, too, at the edge of the city of Benares. Religious devotion, the *rāsa-līlā,* devotional love, sexuality, and auspiciousness all merge and flow through the practice of Benarsi women's Kartik *pūjā,* performed throughout the month on the *ghāṭ*s that run the length of the city along the Ganges' bank. This *pūjā* is the subject of the next chapter.

Chapter 3

Adoring Krishna at the River's Edge: The Practice of Kartik *Pūjā*

> I have been doing Kartik bathing since my childhood, and I used to go regularly for the *pūjā*. I started when I was two years old with my grandmother. I went with her, and by going there and listening, I learned it. So when I came to this house after marriage, there was a tradition that daughters-in-law were not supposed to go outside. So I was not able to go for a while, while my in-laws were alive. After they died, I started doing it again. That was ten years ago.
>
> Muneshvari Devi, Kartik *pūjā* participant from Benares

Prologue

I was sitting on Muneshvari Devi's couch, drinking tea and eating the sweets that she had placed before me as she answered my questions, my tape recorder picking up her words. Muneshvari Devi was one of the women who became to me what is commonly known in ethnographic circles as a "principal informant," a knowledgeable "native" willing to spend time with the researcher explaining the things that the researcher (in this case me) wants to know about. And at this moment, I was asking her about her participation in women's Kartik *pūjā*.

If you have been to the *ghāṭ*s in Benares at morning time during the month of Kartik, you may have noticed the large groups of women that congregate daily by the river's edge to perform Kartik *pūjā*. Then again, if, like me, you tend to be a late riser, you may well have missed the scene entirely, since most of the groups are gone by shortly after sunrise. Although both men and women may engage in ritual bathing and other practices associated with the Kartik *vrat*, this *pūjā* is exclusively for women. Not all female Kartik votaries participate in Kartik *pūjā*, but, as far as I could observe, all Kartik *pūjā* participants are female Kartik votaries.

After bathing in the Ganges River as part of their Kartik *vrat*, *pūjā* participants gather together on the *ghāṭ*s and construct several icons out of Ganges mud. Forming a circle around the icons, they perform *pūjā* while singing devotional songs, called *bhajan*s, particular to this occasion. Many deities are represented and honored, but several songs sung during the *pūjā* focus specifically on Krishna, and a number of informants told me that the *pūjā* is dedicated to Krishna with other deities called to be present chiefly so that they, too, can participate as devotees.

More than half of the Kartik *pūjā* participants I interviewed indicated they consider Kartik *pūjā* to be in some way related to Krishna's *rāsa-līlā*. Some participants maintained that the *rāsa-līlā* took place during the entire month of Kartik, not just the first or last days, and hence ascribed to it special importance throughout the month. Some participants described Kartik *pūjā* as a version of the *rāsa-līlā* transfigured into *pūjā* form, or as a form of worship enacted in commemoration of the earthly *rāsa-līlā* performed in Braj in ancient times. In interviews, a number of informants compared their role in the *pūjā* to that of the cowherdesses, or *gopī*s, who took part in *rāsa-līlā*. Elements of the *pūjā* also suggest this association. Songs sung during the *pūjā*, for example, often invoke the term *sakhī*, "female friend," a term used to refer to Radha's faithful servants who accompany and serve the divine couple Radha-Krishna, and in Kartik *pūjā* circles women refer to themselves and each other with the same term. Popular Krishna traditions equate Radha's *sakhī*s with the *gopī*s, and *pūjā* participants generally do the same.

But what, exactly, should be included under the rubric *rāsa-līlā* in this case? On one level, of course, the term refers to the famous circle dance of Krishna mythology, and this dance is considered by many Kartik *pūjā* participants to be the model for the *pūjā*. Just as the *gopī*s or *sakhī*s gathered around Krishna in a circle in the original circle dance, so Kartik *pūjā* participants gather in a circle around icons of Krishna and other deities; and just as the *gopī*s adored Krishna with song and dance, *pūjā* participants worship him with song and devotional offerings. Muneshvari Devi, who is cited at the very beginning of this chapter, explained it to me this way:

> Krishna-jī did *rāsa-līlā* with the *sakhī*s, and that is why all we *sakhī*s get together and make God (Bhagavan) and put Him in

> the middle. . . . Whatever they did in the past, we are doing the same thing in the *pūjā*. . . . In reality, we cannot get Lord Krishna himself, so we do this. It is the very same thing (as *rāsa-līlā*). God is in the middle, and we are doing *rāsa-līlā* all around him. We say we are Krishna's *sakhī*s and we are doing *rāsa-līlā*.

It was not uncommon, however, for informants to use the term "*rāsa-līlā*" to refer not only to the specific episode of the circle dance, but also to Krishna's entire youthful life in Vrindavan or even his entire life on earth.[1] Some insisted that most or all of the major events of his life occurred during the month of Kartik. Knowing that, for example, Krishna's birthday is celebrated in Benares as elsewhere on the eighth day of the waning fortnight of the month of Bhadrapad, I pursued this point with Lilavati, the first woman I had ever spoken with about Kartik *pūjā* and who had participated in the tradition for many years before deteriorating health had compelled her to give it up. Lilavati explained:

> Krishna was born on the eighth of Bhado (Bhadrapad), but he took another birth in Kartik to perform his *līlā*. So he was born in this month of Kartik, he killed all the demons in this month, he "met" with Radha, and he did *rāsa-līlā*. God did every kind of *līlā* in this month.[2]

Some informants also insisted that every year Krishna spends Kartik in Benares, recreating various aspects of his long-ago *līlā* on the banks of the Ganges. One elderly, high-caste woman who lives on Tulsi Ghat, for example, told me that during Kartik, Radha and the *sakhī*s come to Benares to bathe in the Ganges and sleep by the river's edge, and Krishna stays in Benares to watch over them.

When speaking of Kartik *pūjā* as a practice that imitates or commemorates the *rāsa-līlā*, many informants seemed to have in mind notions of *rāsa-līlā* as referring to not only the famous circle dance, here understood to include both Radha and a host of *gopī*-girlfriends, but also the sum total of all the events of Krishna's early life in Braj leading up to his departure for Dvaraka. Informants also tended to speak of their role in the *pūjā* in relation to both these levels of meaning. Like other forms of Krishna worship, Kartik *pūjā* invites worshipers to envision themselves as participants in Krishna's divine *līlā* and assume the role of his original devotees. In this case, it is specifically the *gopī*s who serve as role models for *pūjā* participants: participants express their devotion to Krishna by replicating the caring bonds that

Krishna shared with the women who loved him during his sojourn on earth in ancient times. The love that the *gopīs* lavished on Krishna in ancient times thus becomes for many *pūjā* participants the prototype for the love they lavish on him in the *pūjā* circle.

I have noted that Bengali Vaishnavism details five basic devotional attitudes and experiences (*bhāva*s and *rasa*s) foundational to Krishna worship. Various legendary characters prominent in Krishna mythology are said to exemplify each of these *bhāva*s. North Indian Vaishnava theologies have upheld the *gopīs* as ideal exemplars of spiritual intimacy with Krishna especially through the amorous (*mādhurya, śṛṅgāra*) devotional sentiment. As models of amorousness, however, the *gopīs* evoke more than one relational possibility. Rupa Gosvamin, a well-known and influential theologian of Bengali Vaishnavism, details two ways that one might experience the amorous sentiment: through direct sexual enjoyment of Krishna, or through vicarious sexual enjoyment of Krishna. Both are models of devotion that human devotees may imitate. In the first case, the practitioner takes on the role of Krishna's lover directly, but in the second, the practitioner assumes a less direct role as the friend or *sakhī* of Krishna's lover, whose sexual engagement with Krishna the practitioner witnesses as a supportive spectator. The former stance is modeled by Radha and some principal *gopīs*, and the latter is modeled by a different type of figure, the *sakhī* or female friend who serves the divine couple but does not strive to enjoy Krishna's sexual embrace directly (Haberman 1988, 81).

None of my informants drew any such distinctions between principal *gopī* and *sakhī*; they used the terms *gopī* and *sakhī* interchangeably. But neither did any of them explicitly describe to me her role in the *pūjā* in terms that emphasized direct sexual enjoyment of Krishna. Some informants denied that Krishna's relationship with the *gopīs* had an explicitly sexual dimension to it. One, for example, insisted that the *rāsa-līlā* involved no sexual congress whatsoever between Krishna and the *gopīs*, remarking, "Whatever *rāsa-līlā* God did, people misinterpret it. *Rāsa-līlā* is a very pure thing. It is just an attitude of love (*prem bhāv*). . . . It is only singing and dancing in the form of devotion, just to please Krishna." It was in fact not uncommon for informants to emphasize singing and dancing as the essence of *rāsa-līlā*.

On the other hand, I observed a lot of sexual joking during the course of the *pūjā*, and other participants not only acknowledged, but also even delighted in describing accounts of Radha and the *gopīs*' sexual intimacy with Krishna. But, while they did not deny the sexual dimension of the *gopīs*' relationship with Krishna, neither did they emphasize it in this context as terribly relevant for *human* devotional posturing. Instead, they spoke overwhelmingly of their own devotional role as contemporary *sakhīs* in terms of loving service (*sevā*), and they tended to stress the *emotional*, not sexual, nature of the *gopīs*' attachment to Krishna as exemplifying devotional ideals. If we understand *mādhurya* as embracing both the emotional and physical dimensions of erotic relationality, then we might say that *pūjā* participants tend to stress the emotional over the physical in speaking of their own erotic stance toward Krishna. None of the women with whom I spoke, furthermore, ever claimed any ability to witness Radha's and Krishna's love play. Instead, informants who addressed this issue tended to stress the ultimately unknowable nature of God's action, noting that while "it is said" that Krishna made love with Radha and the *gopīs*, no one could ever know for sure if this was indeed true.

My findings in this regard contrast with what John S. Hawley has observed in the poetry of Mirabai, the famous female Krishna devotee of sixteenth-century Rajasthan. Hawley notes that Mirabai portrays herself as Krishna's bride, depicting her intimacy with Krishna as "on par with and perhaps in the same world as the *gopīs*" (1986, 241). The difference between Mirabai's devotional stance and that of the women with whom I participated in Kārtik *pūjā* may be attributable to life circumstances; Mirabai allegedly chose to reject family ties to devote herself entirely to Krishna, whereas most of the women who participate in Kartik *pūjā* have human husbands (or anticipate having human husbands) toward whom they direct their erotic energies. The difference may also have something to do with Hindu reform movements of the nineteenth and early twentieth centuries, which formed in response to colonial British criticisms of Indian cultural and religious formations. Reformers tended to be highly critical of elements of Hinduism that they perceived to be crude or unsophisticated, including the sexual aspects of Krishna traditions. It could be that such criticisms have affected the way that contemporary Hindu women consciously perceive the devotional implications of the *gopīs*' erotic stance toward Krishna.[3] Furthermore, in contemporary North India, traditional Hindu morality concerning women's behavior favors chastity, sexual modesty, and service (*sevā*) to others, and it may be that an emphasis on these values makes imagery of sexual congress less overtly attractive to women as a devotional paradigm than some Sanskritic theologies might lead one to believe. Nonetheless, suggestions of physical intimacy do indeed permeate narrative traditions pertaining to Krishna and the *gopīs* and are undeniably part of this tradition of women's worship.

In Kartik *pūjā,* to imitate the *gopīs* also means to assume a parental (*vātsalya*) posture. While Krishna's foster mother Yashodha is the ideal exemplar of the parental sentiment, the many *gopīs* who cared for Krishna as a child, fed him, played with him, and adored him as if he were their own child, also exemplify this devotional stance. Devotion to Krishna in his child form thrives throughout North India; not only is it common in popular religious practice, but it is especially prominent in the Pushtimarg tradition, a sectarian form of Krishna devotion based on the teachings of the theologian Vallabhacarya. The emphasis placed on devotion to the child Krishna in Kartik *pūjā,* while not extraordinary in the context of Hindu devotional religion, clearly reflects the social and emotional significance that Hindu women living in North India tend to attribute to motherhood and the raising of children, especially sons.

The practice of Kartik *pūjā* continuously juxtaposes and mixes amorous and maternal devotional sentiments, both of which are encompassed by a larger diffuse emphasis on loving care and service, all directed toward the same male devotional object, Krishna. In exploring the world of Kartik *pūjā* in this chapter, I highlight the ways that amorous and maternal relationality are continuously brought together. This blending of maternal and amorous emotions has specific social and psychological resonance for Hindu women, as I will discuss further in chapter 4.

Within this form of ritual worship, the parental dimension of devotion entails not just nurturing Krishna from childhood to adulthood, but also fulfilling parental responsibility through the arrangement and execution of Krishna's marriage. The bride in question here, however, is not, as one might suspect, Radha: it is Tulsi. Tulsi is of course important throughout Kartik, in terms of both ritual, the lighting of lamps each night at the base of a Tulsi plant during the month, and narrative, as God's bride born from the milk ocean when Dhanvantari's tears fall into the pot of nectar held in his hands. As noted earlier, the KMSP clearly understands Tulsi's groom to be Vishnu and portrays Tulsi as Lakshmi's co-wife. Several high-caste, religiously educated Benarsi men who discussed Tulsi's marriage with me insisted that Tulsi's groom is Vishnu. But the Devi-Bhagavata Purana associates Tulsi with Krishna, not Vishnu, and for many of the women of Benares, on the day of Prabodhani Ekadashi, Tulsi is wed not to Vishnu, but to Krishna. Such a distinction might at first appear trivial: Krishna and Vishnu are, after all, different forms of the same deity, and the votaries with whom I interacted often referred to Krishna, Vishnu, and Ram interchangeably as "Bhagavan" (Lord or God). However, the women who perform the marriage are quite clear about the groom's identity, and in this context no other form of God will do.[4]

Susan Sered (1992) has observed that in religious traditions that accord more institutionalized power to men than to women, women find a variety of strategies for constructing a meaningful religious life, including the selective appropriation and reinterpretation of normative traditions. In Kartik *pūjā,* women appropriate the month's association with auspiciousness and renewal in ways that highlight what is important to them not only religiously, but also socially, especially marriage and motherhood. In seeing the divine wedding as Krishna's marriage, not Vishnu's, women create an emotionally rich and satisfying context in which this can be accomplished. Vishnu is a regal deity who tends to be distant and somewhat aloof from human devotees, male and female alike. Krishna, on the other hand, is eminently accessible and approachable. He incarnates in human form, and Krishna mythology is filled with stories about his childhood and his relationships with the numerous women who adore him. Furthermore, Krishna devotional traditions invite devotees to identify with characters from Krishna's life story, and they encourage emotional intimacy with Krishna; it is much harder to cozy up to Vishnu. In Kartik *pūjā,* normative traditions concerning both Krishna and Kartik meet and mingle, and in the process, both are transformed.

For many of the women who participate in the *pūjā,* the marriage of Tulsi and Krishna is inextricably woven into the devotional fabric of Kartik as a whole. In addition to likening Kartik *pūjā* to *rāsa-līlā,* for example, some informants also claimed that this *pūjā* imitates a *pūjā* that Tulsi herself performed in ancient times to win Krishna as a husband. Others interpreted food restrictions associated with the Kartik *vrat* as commemorating the fast that Tulsi undertook in ancient times to attain Krishna as a husband. One informant described the festivities associated with Sharat Purnima, the full-moon night that ushers in the month of Kartik, as a celebration of Tulsi's engagement to Krishna, interpreting the sharing of consecrated food (*prasād*) that the holiday entails as an act of sealing Tulsi's engagement to her future husband. It is in the context of the daily women's *pūjā,* however, that traditions concerning Krishna's marriage to Tulsi find their fullest expression.

While Tulsi's importance here is undeniable, she does not fully displace Radha, for the passion that Radha and Krishna share never leaves the ritual circle even as Krishna prepares to meet his leafy bride under their bamboo wedding canopy. Narrative logic informed by the constraints that govern earthly human experience might relegate Radha and Tulsi to different times and places, refusing them shared space;

but such logic does not hold in the devotional sphere, where other logics are at work. Religious traditions may embrace logical inconsistencies when it comes to representations of the Divine, often by invoking the claim that the Divine realm transcends mortal rules and mortal comprehension.

In Kartik *pūjā,* the ring of *sakhī*s facilitates simultaneously both the love play of Krishna and Radha and the marriage of Krishna and Tulsi. Sudhir Kakar notes that for most Hindus the story of Radha and Krisha's love is "less a story remembered than a random succession of episodes seen and heard, sung and danced" (1986, 75), and such episodes acquire a life of their own, combining and recombining in ritual practice with other episodes, other stories, other loves. The logic of devotion here makes room for both Radha and Tulsi. And both goddesses claim their place in the center of the ritual circle.

Setting the Stage, and a Tale of Two Votaries

I participated in Kartik *pūjā* during three years, 1995, 1997, and 1998. There was only one year (1997) when I attended the *pūjā* daily right from the beginning of the month to the end. During the other two years, I was able to attend only fifteen to twenty days of the *pūjā* cycle. When I first began research on Kartik *pūjā* in 1995, I participated in the *pūjā* with a group that met on Tulsi Ghat. Although the *pūjā* takes place on *ghāṭ*s all over the city, participating women tend to go to a *ghāṭ* that is conveniently located with respect to their homes. Tulsi Ghat was a brief walk from the house I was living in, so I continued to do *pūjā* there. Some of the women in my group were from the area around Tulsi Ghat, but most of them were from Kojva, a neighborhood about one or two kilometers west of Tulsi Ghat. The women from Kojva all knew each other, and some of them were close friends outside of the *pūjā.*

When I returned in 1997, I found that the group had split, and a good number of the regular participants had started a new group on a neighboring *ghāṭ*, Assi Ghat. I was told that the reason for the split was the desire of some, but not others, to shift to the larger *ghāṭ* (Assi Ghat is much larger than Tulsi Ghat), since many more *pūjā* groups meet there and the atmosphere is more festive. There may have been other reasons for the split, but if so, I was not able to discover them. What the split meant for me was that either I would have to choose between the two groups, which would certainly alienate those in the group I abandoned, or I would have to try to participate in both. In

1997, I opted for the latter solution. Luckily, the group on Tulsi Ghat tended to meet earlier than the group on Assi Ghat, which meant that I was often able to complete one full round of *pūjā* at Tulsi Ghat before going to the other group and finishing their *pūjā* with them. On several occasions, however, I simply skipped one or the other group. This offended some women in both groups who felt that splitting my time demonstrated a lack of loyalty to their group, but at the time it seemed to me to be a good compromise. In 1998, my research goals included collecting several hours of video footage of the *pūjā*, so I opted to work almost entirely with the group at Assi Ghat for the sake of visual continuity and image quality: since this group tended to begin the *pūjā* later, more of the *pūjā* took place after sunrise, meaning that I could film in the light.

In the course of my research I formally interviewed women from the *pūjā* groups at both Assi Ghat and Tulsi Ghat, and I asked several women from both venues for help in clarifying song texts and explaining to me the *pūjā* and its meaning. In addition, my research associate, Sunita Singh, attended the *pūjā* on Kedar Ghat on several occasions, and we interviewed participants in that *pūjā* group as well. My discussion of Kartik *pūjā* in this chapter draws on these materials and on my participant observations of the *pūjā* on both Assi Ghat and Tulsi Ghat.

In describing the *pūjā*, I translate texts of several of the songs that are sung daily in the *pūjā* circle. It was a challenge for me to arrive at a single version of these songs from the recordings I made. When we listened to my tape recordings, often neither I nor the native Benarsis with whom I consulted could figure out exactly what we were hearing, and even when we did, what was being sung sometimes did not make sense to us. During the *pūjā* itself, several women would be singing at once, sometimes out of synch with one another, sometimes singing different versions of the same song, sometimes humming when they didn't know or couldn't remember the words. Songs would often be sung differently on different days, and, as one informant was quick to point out to me when I asked her about the songs, "There are many words that we (*pūjā* participants) don't understand; we just sing them." There are no critical editions of these song texts, but to arrive at versions that reflected at least some kind of limited consensus, I relied on extensive consultation with a few key informants who were long-term, experienced participants, including two women, Kusumlata and Hem Kumari, whom I describe briefly below. The song texts I have translated in this chapter, therefore, are, in a sense, artificial versions cooked up in sitting rooms and on rooftops all around Benares. I highly doubt that any of the Kartik votaries with whom I performed *pūjā* would be disturbed or shocked by these versions of the song texts, but they well might change a verse here, a word there. In describing the *pūjā*, I offer interpretive comments that reflect not only my own thoughts about these songs, but also the perspectives of several *pūjā* participants who took the time to highlight for me what they perceive to be the most important elements of the songs and explain to me their meaning. I do this knowing that other participants might not agree with these interpretations. Finally, I have chosen to emphasize clarity of meaning over literal translation in my renditions of the songs, but I have appended the original song texts for those who may wish to consult them.

Most of my informants were middle class, although some of them were from poor families. All were high- or middle-caste. When asked, informants tended to insist that caste is no bar to participation in the *pūjā*, and one informant claimed that our *pūjā* group on Tulsi Ghat included low-caste and Untouchable women. If this was indeed true, I was not able to verify it. Only one informant stated unequivocally that low-caste and Untouchable women would not be welcome. In any case, I personally never encountered any participants from the lower castes in my Kartik *pūjā* groups or in the course of my interviews. I suspect that prejudice against low-caste individuals may have been stronger than most of my informants were willing to admit to me, and it is likely that women from such castes would not feel welcome, although many participants claimed that women of any caste could (and should) participate in the *pūjā*.

My informants included unmarried girls, married women, divorcees, and widows. Most of the women with whom I spoke understood the *pūjā* as an expression of both their religious devotion (*bhakti*) and their duty as women (*dharma*), including duty to both family and God. Several insisted that participation in Kartik *pūjā* is really most important for unmarried girls, who perform the *pūjā* to attain a husband like Krishna. Others, however, claimed that the *pūjā* is most important for married women, who tend to perform the *pūjā* to secure family well-being.

Sered has noted that for women, religion often has a lot to do with interpersonal relationships, with an emphasis on the welfare of family members. She includes this emphasis under the rubric "domestication of religion," which she describes as a process in which religion becomes personalized, often involving concern for the health, happiness, and security of particular people, especially kin, with whom one is linked in caring and interdependent relationships (1992, 10). Mary McGee's work on women in Hindu *vrat* traditions highlights the domestic emphasis generally characteristic of such traditions (1987; 1991;

also Wadley 1985, 163). McGee observes that most votaries are women, and for them one of the primary aims of *vrats* tends to be marital good fortune (*saubhāgya*) embodied especially in the form of a good husband, healthy children, and a happy home. McGee notes that "while most women say that their performance of these rites is motivated more by a sense of duty (*dharma*) and devotion (*bhakti*) than by any desire, we cannot overlook the fact that it is the promised fruit (*vratphala*) that most often influences which rite a woman performs," and that this fruit is usually *saubhāgya* (1991, 82). She further observes that the fruits of *saubhāgya* are generally identical with the tasks and goals prescribed for the fulfillment of Hindu women's *dharma*. For Hindu women, then, the performance of *vrat*s simultaneously expresses religious devotion, fulfills duty, and helps attain householder goals that bring joy and happiness to oneself and one's family. In her work on Hindu *vrat* traditions, however, Anne Mackenzie Pearson cautions against an overemphasis on domestic values when it comes to women's performance of *vrat*s, noting that, in her experience, "while women often spoke initially of *vrat*s as being for [maintaining] *suhāg* [Hindi for *saubhāgya*]—the auspicious married state—they also spoke directly or indirectly about the psychological, social, physical, and spiritual benefits for *themselves*. For many women, these were not just residual benefits, but primary benefits" (Pearson 1996, 9). Pearson's observations are important, for they remind us that the rich and varied texture of women's religious lives cannot be reduced to any single set of concerns.

In responding to questions regarding their motivations for engaging in the Kartik *vrat* and *pūjā*, many informants certainly highlighted domestic relationships, marital accord, and family welfare, yet many also referred to other concerns, motivations, and benefits as well. Consider, for example, Kusumlata and Hem Kumari, two of the informants who helped me most in transcribing and interpreting the songs associated with Kartik *pūjā*. In 1997 and 1998 Kusumlata and Muneshvari Devi, who was Kusumlata's neighbor, were the main organizers of the *pūjā* group that split from the original Tulsi Ghat group to meet on Assi Ghat. Kusumlata's family was lower middle-class, and she lived in a dilapidated house with her husband and two of her three children, a boy and a girl, the latter of whom she always brought with her to Kartik *pūjā*. Her third child, a daughter, was married and living nearby in her in-laws' home. Kusumlata was a deeply religious woman who prided herself on the amount of time she spent engaged in worship. Her husband, a quiet, gentle man who helped his wife make costume jewelry to sell in the market, was also deeply religious. Kusumlata grew up in Benares and married into a family from a nearby neighborhood. Her grandmother and mother had also participated in Kartik *pūjā,* and Kusumlata learned about it from her mother. She first began doing the *pūjā* when she was eleven but had to stop during the years she had small children at home. In 1995, when I first interviewed her, Kusumlata told me she generally abstained from eggplant and white radish during the month of Kartik and observed a *phalahār* fast during the five days of the Bhishmapancak.

Kusumlata insisted that one should engage in Kartik observances for their own sake, as expressions of religious devotion. She insisted that one should have no special desire (*manokāmnā*) while undertaking the *pūjā* but should participate without any self-interest. However, she felt that those who are able to "renounce their own desires and take shelter in God" would see benefits flow to themselves and their families because of their selfless devotion. In this regard, she felt that Kartik bathing and *pūjā* are most important for unmarried girls, who participate to attain a good husband. But she noted that married women also benefit by attaining marital good fortune (*suhāg*) and household prosperity.

Hem Kumari also highlighted domestic concerns in describing her reasons for participating in the *pūjā* during an interview I conducted with her in 1997, but she emphasized other motivations and benefits as well. When I met her, Hem Kumari was a married, middle-aged woman from a middle-class, high-caste family. Her husband had worked for the state government's irrigation department but had already retired by the mid 1990s. She lived in a large, airy house that was home to herself, her husband, youngest daughter, eldest son, daughter-in-law, two grandsons, and pet dog. Her eldest daughter was married and living with her husband's family in another part of Benares, and her youngest son was pursuing an advanced degree in Lucknow. All of Hem Kumari's children were college educated, which was a source of great pride for her. Indeed, she and her family were highly supportive of me and my research, and they had a robust appreciation for my academic pursuits that I found to be atypical. Because of her long-term involvement, Hem Kumari had memorized all the *pūjā* songs and could recall them easily at will. I relied a great deal on her knowledge, and she graciously spent many afternoons with me on her rooftop helping me document and interpret *pūjā* songs.

In 1997, Hem Kumari told me she had been observing the Kartik *vrat* and *pūjā* for twenty-one years. When she first began participating in Kartik *pūjā* in the 1970s, she and her husband had been renting an apartment, and her landlord's daughter had brought her to a *pūjā* circle. There had been one year a few years before I met her when she had undergone surgery and hence was housebound during Kartik, but she claimed she had taken part in the *pūjā* every other year since she first became a Kartik votary. In the past she had observed month-long Kartik food restrictions, including abstention from eggplant and white radish, but she no longer did so. By the mid 1990s, the only fasting practice she continued to observe for Kartik was during the five days of the Bhishmapancak, when she maintained a *phalahār* fast.

Hem Kumari felt that all women, regardless of age or marital status, would profit equally from participation in Kartik *pūja*. Whereas unmarried girls might attain a good husband, married women could attain benefits for all the members of their families, and widows, for their children or other family members. There were in fact several widows among my informants, and they did indeed include their children's welfare as one of the main concerns they brought to the *pūjā*. Hem Kumari also felt that her continued participation in the *pūjā* had become for her a way of showing her gratitude to God for having survived an apparently painful and difficult surgery. Like other *pūjā* participants, too, she viewed the *pūjā* as a way of expressing her devotion to and affection for God in a way that she felt would "make God happy." She also claimed that the *pūjā* gave her "mental satisfaction" (*man kī santuṣṭi*) and remarked that in doing the *pūjā,* "I feel satisfied that I have done so much, so much" for God.

Family relationships and the welfare of family members, then, are important concerns that many women bring to the *pūjā* circle, but they are not the only concerns participants have on their minds and in their hearts as they rise in the silent, dark stillness to make their way to the river's edge.

Performing Kartik *Pūjā*

It is usually still quite hot in Benares when Kartik begins, although by the end of the month mornings become rather chilly, often requiring one to wear a shawl. The streets are dark and peaceful in the early morning hours. If you were to make your way from the dense neighborhoods of the city to the Ganges' edge at this time, almost every being you would pass would be sleeping: people, water buffalo, dogs, all slumbering quietly by the side of the road. The first active souls you would be likely to encounter are Kartik votaries on their way to the Ganges River to perform their morning ablutions. There is a Parijata tree on a street corner close to Tulsi Ghat, and it is there that one is likely to first run into Kartik *pūjā* participants on their way to Tulsi or Assi Ghats.

The Parijata tree is one of the items said to have emerged from the ocean of milk when it was churned in ancient times. In Benares, Parijata trees are closely associated with both Krishna and Kartik. One informant, in fact, insisted that the Parijata tree near Tulsi Ghat begins blooming every year on the first day of Kartik and stops blooming on the last day of the month. During Kartik *pūjā,* one is supposed to offer Parijata flowers to Krishna, and this seems to be the only Parijata tree around, so many *pūjā* participants stop at it on their way to the *ghāṭ* to gather its flowers. The fragrant blossoms fall from the tree at night and carpet the earth by early morning. Although one is not supposed to use fallen blooms as religious offerings, many *pūjā* participants take the ones lying on the ground rather than pick others off the tree. Parijata blossoms are delicate, and by the time one returns from the *ghāṭ*s shortly after sunrise, the flowers lying on the ground will already have withered in the morning sun.

While silence reigns along the city streets, it is a very different story at the *ghāṭ*s. From about 3:00 AM on, Kartik votaries come to the river's edge to fulfill their vow of daily, early-morning bathing throughout the month. The *ghāṭ*s get more and more crowded with bathers as the month progresses. One sees both men and women splashing in the waters and dressing discreetly by the river's edge, but one sees mostly women. Men on the *ghāṭ*s tend to perform their morning rituals and then leave, headed to home and work, with only a few men remaining to meditate by the side of the river, drink tea, or watch the goings on. Most of the women, however, stay to participate in the *pūjā*.

During the years I took part in Kartik *pūjā,* I remained ambivalent about whether or not I should bathe in the Ganges before participating in the *pūjā*. One must always bathe before engaging in ritual worship, and I followed this religious prescription faithfully. To do otherwise would have been disrespectful to the women who had welcomed me into their ritual circle. The issue for me, however, was whether or not to wash my body in the river or in my bathroom at home. Those who do the *pūjā* claim that the largest portion of merit comes from the ritual bathing, not from the *pūjā,* so no one would choose to bathe at home and come to the river only for the *pūjā*. The high level of toxins present in the Ganges where it flows through Benares, however, is well documented. Those not accustomed to these pollutants are the most vulnerable to their effects, and I did not want to risk becoming ill and having to abandon my research. Hence I opted to bathe at home before coming to the *ghāṭ*s during all three

Figure 16. Kartik votaries beginning to gather together to perform Kartik *pūjā*

years that I participated in *pūjā* circle. This decision clearly puzzled many of the women I worked with and annoyed some of them, although by my third year as a *pūjā* participant it was no longer questioned openly. Although this was the right decision for me at the time, it was not without cost, and I continue to wonder what affect it had on my relationships with *pūjā* participants.

After bathing and changing their clothes, women begin to gather near the area where their *pūjā* group ordinarily meets. Some of the women bring Ganges mud with them up onto the *ghāṭ* to use for making the icons (*mūrtis*) used in the *pūjā*. When I asked *pūjā* participants, "Why use Ganges mud?" the answer they almost always gave me was that Ganges mud is not only readily available, but also pure, and hence an appropriate substance to use to make divine images. The Ganges is a goddess, and the mud along the river's bottom is continually cleansed by her sanctifying presence. Anyone may participate in the fashioning of the icons, but I found that a few experienced, long-term participants took on this role most of the time. In fact, while participants insisted that there is no formal leader in these groups, one or two women tended to take the lead in a variety of matters, not just in fashioning the icons, but also collecting money to buy needed *pūjā* items, taking responsibility for bringing such items, coordinating special ritual events that take place periodically in association with the *pūjā*, and so forth.

Women begin to gather, yawning, dressing in the damp darkness, braiding their hair, chatting softly, joking and laughing. As participants produce icons from the mounds of mud that appear before them, they place them on a cloth that they lay out to demarcate the altar. Usually the cloth used is yellow, a color that has Vaishnava associations and hence is appropriate for a cloth used in an essentially Vaishnava ritual. Some of the icons are clearly recognizable: the sun-god Surya, moon-god Chandrama, Shiva, the Ganges, Ganesha, and Tulsi herself, embodied in a sprig of the Tulsi plant stuck into a mound of Ganges mud. A few of the icons are in male-female deity pairs. I found there was little agreement about exactly whom these icons embody, but there was consensus that two of the male-female pairs embody Radha-Krishna and Lakshmi-Vishnu. Other icons made include small, round balls and longer tubular rectangles, which, I was told, embody protector deities, family deities, or additional deities not specifically represented in the other icons. As one informant put it, the gathering of icons in its entirety embodies the whole world of the gods (*deva-loka*), but participants tended not to dwell on the particulars of who was who. Lack of theological specificity concerning religious icons is not necessarily all that unusual in Hindu devotional traditions. However, some scholars have noted that when it comes to religion, women tend to be more concerned with ritual specificity than theological specificity.[5] I certainly found that to be the case here with respect to the identity of the images used in worship.

More and more icons appear. By now more women will have gathered, and they begin to set up their *pūjā* items, which include a pot filled with Ganges water, rice, Parijata and other flowers, cotton wicks soaked in ghee for performing the waving of lights, or *ārati*, and a number of other items used as offerings. While the icons are being made, some participants usually begin to sing *bhajans* informally. As the process of fashioning and arranging the images draws to a close, the circle tightens, and the *pūjā* formally begins with a "wake-up" song. This song marks the act of calling the deities forth to come and enter the icons (*āvāhana*), remaining present to worshipers for the duration of the *pūjā*. For Hindu images that are consecrated only temporarily, religious acts that bid deities to enter the icons at the beginning of worship and then dismiss them at the end mark the temporal boundaries of the life of the image (Eck 1985, 50).

Figure 17. Making the icons

Figure 18. Close-up of the icons

Men form the overwhelming majority of temple priests and religious functionaries in Benares, and men control most of the public temple space in the city. The edge of the Ganges River, however, where women's Kartik *pūjā* circles meet, is public space that is not fully controlled by males. The worship groups that women form at the river's edge throughout the month are the equivalent of temples, with the ring of participating women's bodies marking the boundary of these sacred spaces, and men are not welcome in the *pūjā* circles unless they are specifically invited to be present. Indeed, on several occasions during the three years that I joined participants in performing the *puja,* I watched women engage in gleeful verbal abuse of men who dared stray too close to the edge of the *pūjā* circle. In Kartik *pūjā,* women control both the worship space and the devotional practices that occur therein.

The singing of the first song effects the consecration of the images. In the song, the *sakhī*s awaken Krishna, and various goddesses awaken their divine mates so that they, too, can attend the *pūjā.* Gathering around the icons, the women sing:

Figure 19. Women gathered in a circle singing the "wake up" song and ready to perform Kartik *pūjā*

Refrain:[6]
Today, oh *sakhīs*, let's wake up Narayan.
Radha wakes up Krishna; Janaki (Sita) wakes up Raghunath (Ram).
Lakshmi wakes up Narayan (Vishnu); Parvati wakes up Mahadev (Shiva).
Verses:
The *sakhī* who wakes Him up very early in the morning
Gets auspicious sight (*darśan*) of the Ganges and Yamuna rivers.[7] (*refrain*)
The *sakhī* who wakes Him up in the morning
Offers him flowers and Bel-leaves. (*refrain*)
The *sakhī* who wakes Him up in late morning
Offers him a meal of butter and sugar candy. (*refrain*)
The *sakhī* who wakes Him up at noon
Offers him rice, lentils, and *malphua* (a type of sweet). (*refrain*)
The *sakhī* who wakes Him up in the afternoon
Offers him a meal of molasses and nuts. (*refrain*)
The *sakhī* who wakes Him up in the evening
Lights for him a four-wicked lamp. (*refrain*)
The *sakhī* who wakes Him up at night
Puts out for him a mattress, pillow, and carpet. (*refrain*)
The *sakhī* who wakes Him up eight times
Attains the immortal realm of Shiva devotion and feeds a boy-child in her lap! (*refrain*)

The epithet "Narayan" that recurs in the refrain is understood to refer to both Krishna and Vishnu, and the awakening that occurs here evokes a number of associations. As one informant explained to me, in this song devotees perform an act of religious service (*sevā*) to Krishna in waking him up, and all the goddesses serve their mates by doing the same.

On one level, this waking is an ordinary morning occurrence, an act of service that in domestic contexts tends to fall in the female domain. It is one of the duties of married women to awaken their husbands in the morning, and waking one's husband and one's god are homologous devotional activities (Reynolds 1978, 430). Mothers also wake up their children. But imagery of awakening also brings to mind the awakening that occurs on the day of Prabodhani Ekadashi, when Vishnu wakes up from his four-month slumber and the world "awakens" after a four-month period of symbolic dissolution (cf. Reynolds 1978, 429–30). The song further describes the items appropriate to offer

Krishna at different times of the day depending on *when* one wakes him up, as well as the rewards that come from this act of devotion—spiritual immortality and, more concretely, a male child. Hindu norms maintain that women should treat their husbands as their God—Kusumlata, for example, always referred to her husband as "Bhagavan," the same term she used for Krishna—and the image of waking up God so that He can give you a son, along with other things, is rife with sexual innuendo. The reference to the son whom one feeds (*khilānā*) in one's lap, however, alludes not just to human sons, either actual or potential, but also to Krishna, who is worshiped in the *pūjā,* as in other forms of Krishna devotion, as a baby or young child. The song points to a blurring of spiritual goals and yearnings with those that are more concrete and earthly; the desires that performing this *pūjā* might help one fulfill include spiritual immortality, the opportunity to worship Krishna, and the birth of a son. It also points to a blurring of erotic and maternal sentiments in relation to Krishna.

Now that the gods have been awakened, the main work of the *pūjā* begins as participants lean into the circle to bathe the icons with Ganges water. This is the point at which chaos sometimes begins to break out as large numbers of women crowd around the icons, bending forward to offer their *pūjā* items. The circle of bodies tightens as women push and shove, struggling to ensure that the Ganges water they are pouring reaches the mark, and it is not unusual for one's offering to end up on the head, arm, or lap of another *pūjā* participant. The next song singles out Krishna and invites him to wake up, bathe, and eat. As in the previous song, the epithet used here in the opening line, Hari, encompasses both Vishnu and Krishna, suggesting both the daily act of waking that occurs in the *pūjā* and the divine awakening that will take place on Prabodhani Ekadashi:

> Wake up my Hari, it is early morning.
> Brush your teeth, clean your mouth, and bathe.
> Put butter and sugar candy in your mouth; apply oil, flower oil, and mustard paste to your body.
> Let's bathe you in Ganges water.
> Cucumber, *Pāpaṛ,*[8] sweets, and dried fruits—you have these things for your breakfast.
> The *pān*[9] seller brings him the cardamom-flavored *pān*; the flower seller is putting a decorated garland on him.
> And then Krishna's[10] auspicious worship with lights (*ārati*) will be performed.

The offering of Ganges water that accompanies the above song is followed by three substances—turmeric, sandalwood powder, and *roli*, a red powder made of turmeric and lime—that are considered to be auspicious and purifying. Turmeric is sometimes used in bathing, while sandalwood powder and *roli* may be used to make sectarian or decorative marks (*tilak*) on the forehead. Women then offer small pieces of cloth that act as clothing for the icons, and flowers or flower garlands while the next *pūjā* song celebrates Krishna's form, enjoining all the *sakhīs* to focus their gaze on him and enjoy his physical splendor. Krishna devotion tends to emphasize Krishna's physical beauty, and such an emphasis is evident here:

> Having bathed and cleaned himself, good Krishna[11] is walking: look at him!
> He has a golden pot and is offering water: look at him!
> He is playing a golden flute in his hand: look at him!
> He has a golden anklet on his ankle and is making a ringing sound with it: look at him!
> He has a golden basket, from which he is offering flowers: look at him!
> He has a shiny, golden headpiece (*seharā*) on his head: look at him!
> The yellow garment (*pītāmbar*) that he is wearing is flapping: look at him!
> He is chewing *pān* in his mouth: look at him!
> He has put black eyeliner (*kājal*) on his eyes: look at him!
> He is wearing golden sandals and tapping them: look at him!
> Oh Krishna, Oh Narayan, take away my worries!

All of the items associated with Krishna in this song are made out of gold, a substance that is valuable and considered to be purer than other metals, alluding to Krishna's divine, sovereign status. Here Krishna is depicted as wearing a *seharā*, a type of headpiece that grooms wear at the time of marriage. The yellow garment, or *pītāmbar*, referred to in this song is a type of garment associated especially with Krishna, but men's wedding trousers may be yellow. My research associate Sunita noted that in this song, Krishna appears to be decked out in gold and finery for the same reason he is wearing the *seharā*—he is a groom dressed for his wedding.

Having completed the bathing and dressing of the icons, participants offer baskets of sugar and uncooked rice, along with a small amount of raw lentils, fruit, and sweets, still focusing on Krishna in song.

> Hail, son of Devaki!
> Candravati,[12] please bless us so that we might always live at the banks of the Ganges.
> We are scattering rice and pouring water (for you): Oh, Krishna, drink at the bank of the Ganges.
> Ram is fair, and Rai Damodar (Krishna) is dark.
> I am bringing you rice with lentils (*khicarī*), Oh Krishna, and I am happily feeding you.
> Narayan, you eat rice with lentils.
> I worship your body; your power of illusion (*māyā*) is pure.
> Sudha,[13] open the door! Radha is standing outside.
> Hail Govinda, Hail Narayan! Take away the worries of my mind.

The term *māyā,* which appears here toward the end of the song, is often translated as "illusion." In this song it seems to designate Krishna's play, his *līlā,* suggesting that this play is not earthly but divine, and hence completely pure (*nirañjan*).

In commenting on the references to food in this song, one of my principal informants, Krishna Devi, noted that the allusion to rice and water as Krishna's nourishment reflects the very basic nature of Krishna's needs in this area; since he is "hungry and thirsty only for love," he is satisfied with simple fare. *Khicarī,* a mixture of cooked rice and lentils, is considered to be Vishnu's favorite dish, and in the song devotees offer it to Krishna, a cooked version of the uncooked rice and lentils brought to the *pūjā.* But, as Sunita noted to me, *khicarī* has special associations with marriage as well; customarily, bride and groom eat *khicarī* toward the end of the wedding, before the bride is bid farewell from her natal home (cf. Henry 1988, 53). Hence, like the headpiece, or *seharā,* in the previous song, the *khicarī* in this one hints at the forthcoming marriage. *Khicarī* is also one of the foods that mothers favor for children, since it is considered light and easily digestible.

Detailing of specific food items offered to Krishna occurs in several of the *pūjā* songs, suggesting that food symbolism plays a large role in this context. In Krishna traditions, food tends to be synonymous with love (*prema*), and the offering of food generally connotes the offering of devotion. In Braj, Krishna worship entails elaborate practices pertaining to the offerings of food, and ordinarily Krishna is offered food daily on eight occasions (Toomey 1994, 56–57), the same number of times that Krishna is awakened in the "waking" song with which the *pūjā* begins. But imagery of food and feeding has particularly rich social associations for women. Food preparation is women's work, and food references evoke that role. Preparing food and feeding others is both a duty and an act of loving care that women may perform for husbands, children, in-laws, guests, and deities. In many contexts, food preparation also assumes special religious significance for women. Vasudha Narayanan notes that when asked about her reaction to Hinduism textbooks when she first came to the United States, she noted instantly that they lacked any discussion of the types of food her grandmother always prepared for religious rituals (2000, 761). Feeding and eating also have sexual connotations in popular Hinduism. Terms for both eating and sexual enjoyment are derived from the same Sansrit verb (*bhuj*), and one can describe sexual intercourse as the mutual feeding of male and female (Kakar 1990, 91).

Like feeding, bathing, too, has erotic connotations, and bathing can be a euphemism for sexual union. Both bathing and feeding also connote maternal love, for mothers are traditionally responsible for bathing and feeding children (Seymour 1999, 83).[14] Muneshvari Devi, the woman who with Kusumlata coordinated the *pūjā* group I attended on Assi Ghat, remarked that in this form of worship when she bathes Krishna and the other deities with Ganges water, she envisions Krishna as a young child, and she bathes him with the same loving feeling that she had when she at one time bathed her own children. In the context of this *pūjā*, feeding, waking, bathing, and so forth are all acts that have multiple resonances, suggesting simultaneously sexual and maternal intimacy, religious devotion, service, and loving care.

Krishna, now dressed and fed, stands ready to greet Radha, who is waiting for him outside an imagined door. It is notable that the song features Radha, not Tulsi, for it seems to suggest that Radha is in fact the eager bride, not Tulsi. Within the *pūjā*, both Radha and Tulsi are celebrated as Krishna's most beloved consort, assigned special places of honor, and referred to as his wife. Yet while there is a tendency in the *pūjā* to conflate the two as Krishna's blushing bride, the situation also suggests a potential for rivalry between Radha and Tulsi, given the tensions that surely must arise from having to share their beloved mate.

There don't seem to be any clear references to marriage in the two subsequent *bhajans*. In both of these songs, a section dealing with questions of religious merit precedes a section depicting an image from Krishna narrative traditions. In the first part of the next *bhajan*, for example, participants implore Krishna to bless them with the spiritual fruits that they deserve for their meritorious actions and the duties they have had to perform as women. Here, notably, being a woman is given a positive valence, for femaleness is associated with an abundance of religious activity and hence religious merit. The second half of the song focuses on the image of Krishna's foster mother, Yashoda, sitting on a throne surrounded by *gopīs*, who are complaining about Krishna's childish pranks and antics. Yashoda comes to his defense, blaming Radha and the *gopīs* for any difficulties they might experience. The first verse suggests an attitude of subordination toward Krishna, whereas the latter invokes instead the protective, intimate love that this mother feels for her child as she comes to his defense in front of the neighborhood women:

> The sun is rising; the ducks (*cakavā*) are rising.
> All the cows have been untied; Oh Lord, give me beautiful heaven!
> Give me the fruit (*phal*)[15] of my birth as a woman.
> Give us the fruit of bathing.
> Whatever I have done or will do, give me the fruit of that.
> Give me a place to live in Heaven (Vaikunth), Lord, and keep me in your protection.
> Whatever I have done or will do, give me the fruit of that—
> Some from today, some from tomorrow, and some from other days and nights.
> Do service (*sevā*) to Krishna, do service to God (Bhagavan)!
> Krishna's mother is sitting on the jeweled throne.
> All the *sakhīs* are complaining; their complaints increase every day.
> Some complaints are small; others are big.
> She is threatening them with a stick; she says, "It is not my son's fault! *Sakhīs*, it is your fault.
> Go and call Miss Radha! She is the leader of the *sakhīs*.
> *Sakhis*, you are the ones arguing.
> Go and call Miss Radha! She is the leader of the *sakhīs*.
> My son is very good." She takes him in her arms.

The next song is structured similarly in two parts. Again, the first part focuses on concerns regarding religious practice and merit and comments on gender, followed by an image related to Krishna narrative traditions. The song opens with women deploring their gender and questioning whether women are even worthy of engaging in worship. Krishna, however, removes such doubts, telling the women that his feet will be their riverbank (*tīr*), meaning he will help carry them to the "banks" of Heaven. The reference to the cow's tail in the third verse alludes to the belief that at the time of death, one will be required to cross a dangerous river; those who have donated a cow to a Brahmin during their lifetimes will be able to cross the river by holding onto the tail of that cow, who will come to their aid.

(*The women say,*)
With hands joined, we beseech you, Oh Lord, don't give us a woman's birth!
A woman's birth is very bad. How will I wash your feet?
(*Krishna says,*)
Your birth as a woman is good. Wake up daily and worship my feet.
My feet are your riverbank (*tīr*).
(*The women say,*)
We will bathe at the bank of the Ganges, Pancaganga, Beni Madhav, Manikarnika.[16]
We will give donations (*dāna*) on Assi Ghat; grabbing hold of the cow's tail, we will ferry across (the river).
In the middle of the Yamunā, a crow caws. It says,
"You are going to see Krishna today."
Radha is standing there and thinking, "This is very good news."
Krishna went to Radha—and to Rukmini, Satyabhama, and Tulsi—
The one who has beautiful, gem-like eyes.

In the first part of both of these songs, female devotees approach God as supplicants, concerned about reaping the rewards that they, as women, will receive for their devotion. The second section, by contrast, highlights devotional images featuring the women most intimately bound to Krishna—that is, his foster mother Yashoda and his beloved Radha—in nonsubordinate relationships. The juxtaposition of these sections may suggest something about the complexity of the devotional posture that female worshipers maintain before Krishna: while delighting in the intimate erotic and maternal emotions that Krishna traditions evoke, devotees simultaneously retain a sense of servitude (*dāsya*) and subordination.

The second part of the above song paints an image of Radha waiting for Krishna, who comes to visit not just her, but three of his wives as well, including Tulsi, hinting that Radha and Tulsi may potentially be rivals here. The next song, by contrast, celebrates Radha's special relationship to Krishna as his unique mate, joined to him eternally and inseparably. This song locates Krishna in Benares, bathing in the Ganges River, and likens the bond between Radha and Krishna to that of the Ganges and her waters, suggesting that both bonds are equally immutable. The focus on the Ganges here highlights the Benares context and the physical location of this ritual tradition at the River's edge, where the Ganges' presence is difficult to ignore.

> Hari, cleanse yourself in the Ganges; Hari, cleanse yourself in the Mother.
> What is the Ganges like? What is Her water like? What is Krishna's mate (*āncal/acal-joṛī*)[17] like? Radha is Krishna's mate.
> The Ganges is dark, her water is flawless; Krishna is dark, and Radha is flawless.
> Radha is Krishna's mate.
> May Radha and Krishna's love flourish like the Ganges and her water!

As *pūjā* participants are singing these and subsequent songs, some women may come late to the *pūjā* circle, joining in as they are able and pushing to the inner edge of the circle to catch up with other partici-

Figure 20. Performing *ārati* during Kartik *pūjā*

pants. Baskets are passed around, and participants place in them offerings of sugar, rice, coins, and sweets. Several other songs follow, including *ārati* or "light worship" songs to Krishna, the Ganges, Tulsi, Annadev (the goddess of food), and Shiva, respectively. With the first of these songs, participants conduct *ārati*, a form of worship in which light is offered to a deity. Taking in their hands a cotton wick smeared with clarified butter (ghee), they light it and waive it before the icons. The light-worship song to Tulsi, here called Tulsa,[18] praises some of the special qualities associated with her, especially her auspicious qualities as a plant, and celebrates the unique place that she holds in God's heart. Here the name for God is Thakur, "Lord" or "Master," an epithet that is applied to both Vishnu and Krishna. The song alludes to the practice of placing a Tulsi leaf on food offerings to Vishnu and Krishna, who will not accept offerings any other way. The fifty-six types of food (*chappan bhog*) alluded to in the song refers to a type of feast that calls for offering Krishna fifty-six different types of food. The number fifty-six symbolizes all the food in the fourteen worlds of the cosmos. It also connotes maternal care and love, signifying the number of meals that Yashodha supplied to her beloved son every week: eight meals a day for seven days (Toomey 1994, 86).

Oh Tulsa, I am worshiping you with lights.[19]
I am asking you, Queen Tulsa, who is your father and who is your mother?
Rain is your father, earth (*dharat*) is your mother; you are Thakur's beloved.[20]
(Tulsi says,) "If I am on His head, then I provide shade. If I go into the mouth, the whole body will become pure. Because of that quality, I am God's beloved."
She has long branches and green leaves
We offer flowers to Tulsa day and night; we offer flowers and garlands day and night.
We offer Hari fifty-six types of food. Without Tulsa, he won't take even one.
When Tulsa sways (with pleasure), then Thakur (is satisfied and) eats his breakfast—
Honey, dried fruits, and cooked sweets.
We offer this food to Tulsa; we offer this food to our Mother.
The *sakhī* who sings this light-worship song to Tulsi
Will attain heaven; she will have marital happiness (*suhāg*) from birth to birth,
And success (*ṛddhi*), prosperity (*siddhi*), and all wealth will come to her house!

The last three lines of this song form a refrain that runs through the several of the light-offering songs that are sung daily, including songs to Krishna, the Ganges, Annadev (the deity of food), and Shiva. Like the final verse of the wake-up song with which the *pūjā* begins, the refrain points to a blurring of spiritual goals and yearnings with those that are more concrete and earthly.

This part of the *pūjā* ends with a light-offering song to Shiva. There is a playful moment in a section of this song that describes how different deities transport themselves to the *pūjā,* where Shiva's entrance is marked by much clanging on metal *pūjā* vessels, imitating the beat of the Damaru drum he is said to be playing. Then, as the songs draw to a close, the *pūjā* circle settles down, and the narration of devotional stories begins.

Ideally, five stories are narrated every day, although I found that often fewer stories were told, especially if participants were in a rush or were lacking in inspiration. The first story always focuses on Ganesha, Lord of Obstacles, and the Ganesha story is supposed to be followed by four other stories, including at least one story related to the particular day in question. Since Friday is associated with the Goddess, for example, then on Fridays a story related to the Goddess

Figure 21. Kartik votaries listening to a Ganesh story and offering *dūb* grass

is narrated; on Thursdays, a story related to Vishnu is told; and so forth.[21] There is no official storyteller in the groups, but some women are more knowledgeable and outgoing than others and hence tend to tell more stories than other women. Stories narrated include, among others, those related to Kartik, Tulsi, the Ganges, and Krishna, all of which are of vital importance in the *pūjā* itself. In all cases, participants offer substances associated with the deity whose story is being narrated. During the Ganesha story, for example, participants hold in their hands *dūb* grass, which is associated with Ganesha; during a Vishnu story, marigolds or other flowers that are yellow, a color associated with Vishnu; and so forth. On special festival or *vrat* days, narrators recount a story or stories associated with that particular day. On Karva Cauth, for example, narrators tell a Karva Cauth story; on Diwali, a Diwali story; and so forth.

During the three years that I participated in the *pūjā*, I recorded almost a hundred different stories, many of which were repeated several times. Some of these stories were retellings of narratives from epic or Puranic texts, especially the Kartik Mahatmyas. Every day after Kartik *pūjā*, many participants would go to a nearby Vishnu temple to perform *pūjā* there and then listen to the recitation and Hindi exposition of the Kartik Mahatmyas, so several of the women were quite familiar with the stories from these texts. As far as I can tell, however, the majority of the stories were orally transmitted vernacular narratives.

A. K. Ramanujan has drawn a distinction between Sanskritic, "classical" narratives and "women's tales," that is, stories told by women that are also centered on women (Ramanujan 1991, 33). Many of the stories I heard recounted at the *pūjā* were women's tales. Such stories are usually referred to as folk stories, but I am not entirely comfortable with this term, since it sometimes connotes a lack of legitimacy in relation to scripturally sanctioned narratives. Brahmanical Hinduism itself distinguishes between stories that are *laukik* ("worldly") and those that are *śāstrik* or *śāstrīya* ("from scripture"), assigning religious authority only to narratives found in scripture. Jonathan Parry notes the following regarding this distinction:

> For all my informants—whether priests, ascetics, or ordinary householders—there is a sharp distinction . . . between the *shastrik* (or scriptural) and the *laukik* (or popular). Belief and practice are visualized as a composite of both. The *shastrik* elements are *pramanik* ("proven"), eternally valid, and binding on all Hindus, and in their interpretation the Brahman is preeminent. By contrast, the *laukik* is ephemeral, a mere matter of

> local usage to be discarded if it offends against contemporary canons of good sense, and *here it is often the women who are regarded as the repositories of tradition* [italics mine]. Admittedly this *shastrik/laukik* division is itself derived from the *shastrik* domain; but the fact remains that it is internalized by many illiterate Hindus who clearly represent their religious universe as composed of elements taken from two conceptually separable traditions. Debate on theological issues, or on correct ritual practice, always starts from this distinction. (Parry 1985, 204)

Parry further observes that the textual tradition is accorded "an immunity to skeptical scrutiny, while the oral tradition is the focus of continual critical evaluation" (205).[22]

The few high-caste men that I had occasion to ask about the women's stories did indeed distinguish clearly between these stories, which they tended to disparage as mere *laukik* stuff, and Sanskritic textual narratives, which they saw as true. The women I interviewed, on the other hand, did not tend to draw any hard and fast distinction between *shastrik* and *laukik*, prompting me to wonder if Parry's pool of informants on the *laukik/shastrik* distinction included any women, especially women not steeped in traditional Sanskritic learning. My discussions with women also suggest that while women do indeed tend to regard themselves as "the repositories of tradition," they tend not to regard the traditions and stories they preserve as ephemeral, dispensable, or even uniquely for or by women.

Most of the *pūjā* participants I asked about the stories identified them as largely true accounts, preserved in oral tradition, of past events, while some viewed them as largely fictional didactic tales or a mixture of both. But many women from both camps saw the stories as instructive for all persons regardless of gender, focusing our attention on God and teaching us how we should act toward both God and other people. One of the main storytellers at Tulsi Ghat in 1995, for example, an elderly widow named Shyamavati about whom I have written elsewhere (Pintchman, forthcoming), objected vehemently to my suggestion that these stories were primarily for women and invited me to retell them to my husband so that he, too, could learn their teachings. Furthermore, although most of the stories centered on female characters, this was not always the case. In one story that I heard narrated on several occasions, for example, the main human character was a male devotee of Krishna named Bhanu, who serves Krishna faithfully and is rewarded accordingly. The women who participate in Kartik *pūjā* probably tend not to draw distinctions between Sanskritic and non-Sanskritic tales that they tell in the *pūjā* circle because that distinction is not particularly relevant to them, at least in this context. The primary importance they attach to the stories has to do with their ethical force, and any story that emphasizes proper ethical behavior is welcome.

Most of the stories I heard in the *pūjā* circle in 1995, 1997, and 1998 spoke of the merits and rewards of devotion in a variety of contexts, although some of them focused specifically on the merits obtained by observing the Kartik *vrat*. The following story, for example, is one I recorded in the *pūjā* circle in 1995:

> There was an old lady who used to bathe every day in the Ganges during Kartik. And after bathing in the Ganges, she would do *pūjā* to Tulsi. And after worshiping Tulsi she would say, "Oh, Mother Tulsi!" Tulsi would say, "What?" Then the old lady would say, "When I die, provide me (with residence in) Vaikunth, arrange for Krishna to carry my corpse,[23] and provide me with his yellow garment (*pītāmbar*) as my shroud. And arrange for me to be cremated at Manikarnika Ghat."[24] So, Brother, she used to ask this from Tulsi every day, and that old lady used to do *pūjā* to Tulsi every day.
>
> So Tulsi would say, "Okay, fine." And she would think, "I will provide everything else for this lady, but how will I get Krishna to carry her corpse?" So now Tulsi began to get dry from worry. And when Tulsi began to dry up, for that entire month (of Kartik), Krishna came to her every day. He asked, "Tulsi, why are you drying up? This is the month of Kartik, and people do *pūjā* to you, so you should be green."
>
> So Tulsi said, "What can I say? There is an old lady; she bathes every day in the Ganges, and she comes, she does my *pūjā*, and then she asks, 'Oh Mother Tulsi, when I die, provide me (residence in) Heaven (Vaikunth), get Krishna to bear my corpse, arrange a cremation at Manikarnika Ghat, and get me Krishna's yellow garment as my shroud.' So I can give her everything else, but how will I get you to carry her corpse?" So Krishna said, "This is not something to dry up over, Tulsi. I come to you every day, and now I am going to hang this bell here. When you ring this bell, I will come." After hanging the bell, God went away.
>
> In the meantime, Tulsi's *sakhīs* came, and they said, "What is this hanging here, Tulsi?" And they rang the bell loudly. And God came, and he asked, "Did that old lady die, Tulsi?" She said, "No, My Lord. Look, all these *sakhīs* rang the bell. What could I do?" So Krishna said, "Now no matter how

> much you call me now, I will not come." So when the night of the full moon came, that old lady died. And her dead body could not be lifted. Everyone who tried to lift her dead body failed. And then everyone said, "*Bāpre-bāp*,[25] look! We heard that she did lots of meritorious acts. She used to bathe a lot in the Ganges, and in the Yamuna, and she was very religious (*dharmātma*). And now no one can lift up her dead body." So everyone started criticizing her. And when God and Tulsi saw that, they felt very bad.
>
> So Krishna took the form of a child and went there, and he said, "Move away from here!" And it was very crowded, and everyone said, "If this whole crowd cannot lift the body, what could this little one do?" Then the people said, "Although he is small, let's just let him do what he wants to do. Sometimes we should do what children say." So he came, and he touched the old lady with his pinky finger, and the dead body of the old lady became light like a flower. So he lifted her body up on his shoulder, he took her to Manikarnika Ghat, he put the *pītāmbar* on her body, and then a plane (*vimān*) made out of sandalwood came, and the old lady rode on that. And the way the old lady went (to heaven), may all old ladies go the same way!

It is notable that the central character in this story is an elderly woman, whose main request is for boons associated not with the fullness of life, but with death. Indeed, in hearing several of the stories I had recorded in the *pūjā* circle, one Benarsi commented that, according to his observations, there had been a shift over time in the average age of *pūjā* participants, such that more elderly women and fewer young women were now participating in the *pūjā*. He felt that the presence in many of the stories of elderly female characters reflected such a shift. In the *pūjā* circles in which I participated, however, most of the participants were young girls and young or middle-aged married women. Older women tended to be the storytellers, however, probably because they knew more stories than did the younger women in the group, which might help account for the frequent appearance of elderly women in these tales.

Vrat-related narratives tend to be explicitly didactic and to emphasize the rewards that flow from religious devotion and steadfast faith in a deity or deities (Narayan 1997a, 17), a theme that is evident in the story recounted above. In her analysis of several *vrat* stories, Susan Wadley notes persistent underlying themes pertaining to transaction between humans and deities as well as issues of sin and merit. With respect to the first issue, she observes that in *vrat* narratives, gods consistently exercise compassion and provide boons in exchange for human trust, devotion, and service in the form of not only *vrat*s, but other devotional activities as well (Wadley 1985, 81–82). She describes this exchange as modeling "a transaction of the patron-client (*jajmān-kamīn*) variety" (81). This theme was present in most of stories I recorded in the *pūjā* circle.

With respect to the issue of sin and merit, Wadley observes that the *vrat* narratives she explores tend to be quite clear about the relationship between the ethical force of an action and its result: sinful acts lead to sorrow and meritorious acts lead to happiness. In this context, the category of "good acts" encompasses the performance of votive and other devotional rites, which fall under the rubric of *dharma*. Again, these themes are evident in the story above, where the old lady's devotion is rewarded at the time of her death by fulfillment of her requests, and in many of the other stories I recorded as well. Shyamavati summed up for me what she understood to be the main teachings of all the stories she had told in the *pūjā* circle, proclaiming, "If you are involved with God, then God will always give you good results. . . . Do good and you will get a good result, and God will be happy with you. If you believe in God, God will believe in you. That is all."

Both within the *pūjā* circle and in later reflection, storytelling sometimes became a vehicle for the women to comment on their own life circumstances and relationships. For Shyamavati, for example, the stories she recounted in the *pūjā* became a vehicle for attempting to grapple with a great tragedy that occurred in her life, the murder of her grandson and his wife (Pintchman, forthcoming). Other participants also drew parallels between circumstances described in stories and the circumstances of their own lives, in both profound and somewhat less profound ways. In one story recounted in 1995, for example, Ganesha refuses to accept *pūjā* offerings from a woman because the woman's daughter-in-law takes some of the offered rice for herself rather than giving it all to Ganesha. When her mother-in-law scolds her, the daughter-in-law confronts Ganesha and threatens to cut him off entirely after the death of her in-laws. Chastened, Ganesha decides to accept the diminished *pūjā* offerings rather than go hungry in the future. At the end of the story, Ganesha comments to the woman, "Your daughter-in-law is very clever," to which the woman replies, "Yes. The daughters-in-law these days are very clever." At this point, several of the older *pūjā* participants began to comment on the qualities of their own daughters-in-law, sharing their frustrations and affirming what they perceived to be the story's insight that contemporary daughters-in-law are too clever for their own good and less worthy than daughters-in-law of past times. Here the story became for older women a way to bond by sharing concerns and frustrations about their sons' wives. One must wonder, however, what was going through the minds of the younger women in the circle, many of them daughters-in-law themselves, during this incident.

During the three years in which I participated in the *pūjā,* one story in particular became a vehicle for friendly teasing of other members of the worship circle. In this story, which I first heard narrated in October 1995, an old woman wants to bathe daily in the Ganges during Kartik, so she asks her son to accompany her to a hut on the edge of the river, where she will spend the month. Her selfish daughter-in-law prepares food ingredients of very poor quality for the old woman to use to make laddus, a type of sweet:[26]

> So for one month, whenever the old lady would bathe and begin to eat (a laddu that she had made), God (Bhagavan) would come there. And he would say, "Give it to me, Oh Mother!" And she would say, "Take it, my son." So when it came to the thirtieth day, she said, "For all thirty days up to now, God has eaten my laddu. Now this is the last one left. Now I will taste this laddu and see how it is made." Although it was made from bad ingredients and had a bitter taste, nonetheless God would eat it, and he would eat it quietly (without any reaction). So after bathing, when the old woman was about to eat, God arrived and said, "Oh Mother, just for one more day, give it to me." She said, "Fine. Take it, my son." So after giving it to him, she touched him. And the minute she touched God, she was completely covered with gold ornaments—on her hands, feet, in her hair—everywhere, all over her body. And she became young, just like a young girl.

At the end of the month, the son comes to fetch his mother, and they return home. When the daughter-in-law sees what has happened, she becomes jealous. And the next year, she sends her own mother to stay at the river's edge and bathe daily, packing up for her laddus made of the best ingredients:

> So the hut was made for one month for the daughter-in-law's mother, who stayed there and bathed. Whenever she began to eat (a laddu), God would come and say to her, "Oh Mother,

> give it to me!" And she would say, "This is the product of my son-in-law's earnings, and my daughter has made it, so I should eat it. Why should I give it to you?" So when her thirty days were over, she had eaten all the laddus herself. She did not give even one laddu to God. So God thought, "Now it is the last day, so I should see if the old lady is going to say something or not." So again, when she began to eat, he went there and he said, "Today is the full moon (the last day of Kartik). At least today you should give me something!" But the old lady said, "This is the product of my son-in-law's earnings, and my daughter has made it. Should I give it to you or eat it myself?" So now God thought, "What should I do?" So he said to her, "Now you will become a pig for the next seven births." So she became a pig.

God punishes the selfish old woman by turning her into a pig, an animal that many Hindus consider exceptionally lowly and dirty. She makes her way back to her own neighborhood, where she starts ferreting around in garbage. Eventually the man discovers his mother-in-law and returns her to her home; she remains tied up until the next Kartik, when items used in Kartik *pūjā* are sprinkled on her body, releasing her from her pig form.

While much could be said about this story, I recount it here to illustrate how storytelling in the *pūjā* circle is deployed to create mood and affect relationships. On at least two occasions, the storyteller singled out one or more of the women in the *pūjā* circle as the wicked daughter-in-law or mother-turned-pig, much to the glee of the other women in the circle, who joined in the teasing fun. Lesley Northrup notes that in women's ritual practices, narrative can also be performative; as she observes, "beyond the simple telling of stories, it may include the enactment of feelings, occasions, and experiences through a wide range of performative techniques" (1997, 83). Pulling people from the audience into the story frame helps convey a sense of intimacy between storyteller and audience, and in using the story as a vehicle to tease fellow worshipers in a friendly way, the storyteller evokes among *pūjā* participants feelings of intimacy and warmth.

After the storytelling, the *pūjā* draws to a close as it began, in song. During the *pūjā* the sun rises over the river in a warm, orange glow, and by this point it is usually shining brightly. Participants gather up the four ends of the cloth used in the *pūjā*, now laden down with clay icons and *pūjā* offerings, lift it up, and swing it gently back and forth. The women consider Krishna to be still in child form for most of the month, and in swinging the cloth they are swinging the baby Krishna to pacify him. This swinging is accompanied by offerings of milk and a song that alludes to swinging Krishna. As noted previously, feeding has maternal connotations (along with other connotations), and the feeding of milk in particular evokes the image of a mother's care for her baby. In this song, Yashoda protects her beloved son from the *sakhīs*, who appear to be working the powers of the evil eye on Krishna. Yashoda rescues Krishna by removing the evil effects of the *sakhīs*' magic:

> Oh friend, swing Shyam (Krishna) in the swing (*palanā*). (repeat)
> What is your swing made of? What type of string does it have?
> Oh friend, swing Shyam in the swing.
> The swing is made of Agara wood and Sandalwood; the string is made of silk.
> Oh friend, swing Shyam in the swing.
> While swinging, Shyam became obstinate; he wouldn't drink milk or play in my lap.
> Oh friend, swing Shyam in the swing.
> Many *sakhīs* come day and night; they are giving the evil eye to my dear boy; they are performing some magic on my dear boy.
> Oh friend, swing Shyam in the swing.
> Mother Yashoda is removing it with mustard seed and salt. The dear boy is beginning to laugh; he is beginning to play.
> Oh friend, swing Shyam in the swing.
> We brought milk from a *suraī* cow,[27] and my dear boy started drinking it and playing.
> Oh friend, swing Shyam in the swing.
> (Yashoda says,) "Whoever swings my dear boy's swing, I will give her a gem-studded bracelet."
> Oh friend, swing Shyam in the swing.
> "Kanhaiya (Krishna), don't go far to play! Your mother will cry to death if you do!"
> Oh friend, swing Shyam in the swing.
> "You are my one and only son. Play only at home, dear boy!"
> Oh friend, swing Shyam in the swing.
> He has ankle bracelets on his feet and a belt around his waist, and he starts to wander off.
> Oh friend, swing Shyam in the swing.

The parental sentiment (*vātsalya*) permeates this song. The cloth is then laid down gently, and in the next song, worshipers plead with Krishna not to leave them. Krishna here is described as a flute player (*baṅsi ke bajaīyā*), alluding to his form as divine lover, when he uses his flute to call Radha and the *gopīs* to come frolic with him in the forest. The signature line at the end of the song attributes it to Mirabai, the sixteenth-century female Krishna devotee whose own poetry favors the erotic stance toward Krishna over the maternal.

> Stop going, Krishna![28] The flute player is taking my life-breath away.
> Where have the cows gone? Where have the cowherds gone? Where has the flute player gone?
> Stop going, Krishna! The flute player is taking my life-breath away.
> The cows have gone to the forest; the cowherds have gone to the forest; and Krishna has gone to his in-law's house (*sasurāl*).
> Stop going, Krishna! The flute player is taking my life-breath away.
> The cows have come back, the cowherds have come back, but even today, tricky Krishna has not come.
> Stop going, Krishna! The flute player is taking my life-breath away.
> What do cows eat? What do the cowherds eat? What does my Krishna eat?
> Stop going, Krishna! The flute player is taking my life-breath away.
> Cows eat grass, cowherds drink milk, and my Krishna will eat butter and sugar.
> Stop going, Krishna! The flute player is taking my life-breath away.
> He is a very small boy, dark-skinned; he has big, big eyes, and he is exceptionally beautiful.
> Stop going, Krishna! The flute player is taking my life-breath away.
> Mira's lord is Giradharnath, and she got auspicious sight (*darśan*) of Krishna and became happy.
> Stop going, Krishna! The flute player is taking my life-breath away.

This song is followed by another brief song in which devotees wonder aloud when they will finally obtain their beloved Krishna:

Tell me, *sakhīs*, when will I get Krishna?
I won't get him in the evening; I won't get him in the morning; when will I get Krishna?
Tell me, *sakhīs*, when will I get Krishna?
I won't get him today; I won't get him tomorrow; I will get him in the middle of the night!
Tell me, *sakhīs*, when will I get Krishna?

The image of "getting Krishna" in the middle of the night has sexual connotations. In commenting on this song, Hem Kumari insisted that the very first line should state not "When will I get Krishna?" but instead "We will get Krishna in the month of Kartik." According to her, the song states that the devotees will get Krishna at night in the month of Kartik because the *rāsa-līlā* took place during Kartik nights. Knowing that many Benarsis associate Kartik with an increase in sexual activity among married couples, I asked Hem Kumari if there were any "hidden meanings" in the song. She stared at me blankly, but her daughter-in-law, sitting across the room, burst into laughter and exclaimed, "What else? God does the same 'work' (*kām*, a common euphemism for sex) that we all do. God is no different from us!" In response to this point, Hem Kumari shook her head gently and observed, "People will understand the songs however they want. Each person will see them differently."

Figure 22. Preparing for immersion

After singing several more *bhajans*, *pūjā* participants carry the cloth, laden down with clay icons and all items offered during the *pūjā*, down to the Ganges, and they immerse all the materials in the river. Each day, one participant buys, for a few rupees, the opportunity to participate in the immersion; this money is then set aside to purchase items for the day of Krishna and Tulsi's wedding. Many participants linger and sing a few more *bhajans*. The final end of the *pūjā* is then marked with a declaration about the auspicious fruits of Kartik bathing, chanted in chorus:

> Ram told us to bathe in Kartik. So we bathe in Kartik. Why? For food (*ann*), for wealth (*dhan*), for an ever-filled food storage room (*bharal bhaṇḍār*), for marital happiness (*suhāg*), for going to Heaven (Vaikunth).

In this verse we see the juxtaposition of worldly and spiritual goals, boons associated with Kartik religious observances that pertain to both worldly and spiritual auspiciousness.

This basic rhythm defines the course of the *pūjā* for approximately the first twenty days of the month, with little variation. On the fifth or eighth of Kartik's second (light) fortnight, however, there is a shift. After performing the daily Kartik *pūjā*, participants execute Krishna's *janeū*, the ceremony marking his investiture with the sacred thread, which designates Krishna's transformation from child to young man. When I asked about the timing of this practice, Kusumlata explained to me that Yashoda herself performed Krishna's *janeū* on the fifth, but because Gopashtami, a Krishna-related festival, falls on the eighth, one may perform the *janeū* on either day. For this occasion, as for the marriage that will come later, a brass image is used in place of the usual clay one. After finishing the daily *pūjā*, participants clear the *pūjā* space and cleanse it with turmeric and water. As previously noted, turmeric is considered to be an especially purifying and auspicious substance; during *janeū* rituals, it is used to cleanse the body of the initiant, and at the time of marriage, it is applied to the bodies of both bride and groom. During Kārtik *pūjā*, it is used liberally both in this ritual enactment of Krishna's *janeū* and in the marriage ritual that occurs several days later.

Participants sing *janeū* songs before preparing Krishna for his *janeū*. In the following song, which I recorded in 1998, Krishna is set to leave his parents to take up residence in Benares, traditionally the place where high-caste boys would go after their *janeū* to begin their studies with a learned teacher. In the song, Krishna's mother pleads with him not to leave. The song adopts the mother's point of view, giving expression to the pain that she feels at the prospect of her son's leaving home:

> "Mother, give me a laddu made of brown sugar (*guṛ*), coarse flour (*sattū*), and clarified butter (*ghī*).
> I will go to Kashi, Benares, for my education."
> "Oh my son! What will you do with a laddu made of brown sugar, coarse flour, and clarified butter?
> Your father is Vasudeva. Get your education at home!
> Your grandfather is Nanda. Get your education at home!
> Oh my son! What will you do with a laddu made of brown sugar, coarse flour, and clarified butter?
> Your brother is Balarama. Get your education at home!"

Participants begin the *janeū* ceremony by passing the brass image of Krishna around the circle of women, smearing the image with a mixture of turmeric and mustard oil. They then lovingly bathe the brass Krishna in Ganges water. Laying out a fresh cloth, they place Krishna in the middle of it, dress him in finery, and prepare him for the *janeū*, placing offerings of betel nut, chickpeas, and *janeū* threads

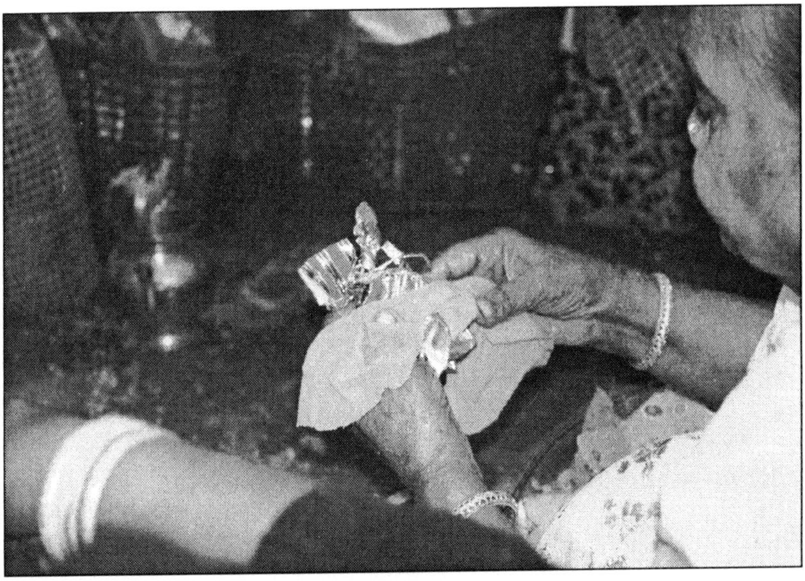

Figure 23. Preparing Krishna for his *janeū*

before him. A Brahmin pundit is called to the circle briefly to utter the mantras appropriate to the occasion, and participants adorn the Krishna image with the *janeū* threads, which they have smeared with the mixture of turmeric and oil.

This is a day of dancing and bawdy joking, for the *janeū* signals Krishna's impending marriage. The *janeū* ceremony is known as a "half-marriage," since it marks a boy's transition from childhood to adulthood; in contemporary India, if a boy who is getting married has not undergone a *janeū*, he will often undergo one just before the wedding ceremony. The connection between *janeū* and impending marriage is implied in a variety of ways. After singing *janeū* songs prior to the *janeū* ritual, for example, participants also sing wedding songs. The mixture of turmeric and mustard-seed oil that participants use to cleanse Krishna's body for his *janeū* is also used to cleanse the body of brides and grooms in this part of India. After the pundit recites the necessary verses, *pūjā* participants smear the brass image of Krishna with a mixture of brown sugar (*guṛ*) and yogurt, a mixture that a bride and groom would eat. And after the *janeū* is performed, participants may sing *gālī*, the verbally abusive, often sexually explicit songs that women sing at Hindu weddings. *Janeū* and marriage are linked in the minds of *pūjā* participants, with both providing an opportunity for sexual teasing. During a *janeū* ceremony on Assi Ghat that I recorded in 1998, for example, the vigorous rubbing of Krishna's body with mustard oil served as an opening for participants to joke about the upcoming wedding night, with one woman complaining that God would be too sore to have sex with Tulsi.

In some *pūjā* circles, the swinging song that is usually sung toward the end of the *pūjā* is no longer sung after this point, since Krishna is no longer a child. Kusumlata observed:

> When we start the *pūjā* from the day of Sharat Purnima, we think that God is in Mother Yashoda's lap. Up to the *janeū*, we consider him to be a child. And when we do God's *janeū*, we think that he is now grown up. Now we should marry him off. So after the *janeū*, we stop swinging him. Some people swing him after the *janeū*, too, but we think that God is grown up now and he will not swing.

In the *pūjā* circle that Sunita attended in 1997, Krishna's transition to manhood after the *janeū* was marked by the reworking of the clay Krishna image from a reclining position to a seated one that explicitly displayed his newly mature male features, accompanied, apparently, by a good deal of laughter and off-color joking. On this day the marriage is considered fixed, and from the day of the *janeū* until the day of the wedding itself women sing marriage songs in the *pūjā* circle before beginning the *pūjā* itself, marking the impending marriage. This practice imitates what is done in human marriages, where women sing marriage songs on the days between the sealing of the marriage agreement (*lagan*) and the wedding day.

In his work on marriage songs from the Bhojpuri-speaking region in which Benares is situated, Edward O. Henry notes what he considers to be the most prominent themes in these songs (1988, 56–61). One such theme is the plight of the bride. In this part of India, male members of the families of the bride and groom almost always arrange marriages, and usually the bride does not know her husband-to-be well—if at all—before her marriage. Girls generally marry at a young age, and at the time of marriage they leave their natal homes to take up residence with their husbands in an extended patrilineal household, where the new bride is subordinate to most of her husband's kin. Hence marriage can be traumatic for girls, who move from the emotional comfort of their natal homes to live with a host of strangers who may or may not treat the newcomer well. A second theme that Henry notes is conquest. The groom's party is depicted as conquerors of the bride's family, emphasizing the dominance of the groom's family in the marital tie.

None of the wedding songs I recorded in the *pūjā* addressed themes of conquest, and the plight of the bride appeared as a relatively minor theme. Other themes came to the fore instead, including the imminence of the marriage, the exceptional beauty of the bride and groom, and the bittersweet anguish of parents at seeing their beloved children grow up and marry. The prominence of such themes suits the ritual context, where participants are anticipating the impending wedding of the exquisitely lovely Krishna, who has now matured from child to adolescent. The wedding songs sung in the *pūjā* are drawn from the larger store of wedding songs in participants' general repertoire of such songs, including many songs that feature married deities. The majority of the songs I recorded featured Sita and Ram as bride and groom, although a few featured Shiva and Parvati or Krishna and Tulsi. Indeed, Sita appears in these songs as the quintessential bride, and Ram, the quintessential groom. Ram and Krishna are, of course, both forms of Vishnu. While the forthcoming wedding is Krishna's, not Ram's, predominant images of Krishna in North India represent him as a playful child or divine lover of Radha and the *gopīs*, not as a husband, while predominant images of Sita and Ram tend to portray them as an exemplary couple. While some of the marriage songs I recorded feature Krishna as the groom, there would not be many such songs in participants' repertoire, whereas songs featuring Sita and Ram seem to be quite popular.

In Kartik *pūjā*, marriage songs are sung during the days between Krishna's *janeū* and his wedding. The marriage of Krishna and Tulsi marks the beginning of marriage season in North India, so themes of wedding anticipation that we find in the songs reflect real feelings of anticipation in the human community. Indeed, this divine marriage functions as a type of "first fruits" offering; just as one should offer the first grains of one's harvest to God before partaking oneself, so the first marriage arranged every season is for God, with humans only partaking afterward. In the following song recorded in 1997, Ram is on the way to his wedding when he stops to pick up a wedding headdress, or *mauṛ*, a type of crown that bridegrooms wear. The flower seller (*mālin*) is surprised to see him, since there have been no weddings for a long while. Ram reminds her that with his marriage, marriage season has now begun. Sita sits waiting for her groom in the nuptial chamber, the *kohabar*, which is a room in the house that is decorated in a special way for the wedding and set up for wedding-related *pūjā*.

> Wake up, flower seller, your husband is waking you up.
> Wake up, flower seller, it is early morning.
> When the flower seller opened her eyes, she saw Ram the groom standing at the door.
> (She said,) "For so long, I have not seen any groom.
> How is it that you are standing at my door today?"
> (He says,) "For so long, there was no marriage season (*lagan*).
> (But) today is a very auspicious day for marriage.
> Oh Flower Seller, at Ram's house there is a marriage,
> So please make a very beautiful headdress for me!"
> (The flower seller says,) "I have never seen such a beautiful groom or such a beautiful headdress!"
> "What will you do with this beautiful headdress?"
> (Someone says,) "Today is my Ram's marriage."
> Oh, flower seller, close by there is a happy gathering of women, and in the middle sits Miss Sita.
> Ram's very lovely sisters-in-law (*sālī*) and the lovely wives of his brothers (*saharaj*) are in the courtyard, and Sita is in the nuptial chamber (*kohabar*).

In another song that I recorded in 1997, Ram is again in a state of anxious anticipation on the way to his wedding.[29] In this song, he stops everyone he meets to ask about his bride, whom he presumably has not seen. All of those who answer him assure him that Sita is beautiful, even more beautiful than Ram himself:

> The king sent invitations all over the country, saying, "Today is my Ram's marriage."
> He is inviting the Sun, the Moon, and Kashi Vishvanath (Shiva).
> He has invited Sarasvati to come from the sky; He has invited Shesh Nag (the king of snakes) from the lower realms.
> The Sun, the Moon, and Lord Shiva all came.
> Sarasvati came from the sky, and Shesh Nag came from the lower realms.
> When the decorated marriage procession (*barāt*) and Ram started to go, The Bard[30] went to welcome them
> (Ram said,) "Oh Bard, I will give you a horse to ride on. Tell me about Sita."
> (The Bard said,) "What can I say about Sita, King Ram?
> Sita is the sun's rays. Sita is more beautiful than Ram. Sita is the shining light of the Dasharath lineage."
> When the decorated marriage procession and Ram started to go,
> A servant carrying a pot came and stood in front of it.
> (Ram said,) "Oh maid servant, I will give you a sari and a scarf. Tell me about Sita."
> (The servant said,) "What can I say about Sita, King Ram?"
> Sita is the sun's rays. Sita is more beautiful than Ram. Sita is the shining light of both your lineages."
> When the decorated marriage procession and Ram started to go,
> The Brahmin came and stood in front of it with a calendar.
> (Ram said,) "Oh Brahmin, I will give you a golden *janeū* thread! Tell me about Sita."
> (The Brahmin said,) "What can I say about Sita, King Ram?
> Sita is the sun's rays. Sita is more beautiful than Ram. Sita is the shining light of the Dasharath lineage."
> When the decorated marriage procession and Ram started to go,
> Sita's little sisters (*sālī*) and her brother's wives (*sarahaj*) stopped Ram at the door.

(Ram said,) "Oh ladies, I will give you a necklace of
precious gems and pearls. Tell me about Sita."
They said, "What can we say about Sita, King Ram?
Sita is the sun's rays. Sita is more beautiful than Ram. Sita
is the shining light of both your lineages."

In this song, the beauty of the bride at the pending wedding is a prominent theme. Other songs celebrate both bride and groom while some focus specifically on the beauty of the groom. Songs that praise the groom's attractiveness make good sense at this divine marriage between the erotically appealing Krishna and his cherished bride. In the following song, Krishna's *sakhīs* are preparing him for his wedding, and he looks so beautiful that the narrator fears he will attract the attention of the evil eye. The song describes him in great detail, while the bride, mentioned only at the very end of the song, appears almost as an afterthought.

Are![31] Don't look at my Krishna! He will get the evil eye.
Krishna, your turban is decorated with fringe, and your
earring, in the shape of the sun, is decorated with pearls
All the *sakhīs* are making perfect the cloth (*cunarī*) (that he
is wearing); he will get the evil eye!
They are giving the final touch to (his) sideburns; he will
get the evil eye.
Are! Don't look at my Krishna! He will get the evil eye.
The wedding clothes[32] that he is wearing are very lovely;
and the Gujarati sash that is around his waist is very
beautiful.
All the *sakhīs* are giving the final touch to his clothing: he
will get the evil eye.
All the *sakhīs* are putting final touches on the sash; he will
get the evil eye.
Are! Don't look at my Krishna! He will get the evil eye.
The socks on your feet are made of velvet.
Your horses that are carrying the wedding sweets are from
Kabul.
All the *sakhīs* are decorating the horsewhip; he will get the
evil eye.
All the *sakhīs* are perfecting the red color applied to the
feet; he will get the evil eye.
Are! Don't look at my Krishna! He will get the evil eye.

The beautiful palenquin carried on the shoulders is very lovely, and the beautiful bride on the decorated bed (*sej*)[33] is very lovely.
All the *sakhīs* are adjusting the curtain (*pardā*); the evil eye will come.
All the *sakhīs* are adjusting the veil (*ghūṅghaṭ*);[34] the evil eye will come.

The following song, which I recorded in 1998, describes Ram's beauty as a groom, only here there is an underlying theme of a young boy who has grown to marriageable age, as Krishna does in the context of the *pūjā*. Ram is sitting on his mother Kaushalya's lap as would a young child, but he is dressed for his wedding, suggesting that Kaushalya's little boy has grown up. Like the previous song, this one too dwells on every detail of the groom's appearance, with the bride appearing only at the end of the song.

Ramchandra is sitting in Kaushalya's lap, and he has become a groom.
On his head, the brocade headdress looks lovely.
A peacock is dancing on the fringe. Ram has become a groom.
Ramchandra is sitting in Kaushalya's lap, and he has become a groom.
The sun-pearl looks lovely on his ear.
A peacock is dancing on his earring. Ram has become a groom.
Ramchandra is sitting in Kaushalya's lap, and he has become a groom.
The saffron clothing looks lovely on his body.
A peacock is dancing on his wrap (*caddar*). Ram has become a groom.
Ramchandra is sitting in Kaushalya's lap, and he has become a groom.
The golden watch on his hand looks lovely.
A peacock is dancing on his bracelet. Ram has become a groom.
Ramchandra is sitting in Kaushalya's lap, and he has become a groom.
The velvet socks on his foot look lovely.
A peacock is dancing on his sandal. Ram has become a groom.

Ramchandra is sitting in Kaushalya's lap, and he has
  become a groom.
The horse from Kabul beneath his thighs looks lovely.
The peacock is dancing on his whip. Ram has become a groom.
Ramchandra is sitting in Kaushalya's lap, and he has become
  a groom.
Janak's daughter with him looks lovely.
A peacock is dancing on her veil. Ram has become a groom.

The image in this song of Ram sitting in the lap of his mother, Kaushalya, even as he prepares to meet his bride on the wedding platform and enter adult life as a husband suggests a blending of maternal and erotic relationality, for Ram is both child and groom. This image also resonates with another theme that runs through these songs: the wistfulness that even a groom's parents may experience when children marry, for marriage is a clear marker of the end of childhood. This theme is in keeping with the ritual context, where *pūjā* participants raise Krishna from childhood to adulthood and complete the process by arranging his marriage to Tulsi. The songs I recorded touched on the anxiety experienced by parents of both the groom and the bride, but especially those of the bride. In this song recorded in 1997, for example, Sita's mother and father refuse to say goodbye to their beloved daughter. The song conveys the sense of great loss that parents may feel when their daughters marry and leave the home:

We will not bid farewell to Queen Sita!
(Sita's father Janak says,) "Who will bring water from the
  Ganges and Yamuna Rivers?
And who will water my garden?
We will not bid farewell to Janak's beloved girl. Who will
  do *pūjā* to my gods?
And who will decorate my *pūjā* things?
We will not bid farewell to Janak's beloved girl!
Who will go to play with the *sakhīs*? And who will call me
  father?"
(Sita's mother says,) "We will not bid farewell to Janak's
  beloved girl!
Who will run around in my house? And who will call me
  mother?
And who will call my name?
We will not bid farewell to Janak's beloved girl."

It is notable here that this song dwells not on the anxiety of the bride, but that of the bride's parents. This does not mean that participants do not identify with the bride and her plight, for they clearly do. But the ritual context here establishes an intention for participants to identify more with the parents of the bride and groom than the bride herself, and this intention is reflected in the emphases prevalent in the songs.

During the days between Krishna's *janeū* and his marriage, *pūjā* participants prepare for the wedding, discussing dowry items and pooling money to purchase gifts and other necessary items for the wedding. The women sometimes take sides at the *pūjā,* assuming the role of the parents of the bride or groom and carrying on as they might in a human marriage, arguing about what to include in the dowry, complaining about the groom's family's demands, and so forth. This is done in fun, and women take great delight in teasing one another. On the ninth of Kartik's light fortnight, the day of Akshaya Navami described in chapter 2, participants exchange invitations to the wedding. As noted earlier, on this day women execute a special *pūjā* in which they construct a ritual diagram consisting of thirty squares and fill the squares with offerings. Kartik *pūjā* participants use this particular ritual to invite one another to the wedding. In Benares, some kind of food gift may accompany a wedding invitation, especially if you greatly desire the person's presence at the wedding. After the Akshaya Navami *pūjā* is completed, participating women offer each other consecrated food (*prasād*) from the *pūjā* as a food gift while orally inviting one another to the upcoming wedding. One Benarsi told me that face-to-face invitations to a wedding are impossible to refuse, so the exchange of consecrated food that occurs on this day obligates all participants to attend the wedding.

When the day of the marriage finally arrives on the eleventh of Kartik's second fortnight, participants celebrate it with great fanfare. After concluding the daily *pūjā,* they clear and purify a space for the marriage platform, arranging bamboo branches for the wedding canopy, as in a human marriage. The women draw auspicious designs on the ground with rice flour. The bride, a potted Tulsi plant with abundant foliage, is brought to the circle, dressed in a red cloth that functions as her wedding sari, and adorned with tinsel, small mirrors, and other decorations. The groom, represented here as in the *janeū* by a brass image, is also brought to the *pūjā* circle, massaged with mustard oil and turmeric, bathed in Ganges water, and dressed in finery. Participants place sweets and gifts before the bride and groom and display dowry offerings, including saris, pots and pans, and jewelry. They also engage in a raucous round of verbally abusive and often sexually crude songs (*gālī*), as they would at a human marriage.

Figure 24. Dressing the bride, Tulsi, for her wedding

As in the *janeū,* a male pundit is called in briefly to officiate. In Hindu marriages, Brahmin pundits officiate at the ritual center of the marriage sequence for what is known as the *phera*. During the *phera,* bride and groom circumambulate a fire seven times and recite marriage vows, before and after which the pundit recites the appropriate verses. In the women's performance of Tulsi's marriage, the pundit comes to the *pūjā* circle only long enough to perform his part and collect the dowry items as *dāna,* while participants recite the seven marriage vows on behalf of the couple while circling a yellow cloth above their heads, symbolically marking the couple's circumambulation around the wedding fire. Then participants sprinkle *sindūr* on the bride's "head" to mark her new, married status, throw puffed rice at the newlywed couple, and offer them yogurt sweetened with brown sugar, a mixture traditionally eaten by bride and groom. On Assi Ghat, in both 1997 and 1998, a food fight broke out at this point, and women started chasing each other and smearing the yogurt mixture on one another's faces and limbs, laughing boisterously and clearly enjoying themselves a great deal. At the end of the celebration, participants gather in a circle singing and clapping while the most extroverted of the married women and widows dance, pulling their coworshipers

Figure 25. Having fun smearing one another with yogurt

into the circle to dance with them. The unmarried girls tend to abstain from dancing, as dictated by conventions of modesty, since the *pūjā* takes place in public space where men are also present.

Krishna's wedding to Tulsi takes place on the same day that Vishnu awakens from his four-month slumber and the inauspicious *caturmāsa* draws to an end. Sanskrit texts highlight these events, and many Benarsis, including many of the women who participate in Kartik *pūjā*, commemorate them in homes and temples all over the city. Yet Kartik *pūjā* does not celebrate them at all, stressing instead the marriage of Krishna and Tulsi. Since women control and shape Kartik *pūjā* traditions, these traditions tend to reflect women's values and concerns. For Hindu women marriage is a highly significant event; Krishna's marriage to Tulsi ushers in the human wedding season in Benares, making it especially significant. In the *pūjā* Krishna's marriage thoroughly eclipses the Sanskritic, textually sanctioned observance of Vishnu's awakening.

Krishna's wedding to Tulsi takes place on the eleventh of Kartik's light fortnight, so the full-moon night that marks the end of the month is still several days away. This is the period of the Bhishmapancak, the five days of Bhishma discussed earlier. During this five-day period, the women's daily *pūjā* continues, although many participants no longer participate, opting instead to undertake their ritual bath during part or all of this period at Pancaganga Ghat, where ritual bathing at this time is said to convey the most merit. Those participants who continue the daily *pūjā* do not make the clay images, since during this period Krishna is believed to be dwelling with his new bride, not his human devotees. Instead, they perform the *pūjā* in curtailed fashion with a plastic or metal box before worshiping the effigies of Bhishma that adorn the *ghāṭ*s, and during these days the stories recounted in the *pūjā* include the stories about Bhishma narrated in chapter 1. One informant described this box as containing all the religious merit that the women earn by ritually bathing and performing Kartik *pūjā* during the month. After completing the stories, instead of singing the usual songs about Krishna, participants all place their hands on the box used in the *pūjā* and chant the following verses:

> She ate no spinach (*sāg*) in Shravan, no yogurt (*dahi*) in Bhado,
> no milk in Kvar, no buttermilk (*mahī*)[35] in Kartik.
> She massaged her mother-in-law and touched the feet of her
> sister-in-law (*nanad*).
> She did not clean her feet by rubbing them together, and she
> sat in the kitchen.
> Shri Krishna's mother did this much religious and ascetic
> activity (*jap-tap*)![36]

These verses describe Yashoda's meritorious actions in past times. The first line describes her as abstaining from forbidden foods during the *caturmāsa*; the second and third, as serving her female in-laws and executing faithfully her duties in the kitchen. The act described in the third line of rubbing one's feet together to clean them is considered inauspicious. Kusumlata explained to me that this verse describes what Yashoda did to obtain Krishna as her son, suggesting that women who are religiously observant and act in a respectful and obedient manner in their conjugal homes will also obtain fine sons like Krishna.

For Kartik *pūjā* participants, the five days of the Bhishmapancak also mark the period between Tulsi's marriage to Krishna and her departure with her new husband to her in-laws' house (*sasurāl*), where the newlyweds are to take up residence, mirroring predominant Hindu conventions pertaining to human marriage in this part of India. Almost all of the *pūjā* participants with whom I spoke understood the in-laws' home to be Vaikunth, the Vaishnava heaven that is usually associated with Vishnu, and almost all of them said that Krishna and Tulsi leave Benares to go to their home on the night of Kartik Purnima. There was no clear consensus, however, on what happens between the couple's marriage and their departure. One informant told me that during that time, Tulsi fasts for the Bhishmapancak, and she cannot leave for her in-law's house until the conclusion of the fast. Another insisted that Tulsi is too young to leave for her in-law's house at the time of her wedding, so she remains at her natal home until Kartik Purnima, which is the night of a rite called *gauna.* A *gauna* occurs when a bride is too young to move to her husband's house at the time of her marriage; when she matures, there is a *gauna* rite, in which the bride is ceremoniously brought from her natal home to go live at her conjugal home.

Several informants understood the five days of the Bhishmapancak as marking the period that Krishna and Tulsi spend in the specially prepared nuptial chamber, the *kohabar.* In many Benares households, after the wedding, newlyweds do *pūjā* and exchange yogurt mixed with brown sugar in the nuptial chamber of the bride's natal home, so some participants imagine that Krishna and Tulsi do the same. One informant, however, told me that in parts of Bihar, where many *pūjā* participants come from, the groom remains at the bride's house for nine days, and bride and groom remain in the nuptial chamber to celebrate the night on which bride and groom consummate their marriage (*suhāg rāt*). For this informant, the image of the bride and groom dwelling in the nuptial chamber during this time implies the consummation of their marriage.

In 1998, just after the pundit arrived to chant the necessary verses for Krishna and Tulsi's wedding, *pūjā* participants sang the following song. It invites Krishna to come to Benares to join his bride in their nuptial bed, instructing him to decorate her body gently (*dhīre se*) with the adornments that mark her new status as an auspiciously married woman (*suhāgin*).

Oh Krishna, go to Benares.
Bring a packet of bracelets for the bride.
Bring them in either your pocket or your purse.
Climb into bed and gently put the bracelets on the bride's wrist.
Oh Krishna, go to Benares.
Bring a packet of *bindi*s for the bride.
Bring them in either your pocket or your purse.
Climb into bed and gently attach one to the forehead of the bride.
Oh Krishna, go to Benares.

> Bring a packet of ankle bracelets for the bride.
> Bring them in either your pocket or your purse.
> Climb into bed and gently put the ankle bracelets on her.
> Oh Krishna, go to Benares.
> Bring a necklace for the bride.
> Bring it in either your pocket or your purse.
> Climb into bed and gently put the necklace on her.
> Oh Krishna, go to Benares.
> Bring a packet of toe rings for the bride.
> Bring them in either your pocket or your purse.
> Climb into bed and gently put the toe rings on her.
> Oh Krishna, go to Benares.[37]

Like any married couple, Krishna and Tulsi presumably engage in sexual relations, and this song seems to describe the circumstances surrounding Krishna's first sexual encounter with his new wife. When I asked specifically about the consummation of Krishna and Tulsi's marriage, *pūjā* participants were quick to remind me that humans would have no access to that information, as God would not allow human devotees to witness him making love with his new wife. As one informant put it,

> Would we be able to see God's marital consummation (*suhāg rāt*)? No. God would never let us do this. When humans are not supposed to see each other (make love), then how should we be allowed to see God doing it? But it is a fact that after a marriage happens, the consummation happens. And no one has to arrange it for them; they will do it on their own. God is the one who makes everyone else's marital consummation happen, so how could we make His happen?

Several informants noted "it is said" or "some people say" that Krishna and Tulsi consummate their marriage on the night of Kartik Purnima, when they depart for Vaikunth. One told me that on Kartik Purnima, in her home she takes a Tulsi plant and a brass image of Krishna, puts them in a cupboard, and closes the door for the night so that bride and groom can enjoy some privacy.

As noted at the end of chapter 2, the Devi-Bhagavata Purana claims that on Kartik Purnima the Ganges joins Krishna in the *rāsa-maṇḍala*, the dance circle where Krishna worships his beloved Radha, and the bodies of Krishna and Radha flow together, commingling in liquid form. For the women of Benares, however, this night is about Krishna's union with Tulsi. As Benares lights up in festive celebration of Dev-Diwali, and as the full moon rises over the Ganges, Krishna climbs into bed with his new bride, decorating her body ever so gently with the adornments of marriage, greeting her body with his own.

Chapter 4

Krishna, Kartik, and Hindu Women's Lives

In his well-known book on Krishna, *The Divine Player: A Study of Kṛṣṇa Līlā,* David Kinsley emphasizes the nature of Krishna as a playful deity who remains eternally unbound by the social and moral norms that condition the human realm. In both his child and youthful forms, Krishna disregards social and moral convention in favor of enjoyment. As a mischievous child, Krishna lies, steals, and bucks authority, all in the name of play. His childish world *is* play, reflecting the nature of the divine world as completely pleasurable, a realm where "fullness and bounty make work superfluous" (Kinsley 1979, 67). The illicit eroticism in which Krishna later engages with Radha and the *gopīs*, whom predominant traditions in North India portray as married to men other than Krishna, is similarly an expression of divine sport, "far removed from the harsh world of work and worrisome duty" (86). Krishna embodies the otherworldly joy of the transcendent realm, and such joy is not, nor can it ever be, subject to the social and moral constraints that restrict the human realm. As Kinsley notes, the call of Krishna's flute to summon the *gopīs* "cares nothing for this world and its moral and social laws. . . . It comes from another world where this-worldly morality and conduct have no place. . . . The world the flute calls [Radha and the *gopīs*] to is . . . a world of ravishing beauty, boisterous carnival, and rollicking play that makes the ordinary world look pale, unexciting, and wearisome in comparison" (99–100).

The world of Kartik *pūjā* embraces predominant imagery of Krishna's behavior as transgressive. But it supplements such imagery with an alternative account of Krishna growing up and marrying Tulsi, reconfiguring Krishna in ways that resonate with householder *dharma*. Hence Kartik *pūjā* does not merely reproduce normative Krishna traditions, but also reimagines them such that a transgressive Krishna persists alongside a Krishna who conforms to human social ideals. Many of the women who participate in Kartik *pūjā* also interpret dimensions of the Krishna traditions celebrated in Kartik *pūjā* in ways that Sanskritic traditions may not emphasize but that resonate with women's everyday values, concerns, and experiences and reflect social and psychological forces that help shape Hindu women's realities.

In her work on women in Judaism, Sered notes that women's religion is not independent of the normative tradition: women's traditions do not exist in a vacuum, and women's beliefs tend not to differ radically from those shared by their male kin. Rather, in male-dominated religions women have a tendency to "subtly alter, elaborate, reinterpret, reshape, and domesticate" normative traditions into forms that are "meaningful to and consistent with their perceptions, roles, identities, needs, and experience" as women living in particular cultural contexts (Sered 1992, 49–50). The world of Kartik *pūjā*, tends more toward being "religiously bilingual," embracing normative, Sanskritic Krishna traditions and women's alterations of these traditions simultaneously, even where the former might seem to contradict the latter. It is the women's traditions distinctive to Kartik *pūjā*, however, and the interface between women's embodied experience and their appropriation and reconstitution of religious imagery that I wish to engage here.

One thing Kartik *pūjā* does is revise predominant narrative traditions concerning Krishna. Religious narratives—that is, myths—articulate cultural paradigms that individuals may appropriate on a conscious or unconscious level to orient their own sense of identity. This may be especially true among the religiously devout, for whom religious narratives tend to carry great significance and importance. Alan Roland argues that myth functions in just this way for many Hindus:

> Adults have deeply incorporated into their preconscious powerful emotional-cognitive images of the vitally alive, richly complex mythology told by various mothering figures during their childhood. The plethora of mythic models and relationship are not only suitable for ego-ideal identifications, but also give norms for correct reciprocal behavior in the complex hierarchical relationships, where the dharma of each is elaborated in the myth. . . . Thus, the powerful incorporation of mythic stories helps to orient the person throughout life. (Roland 1988, 253)

In drawing on Roland's remarks, I do not mean to perpetuate what one scholar refers to as "an Indological myth: the myth of the mythically minded Indian" (Prasad 1998, 17). Certainly it is not the case that all Indians are more "mythically minded" than all Americans or Europeans. I think it would be fair, however, to say that traditional, religiously devout individuals may indeed appropriate religious narrative in ways that help organize their experience of self. Here I am reminded of some conservative Christians in the United States who wear jewelry engraved with the acronym WWJD—"What would Jesus do?" Clearly, such individuals understand narratives about Jesus's life and practices as orienting and providing direction for human beings.

Roland contends that the spiritually oriented self and the human-oriented, especially familial, self are almost always intertwined, and myth helps orient individuals toward the continuity of familial and spiritual identity. He also contends that the tendency to personalize mythological materials may be more pronounced among Hindu women than for Hindu men. For example, he reports that mothers may aspire to embody characteristics of particular mother goddesses in their everyday mothering relationships, using mythic models to integrate familial and spiritual values (1988, 297–98). Roland's claims are consistent with those of Caroline Walker Bynum, who notes in her work on medieval Christian women's stories that women's religious images and symbols tend to continue or enhance women's ordinary experience rather than break with that experience (1996, 74).

While Roland stressed myth, however, one should not neglect the role of ritual action in shaping and bringing together the spiritual and familial identity of individual selves. Recent work on ritual practice emphasizes its nature as a type of performance or set of activities that is constructive, producing through particular strategies specific types of meaning and values. Ritual enables ritual actors to appropriate, modify, or reshape cultural values and ideals that mold social identity (Bell 1997, 82, 73). And ritual engages narrative and theological frames as well. Catherine Bell observes that scholarly work on ritual often has been predicated on a problematic bifurcation between action and thought, with an implicit subordination of act to thought (1992, 49). Subordination of action to thought is especially loaded when it comes to consideration of gender, since women's religious involvement tends to be more heavily weighted toward ritual activity, and less heavily toward theology, than that of men. Observing that rituals may also express complex beliefs, Sered also calls for an abandoning of the action/thought dichotomy (1994, 121).

Much of the Western academic work devoted to the study of Krishna devotional traditions has focused on textual materials, including theological, poetic, and performance texts (e.g., Dimock 1966a,

1966b; Haberman 1988; Hawley 1981, 1983). Traditionally, however, householder Hindu women have not participated to any significant degree in the process of writing authoritative religious texts. Inasmuch as Kartik *pūjā* expresses beliefs and theologies that women participate in shaping, it does writing's work: it helps both articulate and perpetuate a particular vision of reality. And it does so in a medium that engages not just language, but bodily activity as well. The tradition of Kartik *pūjā* comprises religious narratives, activities, and theologies that maintain a dual orientation toward both spiritual and familial selves; the self that is engaged in Kartik worship is engaged as both a spiritual and social being. But selves are embedded in larger frames of cultural knowledge about the divine and social realms, and Kartik *pūjā* engages these larger frames of knowledge as well.

While women shape Kartik *pūjā* traditions, these traditions in turn inform women's social realities. The constructive nature of ritual extends to notions and practices concerning gender, for ritual is an "engendering process" that may both produce and reproduce gender norms (Hancock 1999, 137). Kartik *pūjā* traditions articulate and perpetuate gender norms pertaining to both female and male nature and behavior, and through participation in the *pūjā*, participants come to possess these norms, appropriating them as truths about what is and what should be. Participants reaffirm these norms each time they participate in the *pūjā*.

In this chapter, I explore spheres of symbolism and practice surrounding three prominent figures in Kartik *pūjā:* the *sakhī*, Krishna, and Tulsi. I focus on how each emerges in the context of the *pūjā*, considering ritual activities, song and narrative texts, and theological musings on the part of Kartik *pūjā* participants in the course of my analysis. I contend that constructions of the identity of these three mythic figures in this context engage larger truths concerning women's spiritual and familial selves and women's knowledge about both divine and social realms.

Being a *Sakhī* in Kartik *Pūjā*

> We all make Krishna in the middle and do *pūjā* to him, and we have a good time and tease each other. And we become just like his *sakhī*s, and we feel like we are his *sakhī*s. And we are totally absorbed in him. Nobody even knows if they are wearing their sari inside out, or if they have combed their hair

> or not. All the women get so absorbed in this *pūjā* that they don't care about their body. Just like the *sakhīs* were in His time.

This is how Muneshvari Devi described to me the relationship between the role of the *gopīs/sakhīs* in the *rāsa-līlā* of ancient times and the devotional role of contemporary female devotees, like herself, in Kartik *pūjā*. I have noted that women who participate in Kartik *pūjā* tend to see their role as imitating that of the *sakhīs* who once frolicked with Krishna during his life on earth. Muneshvari Devi describes the ideal in this regard as total absorption in God's play (*līlā*), even to the point of neglecting one's appearance. But Muneshvari Devi's response also reveals an awareness of the collective nature of this form of worship and pleasure that she derives from the company of other women, for, as she notes, "we have a good time and tease each other." Indeed, to be a *sakhī* in this *pūjā* entails focusing loving attention not just on Krishna, but on one's coworshipers as well.

At the close of Tulsi's marriage in 1998, Kusumlata invited me to come see her at her home, reminding me that she would not see me at the *pūjā* anymore since she was going to go to Pancaganga Ghat during the last days of Kartik to bathe and worship there. Gathering up her *pūjā* materials, she hugged the other *pūjā* participants, saying, "Oh, *sakhīs*, we will break for one year; we will meet again in one year. May God keep you well." Later, she told me that she would miss seeing her *sakhīs*.

To be a *sakhī* in the *pūjā* means to worship with other women; as one participant noted, "This *pūjā* cannot be done without *sakhīs*." And to worship with other women brings participants pleasure. On several occasions, in fact, women highlighted to me the enjoyment they derived from collective female participation in the *pūjā*. One worshiper, for example, noted, "Where there are four or five people in a group, then you like doing worship (*pūjā-pāṭh*), singing, dancing. You get so much pleasure. If I sing by myself—say, if you are singing by yourself, then there is no one to listen. If there is no audience, then why sing? . . . And where there aren't four, five, or six *sakhīs*, there is no fun in singing and dancing."

North Indian Vaishnavism stresses the bonds that the *gopīs* share not only with Krishna, but also with Radha, whom they accompany and serve during Radha's love play with Krishna. Kartik *pūjā* participants, however, also tended to stress to me the bonds that participating women share with one another and the pleasure that women derive from gathering together as women. The act of worshiping Krishna in a ritual context that includes other women engages human ideals pertaining to not only devotion, but also friendship and feelings of emotional relatedness among women. When in the course of interviews I asked participants about the meaning of the term *sakhī* as it is used in the *pūjā,* in fact, many participants defined it first in terms of human friendship, bringing up the term's connection to Krishna mythology only at my prompting.

One of the most basic aspects that women articulated to me about being a *sakhī* in the worship circle involves the sentiment of love (*prema*) that such a role requires. As one participant put it, the term *sakhī* means "Love (*prema*). Just love." As previously noted, the *gopīs* typically are held to be exemplars of devotional love for Krishna. However, when participants spoke about the feelings of love associated with being a *sakhī* in this context, they emphasized the term's association not with love for Krishna (although that is certainly important in the *pūjā*), but with love *for one's coworshipers*. While the term *sakhī* has specific associations with Krishna's *gopī*-girlfriends, it is also a commonly used term for "female friend," and in Kartik *pūjā,* women interpret their role as *sakhīs* in social, as well as devotional, terms. For at least some participants, love for fellow worshipers is one of the defining features of what it means to be a *sakhī* in the *pūjā.* When I asked Kusumlata why women refer to each other in the *pūjā* circle by the term *sakhī,* for example, she told me, "*Sakhī* means that there is a lot of love (*prema*) among the *sakhīs*. All of us are going to the Ganges, both younger and older women. Sitting together, talking together, and doing *pūjā* together, we all become *sakhī.*"

But what, exactly, does love entail in this instance? In Indian contexts, love tends to mean something different from what it means in many American contexts. Romantic love in Western cultures, for example, tends to entail an intense emotion directed toward a unique other person whose particular qualities one finds attractive; Indians tend to consider such an emotion dangerous and overly individualistic. Instead, Indians tend to associate love with feelings of interdependence, social attachment, and mutual obligation. Susan Seymour observes that in Indian families, "love is not so much an emotion generated by a specific individual as it is a deep sense of emotional connectedness with the members of one's extended family" (Seymour 1999, 85; cf. Derné 1995, 73–74). While she focuses on family dynamics, she also notes that such "relational love," as she calls it, may be extended to nonfamily members as well, including friends.

In Benares, as throughout India, many people tend not to refer to one another by name, invoking instead relational terms, especially kinship terms. Margaret Trawick observes that the selective use of kinship terms is a powerful way of conveying, igniting, or engendering the sentiments associated with that term (1990, 152). For example, if a person refers to an unrelated male as "brother," the use of that term evokes the feelings that one associates with one's real brother. When participants in Kartik *pūjā* refer to one another as *sakhī* and speak of love among the *sakhīs*, they evoke feelings of relational love that they associate with human friendship. Love among friends, as among family members and between spouses, connotes feelings of connectedness and interdependence. Two particular characteristics pertaining to the meaning of the term *sakhī* in the context of this *pūjā,* however, came to the fore among the participants with whom I spoke: equality, and mutual assistance in conducting the *pūjā*.

"*Sakhī* means that we are equal." This is how one participant, Usha, described to me the importance of using the term *sakhī* in the *pūjā*. Several of the women whom I interviewed gave me similar explanations. As another put it, "All the women, all the girls in the circle, they are all equal. They are all in the same group, they all tell the same stories. That is why (they call each other *sakhī*); they consider everyone to be equal." Indeed, the ideal of equality among women means that they should refer to one another only as *sakhī* during the course of Kartik worship. Ordinarily, women address one another in a variety of ways that often signal relational hierarchy. Young women, for example, generally would not address older women by their names, using instead a respectful term of address, often a kinship term like "older sister" (*dīdī*) or "paternal grandmother" (*dādī*). Older women, however, would often use the first names of younger women, unless they were subordinate to them in another way (e.g., as a servant). In the *pūjā* circle, participants are supposed to abandon all ordinary terms of address in favor of the universal use of the term *sakhī,* which signals a lack of hierarchy. As one informant noted, "If you call me 'Auntie' or 'Mother' or 'Mother-in-Law,' a mother-daughter relationship entails difference. But *sakhīs* are equal. So if you are my *sakhī,* you will sit next to me, and you will be equal to me."

In many contexts, Hindu devotional or *bhakti* traditions have tended to stress the equality of all worshipers before the Divine. Gender and caste distinctions, which mark bodies, and class distinctions, which mark social status, are irrelevant to God, who cares only about the quality of one's devotion. Kartik *pūjā* participates to some extent in this emphasis. However, it is notable that women stressed to me the equality of all worshipers not before God, but before one another. Friends should treat one another as equals. This value is reflected in the physical construction of the worship space as a circle, which grants all participants equal access to the icons used in worship regardless of their social context. It is also facilitated by a pattern of informal leadership, which affords all worshipers the opportunity to participate in construction of the icons and narration of religious stories.

This does not mean that participants abandon all hierarchy in their practice of Kartik *pūjā*. For one thing, as noted earlier, I did not observe any participation on the part of low-caste or Untouchable women, suggesting that they might not be welcome in the *pūjā* circle. Among the women who did participate, however, caste and class, two of the most important markers of social hierarchy in daily life, did not figure prominently within the worship circle. Instead, women tended to grant special honor to age, piety, and religious expertise. In particular, older women whom other participants recognized as religiously knowledgeable and highly devout were accorded great respect, and on many occasions I saw other women touch their feet in the widespread Hindu gesture of reverence to a superior. While elements of hierarchy persist, however, the aspiration toward equality that several participants clearly identified as an important dimension of being a *sakhī* in this *pūjā* remains a central ideal of the tradition.

To be a *sakhī* also entails ideals pertaining to mutual assistance in conducting the *pūjā,* most conspicuously by sharing one's *pūjā* items with other participants. Ursula Sharma observes that, in India, friendships among women are often cemented by small acts of cooperation and mutual aid (1980, 190), and this was certainly evident in the *pūjā* circle. Many women brought extra *pūjā* supplies with them to the worship circle, and I was struck by how these supplies, including flowers, rice, *ārati* wicks, and so forth, were continuously passed around the worship circle. Even when a participant was holding the item to be offered at that moment in her hands, others would nevertheless pass extras on to her, communicating a spirit of sharing that permeated the *pūjā.* One informant, Savitri, commented on this practice, noting, "*Sakhīs* help each other, and in the month of Kartik, when we sit in the *pūjā,* when one of us runs out of something, the others help. In the month of Kartik, if you help someone with the *pūjā* things, this is considered very auspicious." Lilavati made special note of the importance of mutual assistance in promoting equal access and feelings of love (*prema*) among participants, remarking, "If one (of the participants) is poor, another one helps. If I don't have enough to offer, then my *sakhīs* will give materials to me. So this is love (*prema*); you give to me, and I give to you. If someone is running out of *pūjā* items, we share." While some participants commented on sharing as a manifestation of love, some also associated such sharing with the attainment of religious merit. In her comments on the sharing of *pūjā* items, for example, Lilavati continued, "By helping one another, you obtain more religious merit (*punya*)." In a similar vein, Savitri's mother commented, "Doing *pūjā*, offering things, and giving things to other people make someone earn great merit. And that is why people give to one another."

An emphasis on sharing and helping, both as an expression of love for one's fellow worshipers and as a vehicle for attaining religious merit, suggests an ethical valorization of giving and sharing one's resources with others. One of the functions of ritual is to instantiate ethical social relations (Collins 1997, 173–76), although what is meant by "ethical" is, of course, conditioned by context. In this context, women ascribe positive moral value to concrete acts that express care for one's fellow worshipers.

To be a *sakhī* in the *pūjā* also has implications about the stance of the ritual body. Bell has stressed the role of the body in the analysis of ritual practices, noting that ritual entails performing specific bodily actions that in turn impress upon bodies values fundamental to the ritual situation (Bell 1992, 100). In Kartik *pūjā,* conventions concerning the use of one's body reproduce a stress on interrelationship. The continual passing around of worship items throughout the course of the *pūjā* obligates one to constantly direct one's attention toward other participants. I was struck by the amount of touching, chatting, joking, helping, adjusting of other women's clothing, and so forth that continually occurs throughout the *pūjā,* constantly directing one's attention away from the ostensible focus of worship, the icons of Krishna and the other deities who occupy the space at the center of the circle. Indeed, one male Benarsi mocked what he perceived to be women's lack of focus in performing *pūjā,* imitating the stance of a woman leaning over a religious icon and carelessly tossing *pūjā* items on it while gossiping loudly with someone else. But the constant physical and verbal interaction with other women that generally takes place throughout the course of this *pūjā* communicates a particular moral stance. It acts to constantly direct one's attention not only inward, toward the icons, but also outward, toward other worshipers, producing and reproducing an emphasis on the collective nature of this form of worship and one's relationship to one's fellow participants.

Many scholars of Hinduism have stressed the nature of Indian culture as a "group-oriented" culture in comparison with Western cultures. While Western cultures strive to cultivate selves that are autonomous and independent, so the argument goes, Indian culture tends to cultivate interdependence and what Roland calls "we-ness," a sense of self entailing ego boundaries that "remain much more permeable to constant affective exchanges and emotional connectedness with others" and a "heightened empathic awareness of others" (1988, 233). Steve Derné finds that men in Benares conform to the ideal of "we-ness," leading them to be especially sensitive to the demands of others (Derné 1995, 161). Scholars have tended to connect an emphasis on interdependence to joint-family living and childcare practices in India, which engage multiple caretakers, pushing children to rely more on a group of kin than on their individual parents. Stanley Kurtz (1992) contends that the collective nature of child care in joint-family living in India socializes children into a give-and-take with the kinship group, such that both a sense of entitlement to take from the group and a willingness to sacrifice on behalf of other group members "are necessary components of the understanding toward which the bulk of Hindu adult-child interaction is directed" (80). Seymour stresses that in Hindu culture, given the orientation toward group membership, there is a persistent, continual tension between the individual's own selfish desires and the interests of the joint family. That is why, she concludes, renunciation of personal desire is culturally lauded (1999, 270). Seymour rightly cautions that one should not overemphasize the difference between independent Western selves and collectivist Indian selves. She notes that interdependence-independence might best be understood as a "continuum along which cultures fall according to the particular mixture of collectivist and individualist elements that they exhibit at any one time" (269).

What seems to be missing from all these discussions of child rearing and issues of independence/interdependence, however, is thoughtful engagement with the ways that girls and boys tend to be socialized differentially toward autonomy and interdependence both in Western contexts and in India. Carol Gilligan's groundbreaking work on women and morality, for example, demonstrates that for American women, identity tends not to be defined in terms of an autonomous, independent self but is defined instead "in a context of relationship and judged by a standard of responsibility" (1982, 160). American women's selves seem to approach the model of the "we-self" that Roland locates in India. Conversely, I have often wondered about the relationship between the alleged empathetic Indian sense of "we-ness" and stress on renunciation of personal desire as I have watched Benarsi men sit by idly as their wives and daughters scurry around fulfilling their needs and wants, offering tea to family members and guests, caring for children, massaging the bodies of elderly family members, and so forth. While men may value interpersonal bonds, clearly they do not express this value in the same ways that women do. For Indian women, interdependence and "we-ness," especially in terms of family, manifest themselves in repetitive everyday acts of physical care for others that are performed much more frequently by women than by men. Indeed, it seems to me that in terms of the activities that characterize concrete, daily interactions with others, especially familial others, women are under much more pressure than men to subordinate their egos and renounce personal desires for the good of group harmony.

Hence while both men and women may subscribe to an ideology of self that stresses interdependence, subordination of individual autonomy to the group, and renunciation of personal desire, the concrete implications of such an ideology of self play out differently in the domestic arena for men and women. Within the family, for men such ideology may entail things like acceptance of the authority of parents and other male elders or submission to group pressure (Derné 1995). For women, such ideology manifests itself also in the numerous mundane, embodied acts of caretaking for others that characterize women's lives in the domestic sphere.

Certainly in many contexts, not just Benares, women's lives are more apt than men's to revolve around caring for others. In her study of female-dominated religions, Sered argues that women's rituals and beliefs in such contexts tend to reflect strongly the interpersonal orientation of women's familial lives (Sered 1994, 121, 138). Lesley Northrup observes that the theme of "community" is a central aspect of women's worship in many contexts (1997, 34). In the practice of Kartik *pūjā*, participants clearly emphasize mutual dependence and interrelationship among women as coworshipers, not only in terms of the ideals participants express, but also the actions they perform. The term *sakhī* as it is deployed in this context embodies these emphases. Small acts of caretaking within the *pūjā* circle, such as assisting another worshiper with *pūjā* items, function as a female idiom for communicating relational love (*prema*) and reinforce social patterns that encourage women to express love through such acts of caretaking.

The emphasis on friendly interaction among women may or may not extend to the relationships that particular women share with one another outside of the worship context, depending on the persons involved. In Benares, many of women's activities, especially those outside the home, tend to be subject to male control, so women must have the permission of husbands or fathers to attend the *pūjā* in the first place. Participants tend to worship at whichever *ghāṭ* is closest to their home, but that can sometimes entail walking a considerable distance in the early morning darkness, when streets are fairly deserted. Under such conditions, a woman walking alone could be subject to harassment, encounter the possibility of engaging in illicit behavior, or simply become the target of gossip. Hence women are more likely to attain permission to attend, and to want to attend, if they come with other women. This means that participants who have to walk a fair distance to get to the river's edge often journey there with female family members or friends from their neighborhood, joining their companions in the same *pūjā* circle. Indeed, while social conventions mitigate against women roaming or socializing with other women uniquely for their own pleasure, it is perfectly legitimate for a woman to join with other women so that she may attend a religious function. Especially under these conditions, the *pūjā* can serve to facilitate friendships outside the worship circle, for Kartik *pūjā* comes to serve as both a religious and a social gathering.

For women not engaged in sustained relationships outside the worship circle, the emphasis on interpersonal bonding that the *pūjā* promotes stops at the circle's edge. As one participant put it, "We become friends, but after having fun together, we go back to our homes. We do not know where the others live, so this friendship is just for the time of the *pūjā*." Even such temporally bound relationships, however, serve an important social function. Benares and its surrounding regions tend to be conservative regarding marital practices. Women tend to marry fairly young, and when wed, they tend to take up residence in their conjugal homes and live in extended patrilineal families, where they are subject to the control of their in-laws. Social mores pertaining to women's behavior tend to confine women to the conjugal home as much as possible, especially in their early years in the conjugal home as wives and young mothers. In an urban environment such as this one, Kartik *pūjā* affords some women the opportunity to meet other women and forge relationships, however temporary, away from the prying eyes and potentially meddlesome control of family members, where they may ask questions or share concerns that they might not feel comfortable sharing with women in their families or neighborhoods. On one occasion, for example, two women quizzed me about the types of birth-control options available to women who want to prevent pregnancy but don't want their husbands or husbands' families to know. Clearly they perceived me, as a Westerner, to be someone who would have access to this information and would keep their concerns secret. Certainly the roster of Kartik *pūjā* participants does not normally include people like me. But the opportunity to ask for such information arose because these women participate in an activity that brings them together with women from outside their immediate neighborhoods.

Krishna as Lover, Husband, and Son

When participating women liken their role in the *pūjā* to that of the *gopīs* who adored Krishna in ancient times, they evoke both erotic and maternal relationality, along with a diffuse notion of religious service (*sevā*) and devotional love (*prema*). In his research on Krishna *līlā* performances in Braj, Hawley notes that many of the people he spoke with tended not to maintain distinctions between parental (*vātsalya*) and amorous (*mādhurya*) sentiments when it comes to Krishna devotion; he quotes one informant who describes these two devotional sentiments as being like two light bulbs that can be lit up with a common switch of love (1983, 263–64).[1] While sectarian traditions like Gaudiya Vaishnavism sort out and codify the five devotional sentiments (*bhāvas*) with great care, popular religiosity tends to remain largely unconcerned with sorting them out or differentiating one *bhāva* from the other (cf. Toomey 1994, 30). Hence the mixing of devotional sentiments that characterizes Kartik *pūjā* is not in itself remarkable. However, the focus on Krishna simultaneously as child and mate resonates in quite specific ways with Hindu women's concerns, values, and experiences, implicating in particular psychological and social aspects of women's lives.

Sudhir Kakar explores at some length the connections he sees between Indian familial arrangements, psychological drives, and Krishna mythology. Like Roland, Kakar believes Hindu myths articulate cultural paradigms that individuals may appropriate to orient their own sense of identity. He argues that "popular and well-known myths are isomorphic with the central psychological constellations of the culture and are constantly renewed and validated by the nature of subjective experience" (1990, 135). In myth, the wishes and impulses of unconscious fantasy are defused "by the very fact of the fantasy's becoming collectively shared rather than remaining an individual burden, and by the simple device of its being externalized and projected onto mythical heroes and heroines" (Kakar 1978, 145). With respect to Krishna, he proposes that there are separate "masculine" and "feminine" traditions that serve differentially as projective vehicles for the unconscious fantasy of both men and women (146).

Kakar's interpretation of Krishna mythology is rooted in his analysis of the psychological impact of Indian mothering styles on young children, especially male children. He contends that in India, children typically undergo an extended period of infancy that lasts up to four or five years. During this period, the Indian child remains intensely attached to his mother. This attachment is manifested particularly in the physical closeness that young children and mothers share (1978, 80). Young children sleep with their mothers, breastfeed until an advanced age (up to three years), and are carried by them throughout the day (1978, 80–81). Mothers are inclined to totally indulge their infant's wishes and demands, extending this indulgent mothering well beyond the time when the child is ready for independent functioning in many areas (1978, 81).

The impact of such prolonged intimate mothering on the male child in particular, argues Kakar, is ambivalent. As a source of endless nurturing, the Hindu child's mother is a benign, loving figure. This internalized image of the "good mother" manifests itself in Hindu mythology as a number of benevolent mother goddesses, for example, Lakshmi, Sarasvati, and Parvati (1978, 84). At the same time, argues Kakar, the intense closeness of the mother-child bond may become smothering. Indian culture valorizes motherhood very highly, and the status of women in the joint patrifocal family is connected to the production of children, especially sons. He maintains that an Indian mother tends to perceive a son as a kind of savior figure (1978, 88–89). This factor may dispose women to overly valorize the bond between mother and son. The mother may also turn her erotic energies to her son, since marital sexual relationships are not fulfilling for many Indian women, and conventions of joint family living militate against close emotional ties between wives and husbands, especially in the early years of marriage (cf. Derné 1995, Kakar 1990). The internalized image of the smothering, sexually devouring "bad mother" manifests itself in Hindu mythology as female vampires, ghosts, and other rapacious female figures.

Kakar singles out several accounts of Krishna defeating demonic forces as masculine myths that express the male child's fantasy of destroying the "bad"—that is, smothering and sexually devouring—mother. Exemplary in this regard is the story of Krishna's destruction of Putana, a demoness whom Kamsa sends to the child Krishna to destroy him. Putana gives Krishna her poisoned breast to suckle, hoping that the poison will kill him. Instead, Krishna sucks away not all her milk, but her very life, killing her. Kakar interprets the poisoned breast as symbolic of the "Indian boy's critical psycho-social dilemma: how to receive nurturing without being poisoned by it, how to enjoy his mother's love and support without crippling his own budding individuality" (1978, 148). Kakar also points to the theme of threatening maternal sexuality in the myth, for Krishna's eager sucking at Putana's breast "is an act of oral sexual violence that combines both the infant's excitement and his anger. This image may be construed as a fantasied fulfillment of the mother's sexual demands and at the same time a grim revenge on her for making such demands at all" (1978, 149).

The stories that Kakar identifies as particularly feminine—that is, accounts of Krishna as an irresistible though mischievous child and a lover of Radha—echo the same themes from the mother's point of view. He contends that a central feature of the "feminine" Krishna myths is "the infantilization of the god and, implicitly, of the ideal male by Indian women." Women perceive and experience Krishna primarily as an ideal son whose childish playfulness "reflects the deep sensual comfort and security of the idealized bond of intimacy between Hindu mother and son." Krishna is the savior of women not as an adult male but as the son who is "vital to the consolidation and confirmation of a Hindu woman's identity." The stories of Krishna as Radha's lover contribute to the "fantasied fulfillment" of the mother's sexual desire for her son, for predominant Krishna traditions maintain that Radha was many years older than Krishna when she fell in love with him. Hence accounts of Radha and Krishna as lovers illustrate "the Hindu woman's unconscious fantasy of her son as her lover" (Kakar 1978, 153).

Stanley Kurtz (1992) reconsiders the psychological significance of predominant Krishna mythology from a somewhat different perspective. Kurtz calls into question Kakar's emphasis on the centrality of the mother-child bond in the Indian context. A number of scholars note the importance of numerous mothering figures in the widespread Indian practice of joint-family living and the emphasis that Indian culture places on allegiance not only to biological parents, but also to the kinship group as a whole. Kurtz argues convincingly that Kakar confuses the tremendous physical intimacy shared by Indian mothers and children with emotional intimacy. While physical indulgence of children is indeed typical of Indian childcare practices, notes Kurtz, it is coupled with emotional distancing. Such distancing functions to push the child away from an exclusive tie to the mother and "toward a sense of immersion in, or unity with, the family at large" (Kurtz 1992, 60). For example, in joint-family households parents are supposed to remain distant from children in the presence of family elders. A mother may pick up a crying child to nurse him or her, but she is supposed to do so without indulging the child emotionally. Kurtz contends that such a practice exemplifies the psychological push away from natural parents and toward the group (1992, 83); the parent withdraws attention so the child will interact and bond with other family members. Kurtz's findings resonate with those of Seymour, who also notes that according to her observations of childcare practices in Eastern India, a number of techniques are used to inculcate in children a "sense of interdependence—the need to rely on a variety of persons for care and attention, an incipient identification with the extended family as a whole, and the knowledge that elders are in control" (1999, 82–83).

Kurtz does not consider the Krishna narratives that Kakar describes as "masculine"; he focuses only on the "feminine" accounts. Kurtz faults Kakar for ignoring the place of the *gopīs* in stories concerning Krishna as both child and lover. In fact, argues Kurtz, "The particular role of the *gopīs* and the importance of the opposition between them and Yashoda and Radha must be recognized." Kurtz contends that both Yashoda and Radha represent the natural mother, although in Radha's case, "where the sexual element is explicit, the connection is obviously not conscious." The *gopīs* represent the other mothering figures in the patrifocal family, whom Kurtz describes as "in-law mothers." Conflict between the *gopīs* and Yashodha/Radha over Krishna's many antics represents "the struggle between the in-law mothers and the natural mother for the soul of the child" (1992, 145). This conflict is resolved in the *rāsa-līlā* dance, where Krishna dances and makes love with not just Radha, but all the *gopīs* as well. For Kurtz, the *rāsa-līlā* depicts a psychological solution to the incestuous desire that the male child (Krishna) and his mother (Radha) share with one another. The child "gives up his selfish but dangerously precocious sexual desire to have his mother all to himself," moving psychically toward the group and renouncing exclusive attachment to his natural mother. Once he moves toward the group as a whole, "the power of the incestuous attraction" that mother and child share becomes broken. The mother learns to share the child with the in-law mothers, and the child allows himself to be thus shared (1992, 147).

In relation to Kartik *pūjā,* Kurtz draws an important connection between the group focus of Indian culture, the tendency for Indian mothers living in traditional joint-family situations to share mothering responsibilities with other mothering figures in the family, and the multiplicity of adoring, nurturing females in Krishna mythology. The collective nature of Kartik *pūjā* and the ethical valorization of sharing resources and helping one another all suggest an elevation of the group as a whole and a renunciation of exclusivity in participants' emotional and ritual ties to the male child, embodied here as Krishna, as devotees "raise" him from infancy to adulthood during the course of the month.

Other aspects of Kurtz's analysis, however, are not convincing to me. For one thing, Kurtz conflates Yashoda and Radha as embodying the figure of the mother. But why? If myth clearly distinguishes Yashoda from Radha, what indicates that we should ignore that distinction? Kurtz reprimands Kakar for not clearly distinguishing the role of the *gopīs* from that of Yashoda and Radha, but then he himself refuses to distinguish the role of Yashoda from that of Radha. Let me suggest another interpretation that could easily fit Kurtz's larger frame of analysis: a male's relationship with both his mother (Yashoda) and his wife (Radha) must be balanced with one another and with an allegiance to the larger group of family women (the *gopīs*). Such an interpretation fits the pattern of joint-family living, where a man must learn to balance and negotiate sometimes-conflicting allegiances with wives and mothers, and must learn to balance these allegiances with those felt toward sisters and other family women.

Furthermore, Kurtz seems to agree with Kakar that for women Krishna is an ideal male as a mischievous son but not as a mature lover, and mythology of the child Krishna reveals Hindu women's infantilization of the male (Kurtz 1992, 144). I would argue that this point is simply not correct if you look at how women actually conceive of Krishna, as opposed to how some (male-authored) Sanskrit texts represent Krishna. In Kartik *pūjā* traditions, for example, Krishna is a mischievous son who also grows up to become an ideal husband and assume adult, indeed sovereign, responsibilities. He is child, adult husband, and mature lover all at the same time.

When it comes to the conflation of maternal and erotic sentiments in Krishna imagery, furthermore, Kurtz, like Kakar, tends to pathologize the relationship between mothers and sons in a way I find problematic. Both scholars portray the mixing of motherly and sexual sentiments as reflecting an emotionally unhealthy incestuous situation that Kakar explicitly identifies as springing from Indian women's unfulfilled emotional and sexual drives. He argues that sexual relations between wives and husbands in India tend not to be terribly satisfying for women; simultaneously, Indian culture is much more accepting than Western cultures tend to be of having mothers sleep with children, breastfeed them, and indulge in intimate touch, encouraging the transfer of sexual feelings from husbands to sons. Kurtz is less clear about the origin of the "incestuous attraction" that mothers share with their sons, but he does not challenge Kakar's assumption that it is pathogenic.

I wish to reconsider the conflation of maternal and amorous sentiments in the context of Krishna traditions from a woman-centered perspective, focusing particularly on how such a conflation manifests in Kartik *pūjā,* where women have shaped and reinterpreted predominant Krishna traditions to reflect their own experiences and values. One key issue here is that in Kartik *pūjā,* Krishna grows up and gets married; he is a husband as well as a son and lover. Such an explicit, central focus on marital imagery is absent from predominant North Indian Krishna traditions. I would suggest that from a woman's perspective in this context, the conflation of maternal and amorous sentiments might have much less to do with pathogenic incestuous emotions than with normal social, emotional, and physiological commonalities that Hindu Indian women living in traditional patrifocal joint families might tend to experience in their relationships with both husbands and sons.

Women's relationships with both husbands and children in a joint-family situation tend to be physically intimate yet subject to emotional distancing so that these relationships not jeopardize the collective well-being of the extended family. In a traditional arranged marriage, husband and wife usually assume sexual relations well before they have had a chance to get to know one another to any meaningful extent or to allow emotional intimacy to grow. If they live in a traditional joint family, wives are expected to maintain distance from their husbands during the day, refraining from speaking to or interacting with them in front of their in-laws, so that emotional intimacy is not expressed in front of the family (e.g., Roy 1992, 94–100; Trawick 1990, 94–95; Seymour 1999, 98). Hence wives tend to experience their relationships with their husbands as unique and physically intimate but constrained emotionally by the conjugal family and subject to the control of familial others. The same is true with respect to children, who, as discussed above, tend to maintain a uniquely intimate physical relationship with their mothers for an extended period while also being pushed toward interdependence with the family as a whole. From a woman's perspective, both children and husbands are intimate others with whom one shares a distinctively close relationship that is unique in the way it necessitates continual negotiation between physical intimacy and emotional restraint.

While relationships with daughters, sons, and husbands are all subject to similar constraints, women would experience parallels in the bonds they share with husbands and sons that they would not experience in the bonds they share with daughters. Not only are sons and husbands male others who are distinct from the female self, but socially, too, there is overlap between what women share with husbands and what they share with sons. Like husbands, sons remain in the natal home, where they may support parents in later years; daughters marry and leave the household. Bonds that women share with husbands and sons are life-long bonds of mutual dependence; bonds between mothers and daughters are subject to radical break, as girls leave home upon marriage and become members of the families into which they marry. Women also experience husbands and sons, but not daughters, as breadwinners or potential breadwinners whose labors support the family financially. Husbands and sons, more than daughters, are also the predominant focus of women's ritual practices, especially votive rites, which women tend to perform for the well-being of husbands and sons more than any other family members.

With respect to sexuality, too, women may experience continuity in their relationships to both husbands and sons. A growing body of research on maternal sexuality indeed suggests that female erotic relationality tends to be directed toward children as well as husbands or other adult lovers. This is usually not a sign of incestuous pathology, however, nor a transfer of sexual desires from husbands to sons, as Kakar seems to assume, but simply reflects normal tendencies within women's physiological and emotional makeup. The mother/child bond is indeed erotic in nature, not pathologically so, but naturally so. In fact women's sexuality is inherently and normally expressed in both conjugal and maternal relationships, and the erotic nature of the healthy mother/child bond is not detrimental to the child but is instead highly adaptive. Such a view of maternal sexuality as natural, normal, and indeed functional means, as Cristina Traina notes, that "the whole notion of human sexuality must be adjusted to account for this potentially ubiquitous experience of mothers" (Traina 2000, 371).

Freud and the psychoanalytic tradition have, of course, addressed the convergence of the maternal with the erotic. But the way Traina and others address the eros of motherhood depends, as Traina puts it, "less on dubious and highly individual unresolved issues of infancy than on universal, clearly identifiable hormonal connections" (371). Psychoanalytic theory has been slow to accept as normal any convergence of the erotic and maternal realms, tending instead to portray all such convergence as abnormal and harmful, but those exploring the biological connections between maternal and sexual response would hardly find an emphasis on the physical basis of maternal eroticism surprising. Susan Weisskopf observes, "The two groups who have worked on the problem of maternal sexuality, the psychoanalytic theorists and the biosocial theorists, share some common ground but differ dramatically as to what they feel the proper relationship between maternity and sexuality should be. The former say that in mature women sexuality is harnessed for or split off from motherhood; the latter suggest that sexual gratification can and should be an important bonus of motherhood" (768–69). In considering the convergence of erotic and maternal imagery in women's devotions to Krishna, I would suggest that the biosocial evidence should be taken into account.

In an article that considers the interrelationship between sexual response, birth, and breastfeeding, Niles Newton suggests that while male reproductive behavior "is limited to one act—coitus," adult females engage in at least three types of interpersonal reproductive behavior: coitus, parturition (childbearing), and lactation (Newton 1973, 77). Two of these behaviors entail a woman's engagement not with an adult sexual partner, but the woman's child. Newton observes parallels in physical, hormonal, and emotional response involving all three reproductive behaviors, which are physically intense, share a common neurohormonal base, and often trigger caretaking behavior. She concludes that discussions of sexuality in women need to take account "of the marked intercorrelations and interrelationships between coital response, parturition response, and lactation response" (95).

Writing more than twenty-five years later, anthropologist Sarah Hrdy makes a similar observation, reporting that "maternity and sexuality are inseparably linked in ways that just are not true for paternity and male erotic experience" (1999, 538). Nursing mothers know that an infant's suckling at the breast can induce sexual feelings, even orgasm, in the mother. Indeed, Hrdy wonders whether referring to the pleasurable erotic sensations that breastfeeding in particular may arouse as "sexual" is to put the cart before the horse, subsuming maternal physical pleasure under the rubric of sexual pleasure, whereas the truth might be more the other way around. "We might just as logically describe various orgasmic contractions during lovemaking as 'maternal,'" observes Hrdy (537), since the physically pleasurable feelings we tend to identify with adult sexual response were probably originally maternal responses to infant suckling before they had anything to with coitus. Furthermore, the intertwining of maternity with physically pleasurable sensations is evolutionarily adaptive, since it makes a mother more inclined to care for her baby. "Evolutionary logic," contends Hrdy, "is firmly on the side of mothers who enjoy the sensual side of mothering for its own sake" (Hrdy 1999, 538).

Apart from the specific hormonal and biological connections that link bearing and nursing children and female sexuality, the process of mothering a young child is an intensely physical affair deeply connected to libidinal impulses. Traina notes of her own experience of orgasm while nursing her child that parenting is rarely so arrestingly sexual. Yet parenting is often intensely physical and even erotic: "burrowing, kicking, suckling, caressing, hugging, lying languorously entwined—what Noelle Oxenhandler has called 'the eros of parenthood': an upwelling of tenderness, often with a tinge of amazement, that expresses itself primarily through touch" (Traina 2000, 369; quoting Oxenhandler 1996, 47). A committed mother feels a deep desire to touch and caress her baby. The pleasures of parenting a young child are sensual, like dining on a good meal. Indeed, Hrdy notes that she, like so many other parents, referred to her children using metaphors of food, especially sweets, naming them with endearments like "muffin," "cutie pie," and the like (Hrdy, 539; c.f. Oxenhandler, 47). One of my own favorite terms of endearment for my toddler-aged daughter was "sugar muffin," and we used to play a game where I pretended to eat her cheeks and ears because she was so sweet I couldn't resist.

For mothers, the mother/child bond is naturally and normally erotic, assuming we understand "erotic" as a broad category that encompasses the types of maternal physical pleasure involved in healthy, loving, nonabusive parenting. To speak of a mother's erotic pleasure in her children as a result of transference of desires from adult sexual relationships, then, is to assume a male model of sexuality and pathologize that which is not inherently pathological. But what about the child's perspective? Nursing, touching, or cleansing the genitals "all stir erotic sensations in the infant" (Weisskopf 1980, 771); mothers know, for example, that nursing or changing an infant boy's diaper in cultures where diapers are used can cause him to have an erection. But those sensations, too, are biologically adaptive. For children, as for mothers, the early mother-child relationship "is and *should be* erotic" (Weisskopf 1980, 770; italics mine), for it is the erotic quality of the mother-child bond that prepares the child for healthy adult genital love. In fact infants need a good deal of nurturing physical contact in order to grow and develop. Children who grow up "with no one to touch, hold, cuddle, with neither mother nor allomother to reassure them of their commitment to the infant's well-being" develop abnormally, failing, for example, to cultivate the capacity for empathy (Hrdy, 529).

No doubt, the erotically charged nature of the mother/child bond can become pathogenic, and mothers can become sexually overbearing in relation to their children. One must not confuse the normal eros of parenting with pedophilia or sexually predatory behavior. Healthy eroticism in the mother/child relationships tends to promote human growth and flourishing; sexually abusive behavior tends to interfere with human growth and flourishing (Traina 2000, 392). Assuming that a majority of Hindu women living in India are heterosexual, then the mother/son relationship could be more sexually charged and more prone to becoming sexually pathogenic than the mother/daughter relationship. Kakar (1978) suggests that social conditions in India, as opposed to the West, make Indian culture predisposed to such an over-sexualizing of the mother/son relationship. Kakar's arguments in this regard, however, seem to be based on two problematic assumptions. First, he assumes that adult sexual relations within marriage tend not to be at all satisfying for married women, so women have to find another outlet for their sexual desires. Yet some scholars have argued that such a view might well need to be amended. Jyoti Puri, a sociologist who interviewed middle-class women in Bombay, found that in speaking of their own sexuality and sexual relationships, these women often represent themselves as sexual agents who receive and give sexual pleasure (Puri 1999, 103–33). In a similar vein, Ann Grodzins Gold (Raheja and Gold 1994, 30–72) finds that the Rajasthani folklore she collected expresses a view of women's sexuality that "frankly acknowledges women's active, pleasure taking sexuality" in the context of adult heterosexual relationships (66). Indeed, Gold notes that many Rajasthani women's songs link the sexual and maternal aspects of female nature, affirming that Indian women tend to experience the two as inseparable. Second, Kakar seems to assume that adult sexual coitus is the sole appropriate place for the expression of erotic feelings, with maternal sexuality manifest only as a neurotic substitute when adult sexual intimacy breaks down. In other words, Kakar seems to assume that "good mothers do not have sexual feelings in relationship to children, that good mothers are generally asexual," a belief that Susan Weisskopf terms the "ideology of asexual motherhood" (Weisskopf 1980, 768). Clearly the growing body of research on maternal sexuality calls this assumption into question. Indeed, one might well challenge the appropriateness of applying, uncritically, to women received wisdom about sexual norms that seem to be based largely on male sexual experience.

In fact, it is quite possible that social conditions in India give appropriate primacy to the erotic nature of the mother/child bond in an open and healthy way such that Indian women might be more likely than those in Western cultures to accept and enjoy the erotic dimensions of motherhood without repressing maternal or infant sexuality or experiencing it as wrong or shameful, enabling rather than hindering the flourishing of healthy sexuality in both mothers and children. Newton postulates that there may be a correlation between an accepting attitude toward sexuality and an accepting attitude toward breastfeeding (Newton 1973, 83). Contemporary Indian mothers breastfeed at much higher rates and for longer periods of time than women in the United States and Western Europe; perhaps they might also be more relaxed about and comfortable with normal and healthy maternal/child sensuality than women in Western cultures. Indeed, researchers report instances of observing mothering figures play with little boys' genitals or joke about them in loving ways, apparently without feeling guilt or embarrassment (e.g., Raheja and Gold 1994, 71; Trawick 1990, 219). It is telling that sexual abuse is actually more likely to occur in families where there is an absence of healthy physical affection between parents and children and where harshly conservative values and puritanical views about sex predominate (Oxenhandler, 49).

Perhaps, then, the mixing of maternal and erotic sentiments directed toward Krishna in the practice of Kartik *pūjā*, along with a more diffuse emphasis on love (*prema*) and service (*sevā*), should not be viewed through a lens that depicts the maternal and the erotic as inherently incompatible emotions. Rather, the mixing of these sentiments might well reflect normal—not pathogenic or neurotic—social, emotional, and erotic parallels that women experience in their relationships with their husbands and their sons. Such mixing might also point to sexual attitudes on the part of women that are rather open to and accepting of maternal sexuality as continuous with adult-directed female sexuality.

Ritual actions that women perform as part of the *pūjā* also point toward a dual focus on Krishna as both son and husband. I noted in the previous chapter that waking, feeding, and bathing, activities that women perform during the *pūjā* in relation to Krishna, have both maternal and erotic connotations. Women wake and feed both children and husbands. Waking early to serve Krishna parallels women's domestic responsibilities of waking early to prepare for the rising of husbands and children. Feeding Krishna may evoke for women imagery of feeding their own husbands and children, whether real or imagined. The ritual bathing that women undertake before performing the *pūjā* may be experienced as not only a spiritually cleansing bath, but also one that evokes feelings of erotic desire, while bathing Krishna and the other icons may stir up maternal feelings, as it did for Muneshvari Devi, as cited in chapter 3.

The marriage of Krishna, too, implicates women's involvement with both husbands and sons. During the *pūjā*, women "raise" Krishna from infancy to adulthood, performing his *janeū*, arranging his wedding, and marrying him to his eager bride. Krishna is the quintessentially lovable male child, playful, adorable, and irresistible to all the mothering figures in his life. Every year he is reborn, nurtured, and raised once again. When women participate in the *pūjā* they enact a mother's duty, her *dharma*, in relation to a son, producing and reproducing cultural norms in this regard. But women marry, too, and in the context of the *pūjā*, Krishna is also the ideal groom, sexually attractive, potent, and powerful. Most importantly, perhaps, Krishna is devoted to his bride and loving toward her. Several *pūjā* participants stressed to me the special fondness Krishna feels for Tulsi, noting that food offered to Krishna is always offered with a leaf of Tulsi placed in it, and that Krishna allows Tulsi to reside on his head, placing her physically above him in a reversal of normal gender hierarchy. As one participant put it, "Tulsi is loved most by Lord Krishna because God likes her green leaves, so he put her on his head after making her his wife. He doesn't keep Radha on his head."

The image of Krishna as Tulsi's devoted husband forms a counterpoint to that of him as illicit lover of Radha and the *gopīs*. In the context of Kartik *pūjā*, these seemingly contradictory images persist alongside one another, and their contradictory nature is neither reconciled nor denied. They both exemplify the Hindu belief that the most complete expression of God is as a male-female pair, a value echoed in the human world in the ideal of the married couple as two bodies joined into a single unit. Yet they engage diverging spheres of social and devotional meaning.

Radha and Tulsi in Kartik *Pūjā* Traditions

Just as Kartik *pūjā* participants may experience Krishna as homologous to their own sons and husbands, so might they experience Tulsi as homologous to themselves or their daughters, with whom they share gender identity and, hence, a bride's fate. Nancy Chodorow (1974) notes that mothers in general are more likely to identify with daughters than with sons and to experience daughters as continuous with themselves (and vice versa). In India, from the time of a daughter's birth, Hindu mothers identify "anticipatorily, by reexperiencing their own past, with the experience of separation" from the natal family that their daughters will also go through at the time of marriage (Chodorow 1974, 47). In Kangra, Himachal Pradesh, where Tulsi's wedding during Kartik is also performed, some women make an explicit link between Tulsi's life and the lives of human women, identifying Tulsi's marriage and subsequent uprooting with human women's marriage and departure for the in-law's house (Narayan 1997b, 37). In Benares, too, women tend to experience Tulsi's life, including her relationship with Krishna, as continuous with their own lives, reflecting their values and aspirations as well as their fears and concerns.

In addition to being a goddess and a plant with religious associations, Tulsi is also an herb, basil, with decidedly domestic connotations. In Indian Hindu households, women often use Tulsi in cooking and food preparation. Like chicken soup in the United States, Tulsi is also a form of domestic medicine, and many home cures that women take or give to family members involve Tulsi. As a form of Vrinda, Tulsi is the quintessential devoted wife (*pativratā*), embodying Lakshmi's qualities of wifely auspiciousness. On many occasions, *pūjā* participants stressed to me how completely devoted Krishna and Tulsi remain to one another as husband and wife, bound together by the profound love that each holds for the other. While there is sometimes a tendency to conflate Radha and Tulsi as Krishna's blushing bride within the context of Kartik *pūjā*, the structure of the *pūjā* clearly distinguishes one from the other, and the two clearly inhabit different worlds.

Many of the participants whom I interviewed insisted both that Kartik is the time of *rāsa-līlā* with Radha and the *gopī*s and that Krishna leaves Radha for the month to spend the time with Tulsi and then marry her, apparently without feeling that these two versions of events might be mutually incompatible. Yet some of the songs and stories associated with the *pūjā* suggest otherwise, painting a picture of irreconcilable tension between Radha and Tulsi and describing their competition over Krishna. This rivalry is richly conveyed in a story that I heard women tell numerous times in relationship to Kartik. This story communicates both the exceptional nature of the Tulsi-Krishna bond in comparison with the commonly acknowledged bond between Radha and Krishna, as well as its special association with the month of Kartik. In the story, Krishna colludes with Tulsi to assure that he will always be able to leave Radha behind during the month of Kartik and spend it with Tulsi, returning to his beloved Radha only after the month comes to an end.

> There was Radha and there was Mother Tulsi. They used to see each other every day before Kartik. And when the full moon night came, then Tulsi said, "Oh Radha, give me Krishna (Bhagavan) for one month." And Radha said, "Look. How can I give him to you? I love him like my own life. I cannot give

him to you for one month. I will never give him to you." So Tulsi said, "All right, you won't give him to me?" Radha said, "No." So Tulsi went to Krishna and she said, "Look, I asked for you for one month, but Radha won't give you to me. If you were to come with me, that would be great." So God grew happy and said, "You are right. I should be with you for this one month. Okay, I will come on my own. You go home—I will come."

So when night fell, he went home. And he laughed a lot and had a lot of fun. And he spoke with Radha and made her very happy. And they both went to sleep. At midnight he got up and said to Radha, "Oh Radha! My stomach hurts a lot." She said, "Oh Lord, are you in severe pain? What medicine should I give you?" So God said, "No medicines." He started thrashing around, and this went on for hours and hours. And then she asked, "Now what should I do, Lord? Tell me what remedy I should give you." He said, "Go and bring me some water." So she brought him some water, and whatever water she had, he drank it all. So when Krishna finished it all, Radha went into the village asking everyone for water, but there was none. She said, "The water was supposed to be filled in everyone's house. Now what is this mystery that everyone's water has been used up, and my water has also been used up? Krishna, where should I get water from to give it to you?"

Radha went and knocked on Tulsi's door. Tulsi came and opened the door, and she said, "What is the matter, sister? Why are you asking me to open the door at this time of night?" Radha said, "What can I do? Today my Krishna is going to die. I cannot get water anywhere. That is why I came to you, to ask for water." Tulsi said, "When I asked you to give me God for one month, you would not give him to me. Now why should I give the water to you?" Radha said, "I only need a little bit of water." And Tulsi said, "I only asked for God for one month!" So they got into an argument. Radha said, "My Krishna will die, and then the entire cosmos will be destroyed."[2] Tulsi said, "Fine. Let it happen. I won't give the water unless you give me God for one month." So, with deep regret and much bad feeling, Radha finally agreed to give her God for one month. And so God lives happily with Tulsi for one month, and has the *pūjā* done to him. And then he goes back on the night of Kartik's full moon.[3]

The following song, which I recorded from the *pūjā* in 1997, also details the rivalry between Radha and Tulsi. In this song, Krishna appears wearing the garb and ornaments of a groom, and Radha becomes suspicious that he has married another woman. When she discovers that he has wed Tulsi, she is furious and locks Krishna out of the house. Krishna tries to appease Radha by assuring her that Tulsi will be her servant.

> Oh, my heart, sing to Krishna.[4]
> Laughing, sweet Radha asked, "Krishna, how did that red mark (*tilak*) get on your forehead?"
> Krishna said, "Listen, dear Radha, I got this mark when I went to bathe in the Ganges River."[5]
> Laughing, sweet Radha asked, "Krishna, how did that eyeliner (*kājal*) get on your eyes?"
> Krishna said, "Listen, dear Radha, when I picked up a pen, the ink (from the pen) got on my eyes."
> Laughing, sweet Radha asked, "Krishna, how did that red color get on your mouth?"
> Krishna said, "Listen dear Radha, my friends fed me *pān*, and because of that my mouth has gotten red."[6]
> Laughing, sweet Radha asked, "Krishna, how did that red color get on your feet?"
> Krishna said, "Listen, dear Radha, my heel got red from walking on a henna-leaf."
> Laughing, sweet Radha asked, "Krishna, how did your garment (*dhoti*)[7] get yellow?"
> Krishna said, "The washerman (*dhobi*) must have changed the garment."
> When sweet Radha heard these things, she called the washerman immediately.
> "Listen to what I have to say, Washerman: How is it that Krishna's garment got exchanged for this one?"
> The washerman said, "Listen, sweet Radha, Krishna and Tulsi have gotten married."
> When sweet Radha heard these words, she bolted the door from inside.
> Krishna said, "Dear Radha, open the door! Tulsi will be your servant (*dāsī*)."

Another song, which I also recorded during the *pūjā*, is even more explicit about the tensions between Radha and Tulsi. Here, Tulsi assumes her plant form, and Radha threatens to destroy her. In exchange, Tulsi taunts Radha, claiming that no matter what Radha does, Tulsi will always remain with Krishna and serve him.

> In back of me, there is a clove tree; cloves fall down from it all night long.
> My father cut down that clove tree and made a bed frame,
> And father wove a bed out of silk.
> The groom Shri Krishna and Queen Rukmini sleep on that bed.
> Radha and Rukmini sleep there, one on each side, and Krishna sleeps between them.
> Radha asks, "I am asking you, Sister Rukmini, what is it that I smell?"
> Krishna is talking and laughing; Tulsi stands at his head.
> (Rukmini says,) "That is Tulsi's fragrance wafting in."
> (Radha says,) "If I get a hold of Tulsi now, I will pull her out by the roots, and I will throw her into the Ganges River! Then all of my troubles will go away!"
> (Tulsi says,) "Go ahead, Radha, go to the Ganges River (and throw me in); Krishna will bathe in the river. I will touch Krishna's feet, and my life will be fulfilled."
> (Radha says,) "If I get a hold of Tulsi now, I will pull her out by the roots, and I will throw you, Tulsi, in the cooking fire. Then all my troubles will go away!"
> (Tulsi says,) "Okay, go ahead and throw me in the cooking fire. Then I will become fire in the month of Magh. In Magh and Paush, everyone is cold.[8] Krishna will warm himself by that fire, and my life will be fulfilled."

What are we to make of these accounts of rivalry between the two goddesses in the context of this devotional tradition? Some of the Kartik *pūjā* participants with whom I spoke drew explicit comparisons between these songs and the practice of polygamy, once legal but now outlawed for Indian Hindus. Kirin Narayan notes that women's versions of stories about Tulsi that she recorded in Kangra, Himachal Pradesh also tend to show empathy toward the anxieties of co-wives (1995, 488). But Narayan implies that such plural marriage is a thing of the past. In his exploration of marriage songs from this part of India, Edward Henry also remarks that while some marriage songs still refer to co-wives, it is rare for a contemporary man to take a co-wife (Henry 1988, 27). The few women in Benares with whom I discussed the practice, however, claimed that it is still not all that uncommon for a Hindu man, especially a man of means, to take more than one wife illicitly, often with his wife's knowledge but rarely with her consent. One informant told me the following story:

> My sister's elder brother-in-law, he took two wives. He married for the first time when he was a student. Then he became an engineer in the navy and went abroad. When he came back, he was no longer happy with his first wife, so he married a second time, but he did not leave the first one. The first one had a girl, and the second one had a boy. And then he had an operation because he thought, "I have a girl and a boy; that is enough." In the end, something bad happened, and the younger wife stopped talking to the elder one. One wife lives in the village, and the second wife lives in Lucknow in a big bungalow. So if there are two wives, they don't ever get along.

Another Benarsi female told me that in addition to the continuing existence of co-wives (*saut*), there is also a tradition of wealthy or important men maintaining "kept women" (*rakhel*) or mistresses. She claimed that several Benarsi men have such mistresses, including her neighbor and several professors at Benares Hindu University. Such a practice is a matter of honor or prestige for the men and a matter of shame and loss of honor (*izzat*) for their wives. When I mentioned the issue of co-wives to one of my close friends in Benares, a middle-class Brahmin woman, she confessed to me that her brother has two wives, one in his natal village and one in an apartment in Benares. She also commented that many women of all classes and castes worry when their husbands go out without telling their wives where they are going, fearing that a husband might be cultivating a relationship with another woman.

Hence on one level, songs and stories that describe Radha and Tulsi competing for Krishna's attentions seem to resonate with at least some women's reported experiences and fears concerning husbands' extramarital relationships with other women, signaling a shared anxiety about male infidelity. But the tension between Tulsi and Radha that pervades these materials has larger symbolic significance as well, for Radha and Tulsi represent diverging paradigms of female sexual potential. As already noted, in Kartik *pūjā*, imagery of a transgressive Krishna persists alongside imagery of a Krishna who conforms to human social ideals concerning marriage and human householdership.

Kartik *pūjā* supplements popular Krishna imagery, which embraces Krishna's otherworldly, transcendent nature and the illicit nature of his relationships with Radha and the *gopīs*, with ritual activity that domesticates his sexuality in marriage. Krishna's proper marital relationship to Tulsi, culminating in their departure for Vaikunth, forms a counterpoint to the relationship between Krishna and Radha, whose love play in Vrindavan is widely understood in contemporary Hinduism as always remaining outside the bounds of marriage. In Vrindavan, Krishna is eternally at play, and his erotic sport is not bound by *dharmic* conventions (Kinsley 1979, 56–121). Vaikunth, on the other hand, where Krishna and Tulsi are widely believed to go when they leave the earthly realm at the end of Kartik to take up residence as husband and wife, is the domain of Vaishnava kingship and marriage, both of which are subject to the demands of *dharma*. When Krishna marries Tulsi and becomes her proper husband, he counts Vaikunth, not Vrindavan, as his home.

Krishna devotional traditions throughout North India portray the relationship that Krishna shares with Radha and the *gopīs* as tumultuous, passionate, intense, and, of course, illicit. Predominant religious interpretations of these materials understand the adulterous nature of their love to be symbolic of human passion for God. Yet these materials also have a "dark side," for they embrace imagery of a God who lies, steals, and sleeps with the wives of other men, as well as women who neglect their husbands and children to engage in illicit sex with their lover. The notion of a deity engaging in self-indulgent and seemingly decadent behavior, especially with respect to sexual morality, has seemed problematic to at least some Krishna devotees. Vaishnava theologians have "tied themselves into knots" to explain their relationship with Krishna, since the idea of "trysting with the wives of other men" is unsavory to many Hindus (Dimock 1966a, 200; 1966b, 55). Within Gaudiya Vaishnavism, for example, Vaishnava theologians debated at length whether the *gopīs* were women who were married to Krishna (*svakīyā*) or women who were married to other men (*parakīyā*). Rupa and Jiva Gosvami, two of the foundational theologians of Gaudiya Vaishnavism, argued for the former doctrine, claiming that Radha and the *gopīs* were in fact manifestations of Krishna's own *śakti* and hence were really his. Rupa Gosvami even concluded that the *gopīs* never consummated their marriages to their alleged earthly husbands, for Krishna had used his power of illusion (*māyā*) to create shapes like the *gopīs* that had slept with the *gopīs*' husbands in their place (Dimock 1966a, 202). The latter doctrine that the *gopīs* were married to other men (*parakīyā*) eventually prevailed, however, and has come to shape popular Krishna devotion in contemporary North India.

Perceptions of Krishna as the divine lover unfettered by social conventions permeate the world of Kartik *pūjā,* where participants assume the role of the *sakhīs* and, in their hearts, frolic with Krishna on the banks of the Ganges. Yet the devotional realm of Krishna's carefree sport is far removed from the realm of real human relations that tend to occupy the space of Hindu women's lives. Indeed, on the level of earthly male-female relationships, Krishna's lying and cheating behavior falls short. The women with whom I spoke rarely drew comparisons between Krishna and human men, but when they did, the comparisons tended to focus on Krishna's antinomian behavior with Radha and the *gopīs*, and they were not favorable. In the course of discussing the song detailed above in which Krishna marries Tulsi on the sly, for example, one informant complained, "God has lied, and that is why men lie. They don't lie? They say, 'I went here,' then they say, 'No, I didn't go here, I really went there.' It is like that in every house." Another noted that since God took many lovers, so do human men. Yet she also lamented, "It was important for God, but when men do this, there is no importance to it." For these women, the frolicking, rogue Krishna is certainly not a male that human males should emulate. But what about Krishna the groom? His marriage to Tulsi, celebrated so enthusiastically on the banks of the Ganges, reflects the world of values and conventions that shape and inform human conjugal relations. When Krishna comes to Benares to adorn his new bride with the ornaments of a *suhāgin,* a properly married woman, he enters that world.

I have noted that Kartik *pūjā* participants tend to employ the term *prema,* "love," in the *pūjā* to refer to the friendly affection participants are supposed to feel for and express to one another. In the context of Krishna devotion, the term *prema* has other connotations as well. Krishna's relationship with Radha and the *gopīs* has been characterized as one that shuns the form of love known as *kāma* in favor of a more spiritually pure form of love known as *prema* (Dimock 1966a, 161–64; Hawley 1981, 158–62; Hawley 1983, 275–78; Marglin 1985a, 201–206). *Kāma* is love tinged with personal desire, including the desire for family and children. *Prema,* on the other hand, is selfless, desireless love that is aimed only at pleasing the loved one and does not aim to attain anything for oneself. When participants model themselves on the *gopīs*, they understand the *pūjā* as an expression of their desireless love for each other and for God. But the extraordinary nature of Krishna's relationships with his *rāsa-līlā* partners makes them unlikely models for conjugal relationships confined uniquely to the human realm. In this regard, informants tended to emphasize Krishna's union with Tulsi as one that parallels human marriage and is equally characterized by values generally associated with *kāma*. As one participant put it, "Just as God gets married, I got married in the same way. It is the same. God's *janeū* took place, and then his marriage took place. We do the same things." In stressing Krishna's proper marital relationship to Tulsi as one that parallels human marriage, women's Kartik *pūjā* traditions reflect values that are grounded not only in devotional ideals, as Krishna's relationships with Radha and the *gopī*s are often understood to be, but also in women's social realities, which lie outside the *pūjā* circle and hence are subject to the pull of *kāma* and all that it represents.

The imagery surrounding Krishna and Tulsi that is invoked in the *pūjā*—raising Krishna to marriageable age, then arranging and participating in his wedding to Tulsi—has deep social resonance for Hindu women, whose lives revolve to a great extent around their roles as brides, wives, and mothers. The child Krishna frolics eternally in Vrindavan; yet the sons and daughters of women who participate in Kartik *pūjā* grow up, and when they do, their weddings have to be arranged. The erotic love play between Radha and Krishna expresses the yearning of the soul for intimacy with the Divine; yet human women marry, and when they do, they yearn for a proper husband with whom they can share the earthly joys of marriage and family. Like Tulsi, many of the married women in Benares who participate in the *pūjā* were also carried off after marriage to an uncertain future in their in-laws' house; their daughters, similarly, grow up and leave their natal homes to take up residence in their husbands' villages and towns. As one informant noted, "Just as we sometimes cry when we bid farewell to our own daughters when they marry, so we do the same thing in our homes—we cry for Tulsi." The marital drama unique to women's Kartik traditions is continuous with the norm of women's lives, representing in ideal form the marital destiny of numerous Hindu women in contemporary India.

The privileging in Kartik *pūjā* of the *dharmic* but staid conjugal bond between Tulsi and Krishna over the sexually passionate but tumultuous one shared by Radha and Krishna may reflect particular tendencies in women's romantic longing in traditional Hindu culture. Kakar (1990, 83–84) notes the centrality in Hinduism of imagery surrounding the unified male-female pair or couple, the *joṛī*, as two persons joined together in a harmonious, interdependent, and mutually fulfilling oneness. This ideal of a "single two-person entity" is captured in the image of Ardhanarishwara, Shiva in his form as half-male, half-female. Kakar contends that this "wished-for oneness of the divine couple" is especially important to Indian Hindu women and represents their idealized image of marriage. The desired intimacy implied in the *joṛī* remains for women a romantic longing that, says Kakar, tends to manifest itself as yearning not for "the depths of erotic passion," such as we find in so many of the stories of Radha-Krishna, but for the "much quieter affair" of husband-wife intimacy, affection, and fidelity. This, contends Kakar, "is the real *sasurāl*—the husband's home—to which a girl looks forward after marriage" (1990, 23). Kakar downplays female sexual desire here in ways that are probably not accurate. But my own work among Benarsi women leads me to agree with Kakar that emotional intimacy, mutual affection, and fidelity are certainly qualities that women desire strongly in marriage.

As Tulsi departs for her own *sasurāl,* the in-law's home, on the night of Kartik's full moon, she and Krishna become that seamlessly harmonious couple forever joined in a blissful heaven that is the idealized *sasurāl.* Or do they? Most of my informants were quite clear that at the end of the month of Kartik Krishna leaves Tulsi, despite the love and devotion he allegedly feels for her, to return to his beloved Radha, as the story of Krishna's feigned stomachache clearly articulates. Jonathan Z. Smith observes that ritual "is a means of performing the way things ought to be in conscious tension to the way things are." He accentuates the idealization of events embodied in ritual, arguing that "ritual relies for its power on the fact that it is concerned with quite ordinary activities placed within an extraordinary setting, that what it describes and displays is, in principle, possible for every occurrence of these acts. But it also relies for its power on the perceived fact that, in actuality, such possibilities cannot be realized" (1987, 109). In Kartik *pūjā,* however, the idealization of Krishna's bond with Tulsi is disrupted silently from the margins. Do Tulsi and Krishna live happily ever after in harmonious oneness, or does Krishna return to his beloved mistress, interrupting the blissful harmony of the conjugal bond? The ending is ambiguous, as is the "ending" of human marriages. Tulsi's marital fate, like that of human brides, is not entirely in her control. In Kartik *pūjā,* the complex, ambiguous, and frankly contradictory nature of marital and sexual imagery both expresses and functions as a vehicle for women to experience collectively the wishes, desires, and hopes, as well as fears, anxieties, and disappointments, that surround the conjugal bond.

The practice of arranging and executing the marriage and the teleology toward marriage inherent in Kartik *pūjā*—Krishna is raised to be married, and his marriage to Tulsi followed by their return to the in-law's home is the goal toward which the entire tradition is directed—produces and reproduces cultural norms that place marriage at the center of women's lives. Simultaneously, however, the focus on marriage reflects women's active reshaping of Sanskritic Kartik traditions in ways that highlight their own concerns and values. Marriage effects a significant transformation on the identity of a traditional Hindu bride, who leaves her own home for a new one, exchanging her natal family for her husband's family. Men do not move or leave their families behind; nor is male identity marked by marriage in the same way that female identity is. Hence marriage is not nearly as transformative for men as it is for women. As marriage is the focus of women's lives, in Kartik *pūjā* Tulsi's wedding becomes the focus of the entire month—not just one manifestation of the auspiciousness associated with Kartik, but the central, all-encompassing one.

In women's Kartik *pūjā,* the marriage of Krishna and Tulsi does not just supplement imagery of Vishnu awakening from a four-month slumber or vanquishing demonic forces as marking the return of cosmic auspiciousness, as we find in Sanskritic traditions; it supplants such imagery, yoking symbolism of renewal primarily to that which is of central importance to women: marriage and motherhood.[9] Recreating the world is not the work of muscular and transcendent male deities but of immanent deities joined in wedlock, their union embodying the end of inauspiciousness and the reawakening of the world.

Concluding Remarks

At the end of the description of Krishna's love play with the *gopīs* in the tenth book of the Bhagavata Purana, the narrator, Shuka, warns us that Krishna's sexual antics with the *gopīs*, who are after all the wives of other men, are not exemplary for human action and are not to be imitated by mortal beings (cf. Wulff 1984, 6). In her exploration of dramatic performances of Krishna and Radha's transgressive love that she witnessed in Braj in 1992, A. Whitney Sanford notes that the constructions of gender embodied in these materials are clearly meant for the "otherworldly" (*alaukika*) realm and are not meant to be enacted within the social realm. "In other words," she notes, "the gender constructions exemplified in this context are clearly presumed to be left in the realm of the ideal and not to be enacted in the so-called real world" (Sanford 1997, 180). Again and again, we find affirmation of

Kinsley's observation that Krishna's *līlā* "cares nothing for this world and its moral and social laws."

I would suggest, however, that in fact diverse notions about Krishna's *līlā* and its meaning exist. Predominant Sanskritic discourses about Krishna's divine play may well locate it clearly in the *alaukika* realm, but there are other discourses. In Kartik *pūjā,* perceptions of Krishna's *līlā* as unrelated to this-worldly realities are joined by other perceptions of it as partaking of the values of the worldly realm. Such grounding of Krishna imagery in the "so-called real world" is fitting with larger observations regarding how women tend to theologize and engage religion, assenting to predominant traditions but simultaneously reshaping or reinterpreting them in ways that render them more meaningful to women and more allied with the concerns, values, and experiences that remain central to women's lives.

Chapter 5

Kartik *Pūjā* Traditions and Women's Empowerment

In September 2000, my husband, five-month-old daughter, and I left Chicago for Cambridge, Massachusetts, where I spent the academic year as one of five research associates affiliated with Harvard Divinity School's Women's Studies in Religion Program. I had originally been selected as an alternate in the program, so when one scholar pulled out at the last minute, I was offered the fellowship instead. When the phone call came in late April, I hesitated, apprehensive about uprooting my family for the year, especially since I was a new mother struggling with the demands of parenting a newborn for the first time. Nevertheless, at that point I had only managed to produce drafts of the first two chapters of this book, and I was eager to complete a draft of the entire book while I had the momentum going. Harvard was offering me a year in which my only obligations would be to teach one graduate course and work on this project. My husband supported the idea. So off we went.

During that winter the advisory committee for the program gathered on campus and met with us to discuss our projects and hear about our progress. After my presentation, there were some questions. My recollection of exactly what was said has faded, but as I recall, one member of the committee asked me what I had concluded about how this ritual tradition might help or hinder Hindu women in their struggle for gender equality. To me the question sounded loaded. As a scholar of South Asia, I am keenly aware of American stereotypes of Indian culture that portray it as wholly oppressive toward women and contrast it unfavorably in this regard with the "liberated" West. There is a great deal wrong with this stereotype, and I felt that it was driving the question put before me. I responded that the aims of my project were primarily interpretive, not evaluative. I felt comfortable interpreting the tradition using the scholarly methods in which I was trained, but I did not feel it was my place to judge whether the tradition is "good" or "bad" for women.

What followed was what some might call a spirited interchange. The advisory committee member who raised this issue seemed to me to be interested primarily in conclusions regarding theologies, actions, and policies that would directly advance women's social, political, and economic power as defined by criteria articulated in contemporary Western feminist discourse. She viewed my project as merely descriptive, and she didn't seem to think it had much of a point. I was concerned about imposing Western feminist values on women who did not seem to me to have any desire to have such values imposed upon them and judging their religious traditions against such values. We reached an uncomfortable impasse.

There is no doubt, however, that recent scholarship on ritual practice, especially women's forms of ritual practice, is centrally concerned with issues of women's power and empowerment. In this chapter, I would indeed like to take up the issue of women's religious empowerment and ask, is this ritual tradition empowering to women? If so, in what ways might it be empowering? Having had much more time to reflect on these issues, if I could go back in time and return to that room and that meeting, what would I want to say to the scholar who challenged me so vigorously to enter into this conversation?

One way to think about issues of power in relation to women's ritual practices, especially in patriarchal contexts, is in terms of hegemonic and subordinate groups and the struggles that can emerge between them. What I have chosen to highlight in this book is how Kartik *pūjā* functions not as a medium for the reproduction of social power relations or resistance to these power relations, but rather how it functions as a medium for women's religious revision. Nevertheless, issues of social power are important to consider. Many scholars of South Asia would probably agree that predominant structures and ideologies in Hinduism and Indian culture, like other religions and cultures, are largely patriarchal and tend to discriminate against women in a number of ways. Scholars who work among Indian women also know that these women may circumvent, subvert, manipulate, or contest male authority in a variety of ways, even when they do not openly challenge the legitimacy of that authority. The last dozen years have given rise to a flood of scholarship about women's resistance to patriarchal ideologies and structures of male power in not just Hinduism and India, but in a variety of traditions, cultures, and contexts, through songs, stories, and other forms of speech as well as through religious practices (e.g, Raheja and Gold 1994, Kumar 1994, Abu-Lughod 1990, Griffith 1997).

While concerns about struggle or the dynamics of social dominance/resistance to domination certainly can be helpful for thinking about women's empowerment in traditional religious contexts, however, I would argue that the term "resistance" has been used overly broadly and in an unnuanced way to encompass too many types of discourses and practices. In particular, discussions of "resistance" tend sometimes to lump together alternative discourses, practices, representations, ideologies, and so forth, that do not conform to those associated with institutionally dominant groups with teleological discourses and practices that concretely envision or advocate an end goal of social change.[1] More subtlety may well be warranted here. Scholars of women and religion in many contexts have observed that women tend to reinterpret or reconfigure predominant religious practices and ideologies in ways that reflect women's specific values and experiences (e.g., Sered 1992, 1994; Northrup 1997). But to refer to most or all of such reconfigurations as "resistance" is, I think, to dilute significantly the meaning of that term.

Issues of gender hegemony, furthermore, including questions of compliance with and resistance to male authority and hegemonic structures and codes, are rarely straightforward. They are certainly not straightforward when it comes to Indian culture. The model of male dominance/female subordination is too simple and unnuanced to be applied across the board to all situations; frequently what is going on in gender relationships in specific, lived contexts is much more complex. Lina Gupta observes that Hindu women's status is influenced by many variables, so it is problematic to apply any pat dichotomy to issues regarding Hindu women and power (1997, 85). Usha Menon (2000, 90–92), for example, notes that women who are senior within a family often enjoy a good deal of authority, and they may with impunity engage in certain displays of discontent and refusal to cooperate with male family members. Menon describes these displays not as acts of resistance by dominated individuals but as "explicit expressions of power by dominant women" (91). Economic status, individual personality and living situation, caste, age, and other factors all come into play in diverse contexts. Furthermore, issues concerning resistance to/compliance with dominant social codes are frequently complex and intertwined, so it is sometimes misleading to classify particular actions or behaviors as either compliant or resistant whole-cloth. In her work on Hindu women's domestic rituals in South India, for example,

Mary Hancock explores ways that domestic ritual practice acts, simultaneously, as a site for both "reproduction of and resistance to hegemonic images of female subjectivity" in Sanskritic Hinduism (32).

As I have noted, the world of Kartik *pūjā* embraces predominant traditions pertaining to both Kartik and Krishna while simultaneously allowing Hindu women to rework and appropriate these traditions in ways that tend to express and celebrate female-centered concerns and values. For example, conceptions of Krishna as promiscuous lover, while not rejected, are compelled to share space with conceptions of him as a devoted husband who cares deeply for his beloved wife; the *gopīs*, while still understood as devotees of Krishna and hence subordinate to him, are interpreted as exemplars of female-female friendship as well, embodying values that are of importance to women in their own interpersonal relationships. In terms of traditional gender roles in Indian society, Kartik *pūjā* is a socially conservative tradition that does not challenge the central importance of the wife and mother roles in Hindu women's lives, instead reinforcing the importance of these roles. Judith Butler has argued that gender is primarily performative, and that gender identity is constituted through a stylized repetition of acts (Butler 1990, 171–80). In this regard, Kartik *pūjā* functions to affirm traditional ideals of Hindu womanhood that emphasize an alliance between women and the domestic sphere. Simultaneously, however, it affords women an opportunity to gather outside the home in a public space that is female controlled, and it provides women nearly exclusive liturgical authority within this space. In such ways, one could understand Kartik *pūjā* traditions, like the domestic rituals that Hancock explores, to be acting simultaneously as a site for both "reproduction of and resistance to hegemonic images of female subjectivity" prevalent in Sanskritic Hinduism.

Power is a malleable concept; power takes many forms, and religion may empower women in a variety of ways that are perhaps not always best described in terms of struggle or resistance. For example, Susan Wadley explores five rituals that Hindu women practice in Karimpur, North India, concluding that such rituals "may give psychological support to the women themselves because they allow women to have active control of events rather than depend completely on their male kin. . . . The rituals performed by Karimpur's women clearly reflect the women's social world—the world of the family and household. Their attempts to have active control over these most important facets of their lives may in fact be most critical for our understanding of Karimpur's women's rituals" (1989, 109). Wadley does not use language of empowerment specifically in speaking of

Hindu women's religious rites, stressing instead the "psychological support" they offer in enabling women to feel they have active control over events that are important to them. In her work on women's rituals, however, Anne Mackenzie Pearson does specifically invoke language of empowerment. Pearson explores in particular Hindu women's *vrats*. Like Wadley, Pearson concludes that "women use *vrats* as a way to gain control over their own lives." But she goes on to argue that *vrats* are indeed a source of empowerment for women in two ways: first, by providing them with a degree of personal autonomy; and second, by tapping into traditional religious notions of power (*tapas* and *śakti*) cultivated through ascetic practice (1996, 10). Hindu women, "traditionally denied access to formal aceticism, have found a way to tap into this powerful realm for their own benefit through the performance of *vrats*" (11).

In speaking of the interface between religious practice and women's empowerment, some scholars address explicitly what they mean or do not mean to circumscribe when they invoke "power" language, being careful to limit their claims. In an essay exploring the life of Tara Devi, a woman who becomes a human vehicle of the Goddess, for example, Kathleen Erndl emphasizes that the type of power she wishes to address is specifically spiritual or religious power. As the Goddess's vehicle, Tara Devi becomes a "vehicle for dispensing the Goddess's grace and healing power" with a "never-ending stream of pilgrims, most of whom hear about her through word of mouth, showing up at her door" (Erndl 1997, 27). Erndl concludes that Tara Devi gains "immense personal power" through her relationship with the Goddess, a power that "does not end with a sense of personal self-worth," which Wadley emphasizes, but is "also acknowledged in the community" (30). Nevertheless, Erndl notes that her own emphasis on Tara Devi's religious empowerment does not intend to "downplay the subordination of women either in Hindu hegemonic discourse or in the economic, social, or educational realms of Indian society" (19).[2] In a similar vein, Ann Gold explores a cycle of springtime rituals in which, she maintains, Hindu women celebrate female power, both "demonic and divine," and in so doing "make claims for female worth and community that run counter to male-authored devaluations and fragmentations" (2000, 213). She describes conceptualizations of gender evident in women's celebrations as "counterpoints" that offer "both blunt and subtle denials of a dominant male-authored discourse of female devaluation and subordination" (226). She notes, however, that it is not her intention to argue that "women's counterpoint claims give them any significant advantages in economic or political realms" (227).

Gupta contrasts notions of power that denote physical or sociopolitical power with the traditional Hindu concept of power as an inner, spiritual power essential to human evolution (1997, 85–86).[3] She argues that Hindu women's performance of prescribed rituals functions to cultivate and augment such inner, religious power, increasing women's power overall.

Clearly when scholars of women and religion speak of power and empowerment in these contexts, they refer to a wide variety of forms that power may take. They may invoke, among other things, notions of divine or transcendent power, inner spiritual power, enhanced prestige or influence in the community, increased autonomy, sense of personal or collective female self-worth, or special authority in relation to a specific religious tradition or sphere. The term encompasses a range of meanings, and it is important to remember that empowerment in one sphere might have no effect on, or might even diminish, power in another sphere. Women may derive a sense of empowerment through religious practice even when that power has nothing to do with resistance to patriarchal structures or women's economic, social, or political advancement in the public sphere; or feelings of religious empowerment might even mitigate against social or economic empowerment rather than contribute to it. What kind of power matters most to an individual might depend more on that person's most cherished values and commitments than on a "correct" understanding of what constitutes "real" power. Hence a religious conservative may legitimately profess to feeling empowered by a practice that a secular feminist experiences and interprets as profoundly disempowering. The two would likely be operating out of completely different value systems, priorities, and commitments regarding women's empowerment and hence would have fundamentally different descriptive accounts of what constitutes real or vital power.

In making such claims, I do not wish to imply that anything goes when it comes to questions of women and power. Women's reports of feeling empowered by religious practice do not, and cannot, override or compensate for a lack of social, economic, or political empowerment, and it would be misleading to invoke such reports to conceal, ignore, minimize, or deny specific forms of women's oppression in spheres where such exists. On the other hand, even within contexts marked by institutionalized male hegemony, such reports should not simply be dismissed as forms of "false consciousness" or self-delusion, which would indicate a lack of serious engagement with women's experiential claims.

Marjorie Proctor-Smith makes an important distinction in this regard between what she calls the emancipatory function of religion with respect to women, in which religion helps women transcend existing social restraints and behave in ways that are contrary to social expectation, and a sacralizing function, in which religion serves to affirm women's traditional roles and experiences as sacred (1993, 25–28). While the sacralizing function can serve to justify traditions that limit women's power and freedom in both public and private spheres, at its best it may serve to reveal "the dignity and holiness of women's work" (28). By sacralizing women's roles, religious practices may function to enhance women's self-esteem and feelings of self-worth, empowering women psychologically, emotionally, and spiritually even when the emancipatory function is largely or completely absent.

My own engagement with these issues leads me toward prizing thick description when it comes to women, religion, and power, approaching questions of power in ways that respect women's experiential claims while situating them in descriptive and analytic frameworks that recognize power as multidimensional, situational, and shifting. Here I find helpful A. K. Ramanujan's well-known description of Indian culture as tending to be "context-sensitive" more than "context-free" (Ramanujan 1989). Ramanujan borrows this formulation from the rules of formal grammar. While some grammatical formulations are context-free (e.g., all sentences must have a subject and predicate, regardless of the context), others are context-sensitive (e.g., how to indicate a plural depends on the particular term: "dog" becomes "dogs," but "child" becomes "children"). He concludes that Indian culture tends to be governed more by context-sensitive rules than by those that are context-free (47). I would suggest that women's power, too, manifests itself in Indian culture and Hindu religious practice in ways that tend to be context-sensitive, and claims about women's empowerment are most persuasive when they are qualified and richly contextualized. The challenge to scholars is to situate clearly and describe adequately the nature of women's power in diverse particular contexts, including the boundaries and limits of that power.

In terms of Kartik *pūjā,* certainly not all women who participate in this tradition feel empowered by it. Indeed, at least one of the participants I observed over the course of my research appeared to have been dragged along by female in-laws and did not seem the least bit interested in participating in the *pūjā* in any meaningful way. This participant may well have experienced the *pūjā* as overwhelmingly disempowering, since she seemed to be participating largely against her will. But, I would argue, some participants may well experience

Kartik *pūjā* as empowering in a number of ways. In making such a claim, I find myself confronting directly my own biases about women's relationship to power. I consider myself a secular feminist, and as such I am mostly interested in questions of women's social, economic, and political empowerment. I have a rather deep mistrust of conservative religion, especially in contexts where religious conservatives attempt to impose their values on those, like me, who do not share their values. Yet the women of Benares who so warmly welcomed me into their world have taught me a great deal about my own limitations. In taking seriously the experiences, ideas, and needs of the women who dedicate themselves year after year to celebrating Kartik *pūjā*, I would maintain that many do so because they find this tradition not only enjoyable and meaningful, but also, in some ways, empowering.

Kartik *pūjā* provides a forum for sacralizing women's values, roles, and experiences as potential or actual brides, wives, and mothers. The tradition as a whole helps render these values, roles, and experiences especially significant by enacting them on a sacred stage, relating them to a transcendent model. It provides women with a ritual space in which they may experience collectively emotions surrounding family and marriage in a way that acknowledges and honors the importance of these emotions and their centrality in women's lives. Extradomestic ties with other women tend to be an important source of power and value for women in societies that hold to a firm division between male and female roles (Sered 1994, 259), and Kartik *pūjā* facilitates the creation of such ties by enabling women to meet other women from around the city. The *pūjā* also provides women a chance to exercise religious agency and expertise outside of the home, and it affords women the opportunity to assume positions of ritual authority.

The women who celebrate Kartik *pūjā* function in a highly gender-segregated world, and the separation of the sexes seems to contribute to women's experience of empowerment in this context. In her study of women's religions, Sered proposes that downplaying gender difference may actually result in a devaluation of women. She observes that female-dominated religions tend to stress rather than play down gender differences, accepting nonegalitarian views of gender. In such contexts, however, women tend to reinterpret prevailing views of gender differences, considering the sphere that women control to be as good as or even better than the male sphere (1994, 205, 210). In religions that tend to be dominated institutionally by men, patterns of gender segregation may function similarly to provide women with clearly delineated spheres of responsibility, influence, and control, which may in turn help enhance women's sense of significance and self-worth (cf. Seymour 1999, 101, 277–78). Brenda E. Brasher, for example, notes that while congregational life in the two American fundamentalist Christian congregations she explores is male dominated overall, women participate in women-only ministry programs that establish and nurture "female enclaves, separate, sociocultural networks of women" (1998, 13). These enclaves, Brasher concludes, thrive because they serve to "empower women" by establishing a parallel symbolic world in which women can be "fully contributing participants" (27). The type of power to which she refers is, says Brasher, both personal and congregational (8–9).

In a similar vein, I would propose that Kartik *pūjā* traditions, like many other Hindu *vrat* and devotional traditions, function to empower women religiously by providing women with a clearly delineated sphere of meaningful religious responsibility and authority that they and they alone control. Kartik *pūjā* traditions also function to enhance many women's sense of gender virtue, affirming the value of what participants tend to perceive to be both women's ordained sphere of labor and women's inherent nature. I make this latter claim based on formal interviews that I conducted with *pūjā* participants. One of the questions I asked was "Why is the *pūjā* for women only? Why don't men participate?" When I asked this question, I expected to be told that only women do this *pūjā* because the *gopīs* who serve as the role models for participants were female, so those humans who participate in the *pūjā* must also be female.[4] However, among the thirty-six informants who responded directly to this question, only seven invoked the *gopīs'* femaleness, and of these seven only two emphasized it. More informants (eleven) emphasized the division of labor between men and women in the family. But the largest number—twenty-four respondents (67%)—invoked differences between men and women's natures in ways that clearly favored women as the superior gender. For many *pūjā* participants, the fact that women and not men engage in this form of religious practice has to do with the inherent differences between women's and men's natures and social roles, differences that affirm women's worth and the seriousness of women's responsibilities over those of men.

With respect to the division of labor between women and men, some of the women I spoke with emphasized the role of men as breadwinners. When I asked, "Why don't men participate in Kartik *pūjā*?" I was told that men are busy in their jobs, which is their main sphere of concern, and hence do not have time to devote to things like household matters and religion. Religion is the job of women. Some informants also related this division of labor to the widely held notion that women's husbands reap the benefits of their wives' religious actions. Since men have to work, women attend to religious matters and transfer half of the benefit to the men. This way, both can gain religious merit without any disruption to the man's job.

Women who invoked this division of labor to explain men's lack of participation in Kartik *pūjā* tended to say little else about it. Some, however, expressed impatience with what they perceive to be an unequal distribution of the workload that places too much responsibility on the shoulders of women. One young widow from Rajasthan whom I interviewed in 1997 clearly thinks that men have it too easy. She told me, "Men go and earn outside and bring the money home. But who manages it? Women manage it. Whom will a woman feed first? The elders in the family, her husband, her son, her daughter, and guests if there are any, a beggar if there is one. If a man has money, he will go and eat in a restaurant. He cannot deal with all this stuff. So this is why women are superior, because God did not give men as much strength (*śakti*) as he gave [women]." This participant portrays men's role as breadwinners as only one link in a lengthy chain of responsibility in caring for others. Women have a much more burdensome task in managing the rest of the process and attending to all family members and others in need, tasks that men are incapable of performing, and she perceives women's ability to carry out these tasks as signs of their inherent superiority. Similar sentiments were also expressed by another informant who claimed, "Men cannot do as much work as women can do. For example, suppose you do your housework properly in your home. Then suppose that for one day you leave your house; a man cannot keep the house properly. He will just eat and then go and earn money. Men cannot do what women do. God has made them like this."

Another *pūjā* participant, Savitri, also expressed impatience with what she seemed to perceive as an unfair division of labor between men and women. At the time that I first interviewed her in 1995, Savitri was sixteen years old and unmarried (she was still unmarried when I last saw her in February of 1998). She had been observing Kartik *vrat* and *pūjā* traditions since 1990, primarily for the purpose of obtaining a good husband and family of in-laws in the future. In responding to my question about male nonparticipation in Kartik *pūjā*, she remarked, "Girls will have to look after a house, a family—they have to take care of the entire household. Right now girls (my age) are free, but later on, this and that keep coming, and they have to take care of this and that. And what do the boys have to do? Their only concern is to work and earn. Besides this they have nothing else to do." Savitri appears to think that working a job to earn money is not very burdensome. Women's work, on the other hand, is much more onerous. Not only must women care for the entire household, juggling "this and that" at every turn, they must also undertake *vrats* and other rituals in order to insure the well-being of the entire family. While Savitri seemed happy to leave the workplace to men, she did express concern that men do not take enough responsibility for the religious activities that ensure the well-being of the family. She went on to tell me, "Men ought to help somewhat in religious work. The thing is that within the family, they separate the tasks. If you do lots of *pūjā,* then the effect can benefit the children . . . (so) both men and women should do a little bit, so that our children will be well."

Savitri's response highlights the connection between women's performance of *vrats* and *pūjā*—which can bring benefits to self, spouse, and children—and a general concern for the well-being of family and household. Gayatri, an older woman who has observed Kartik *pūjā* for most of her adult life, also makes this connection, and conversely sees in men's lack of participation in such rituals a lack of concern for the domestic sphere. She remarks, "Every woman has the desire that 'I should get a good husband, he should be well, I should have sons, and the sons should live. I should get wealth.' Men don't care about these things that much. Men don't think, 'I should have this kind of wife,' or 'I should have a son or a daughter.' They don't think about these things that much. Women care more about everything."

The *pūjā* participants quoted above see men's lack of participation in Kartik *pūjā* primarily in relation to a division of labor in the family that some view as problematic, letting men off the hook too easily. For other women, however, the fact that men do not participate in Kartik *pūjā* is directly related to their inherent laziness, their lack of discipline in getting up early in the morning, and their inability to sit patiently for long periods of time—all qualities that mitigate against their ability to participate in this form of worship. When I asked Kusumlata why men did not participate in Kartik *pūjā,* for example, she told me simply, "in Benares, men are lazy. They cannot get up early, and they will say, 'We are not going to do this hypocritical crap (*prapañch*).' " In a similar vein, one older woman, a long-time observer of Kartik, threw her hands into the air in response to my questions and asserted: "The way women sit down and do *pūjā*—men will not do this much. Men cannot sit that long. They will say, 'Let's go home' (*calo—ghar*!). The most they will do is offer water. But we offer Bel leaves, water, turmeric, sandalwood paste, rice, and flowers. Men would not offer that much."

Other women invoked additional shortcomings that prevent male participation as well. One participant, for example, complained, "Men can't sing. Men can't tell stories. Women do all this. . . . (Men) don't care about singing songs. So you won't see any men in this *pūjā*. It is ours. Men will just get up in the morning and bathe, and then they will say, 'Give me food; I have to go to the office.' That's it (*bas*)." Speculating about what would happen if men did participate, another informant, Sashikala, expressed similar concerns about male lack of skill and creativity, noting, "Suppose that they made their own group—then they couldn't sing, because men cannot sing properly, and they can't tell stories. They can only read books and do *pūjā* outside [in temples]."

Other women I interviewed also claimed that men are inherently less religious than women or just lack appreciation for religion and religious ritual in general. One Kartik participant for example, stated to me flatly, "Men don't have as much interest in *pūjā* as women have. Men are like dolls. They just stand there." Kusumlata, the participant who assured me that "In Benares, men are lazy" also proclaimed that "In India, women are more religious (*dharmic*)" than men, a view that is widely held by Hindus living all over India. Another participant confirmed men's irreligiosity in stating, "Men don't believe as much as we do. They won't do as much *tapas* (austerity) as we do." And a housewife named Kamlesh told me, "Men do not have any feeling (*bhāvanā*) for religious worship (*pūjā-pāṭh*). Some men who have some feeling come and do some *pūjā*, but most men are unable to sit still."

Several participants explained the differences between men's and women's religiosity by correlating qualities that women develop in their domestic roles with their heightened religious sensibility. Seymour (1999) notes that Indian women tend to view life as a progression of changing roles in which " 'personal growth' constitutes becoming increasingly embedded in familial relationships and responsibilities, not in achieving autonomy and independence from others" (279). In this regard, several of the women I interviewed correlated ability and willingness to be responsible for familial others with enhanced religious virtuosity. Tulsa Devi, for example, notes, "Women get married, they have kids; men do not invest any time in household things. The same thing with *pūjā*. Men go there, but they will stand outside with hands folded; they will not do the *pūjā* like us. Men don't like *pūjā* very much." Bhagavanti compared motherhood to doing *pūjā*, explaining, "We give birth to a child, we put oil on the child's body, we massage the child. Men can't do all this. So *pūjā* is like this. Men cannot do as much as we do. They cannot do it according to the rules." Hem Kumari portrayed motherhood and concern for children's welfare as the source of women's religiosity, noting "Mothers are considered supreme because they give birth to children, nurture them, bring them up, and teach them how to walk. . . . That is why mothers are always supreme, because they take so much trouble to bring up children, and they give birth. That is why God is always behind them, to protect them. (And) that is why (they are more religious), because women have to bear most of the pain. If a child gets sick, they are the ones who bear the brunt of it."

Whereas Savitri and Gayatri, quoted above, lamented the fact that men do not take much of a role in the religious activities like Kartik *pūjā* that would enhance their families' well-being, those who communicated a negative view of men's religious discipline tended to portray men as "wet blankets" who would only spoil the *pūjā* for the women if they were to participate. One day in 1995 when I was having tea with two participants, Kamlesh and Tulsa Devi, I asked them if they found it convenient (*suvidhā*) that men do not participate in Kartik *pūjā*. Kamlesh noted, "Yes, if the men don't take part in the *pūjā,* this is very convenient for us. If men sit with us, there are constraints. They say, 'Hurry up! Let's go!' and we feel anxious." Tulsa Devi affirmed Kamlesh's remarks, noting, "You feel like walking around, and your husband is there, then he says, 'Hurry up! Let's go! Let's go, let's go!' So here's the thing; when the men are with you, they do what they want to do. We cannot do what we want to do." Kamlesh then responded, "So, for example, if men are sitting there, and we feel like dancing or singing, and men are sitting there, then how can we do it? If men were there, how could we dance? We'd be repressed, afraid, and ashamed. And if you are by yourself, then you sing, jump, and dance a lot."

On one level, as Kamlesh notes, they like the fact that men are not around because women are freed from constraints imposed by modesty, and they are able to act in ways that they could not if men were observing them. But this is not the only reason. Underlying their remarks appears to be an understanding that men are impatient and lacking religious feeling, and they predict that if men were to participate, they would force their wives to cut the *pūjā* short. Another informant echoed such sentiments in a different conversation, remarking: "With men, there is pressure. There is a burden. They would keep interrupting us, saying, 'Hurry up! Hurry up! Let's go!' " Chandni Devi gave a similar response when I asked her, too, if she found it convenient that men do not take part in the *pūjā,* only she emphasized the demands that men place on women with respect to domestic chores. With an enthusiastic "yes," she explained to me: "The reason is that women think, *There are no men, so let's sing together, and play together.* Otherwise at home men always scream, 'You go and spend so much time in your *pūjā,* and we don't get our food on time—our lunch and dinner. None of the work in the house is getting done on time.' This is what they keep screaming. All the men scream, 'You were late, you were late (last time)! Come back quickly (this time)! The children have to go to school.' " Chandni Devi appears to think that men care more about their meals and schedules than they do about religious observance.

Of the thirty-six informants that I interviewed, only two described perceived distinctions between men and women's attitudes and behaviors as primarily a result of custom (*rivāj*) or habit (*ādat*). Among the informants who addressed this issue, most attributed such distinctions to differences in men's and women's inherent nature (*svabhāv*). One informant, for example, Ramavati, in describing why women like *pūjā* more than men responded to my question "Is this just habit?" by insisting, "This is not habit; this is how it has been inscribed in the house of God (Bhagavan)." Similarly, Tulsa Devi commented, "Men are more attached to their business and earning so they give less time to *pūjā.* This is their nature (*bhāv*)." Another informant, in explaining why men don't do like to do *pūjā* proclaimed, "From the very beginning it is like that. Men are like that from the beginning (of their lives). That is their nature (*svabhāv*); it has always been like that." When my research associate, Sunita, then asked, "Are women by nature more religious than men?" she responded, "Yes, yes, yes! Women always walk on the path of religion (*dharma*) more than men. By nature (*svabhāv*), men don't have as much religious feeling as women do. By their nature women will do *pūjā;* even if their husbands forbid them, they will do it."

Sered notes that in female-dominated religions, widespread sexist ideas concerning gender are reinterpreted "as evidence of women's greater interest in, or talent for, religious activity" (Sered 1994, 197). This seems to be the case also with respect to Kartik *pūjā.* For the women I interviewed, there are two primary ways to explain men's lack of participation. Several women suggested that within the family, the primary role of men—their *dharma* (duty) as husbands and fathers—is economic; they are wage earners, and making money has nothing to do with votive rites or religious devotion. A majority, however, associate men's absence from the *pūjā* with inherent male traits, which they contrast—explicitly or implicitly—in a rather negative way with women's traits; men are lazy, too lazy to get up for an early *pūjā* (but, it is implied, women are not lazy, since they do in fact get up early for the *pūjā*); men are impatient and hence lack the discipline to sit through a long *pūjā* (which, by the way, women manage to sit through every day for a month); men are unable to sing or tell stories, basic skills required in many forms of Hindu religious devotion (but women can do this); men are not religious (but women are). These descriptions of men's nature are critical in tone, suggesting that at least in the area of religious observance, men are flawed, and the inherent nature of males renders them less capable than women.

Had the context been different—had I asked directly, for example, "What are men like?" or "What are women like?" without connecting such questions to issues of religious observance—I may well have gotten completely different answers. We all hold multiple and frequently contradictory views of the opposite gender, and different contexts might evoke differing proclamations about what the other gender is like. Hence the views that emerged in response to my questions are probably not the only perspectives on men that these women have to offer. But informants who responded to my questions took their cues from the context. Those who participate in Kartik *pūjā* value it highly. Since observing Kartik *pūjā* is such a good, and yet only women do it, it seems reasonable to assume that there is some inherent defect in males that helps explain why they don't also take part.

In her book *Pierced by Murugan's Lance*, Elizabeth Collins reminds us that "social relations encoded in ritual are not simply relations of domination; rituals also represent conceptions of respect and communality and moral obligations that those of high status may have to care for their dependents" (1997, 173). In other words, rituals have to do not just with relations of social power, but also with ethical values. Many women who participate in Kārtik *pūjā* clearly describe their participation as an ethically valorized activity that expresses and reflects the inherent virtue and strength of their gender. Their proclamations of female value provide a moral framework of self-evaluation in which women claim superiority for themselves.

There is little doubt that women in India, like women around the world, do not enjoy the same political, economic, social, or educational advantages that men in India enjoy. Indian women, like women around the world, tend to suffer forms of material oppression that are gender based. Many of the scriptures, institutions, and traditions of Hinduism, like those of many other religious traditions, tend to reflect male biases that devalue women, marginalize them, or exclude them from positions of institutional power and authority. But this does not mean that Hindu women living in India, or that women from other cultures and religious traditions, merely reproduce male hegemonic norms and ideologies, nor does it mean that they experience their traditions as monolithically oppressive. Culture helps organize human experience, but it does not wholly determine people's actions and thoughts; rather, it serves as a context in which subjects act (Collins 1997, 182; cf. Geertz 1973, 14), and subjects "are capable of interpreting and reconstructing their identities within the cultural discursive contexts to which they have access" (Kapadia 1995, 7). Through their participation in Kartik *pūjā* traditions, Hindu women construct and reconstruct their own identities as strong, valued beings, empowered by both their cultural traditions and their female natures.

Appendix: Transliterated Song Texts

Chapter 3

1. (page 107)

Refrain: āj sakhī nārāyaṇ jagāvaiṅ, rādhikā śrī Kṛṣṇa jagāvaiṅ, jānakī raghunāth jagāvaiṅ, lakṣmī nārāyaṇ jagāvaiṅ, pārvatī mahādeva jagāvaiṅ

jo sakhī baṛebhore jagāvaiṅ (2X),
gaṅgā jamunā kā darśan pāvaiṅ (2X)
jo sakhī savere jagāvaiṅ (2X)
mālā phūl belpatra chaṛhāvaiṅ (2X)
jo sakhī din caṛhale jagāvaiṅ (2X)
mākan/makkhan miśri kā bhog chaḍhāvaiṅ (*or* lagāvaiṅ) (2X)
jo sakhī dupahariya jagāvaiṅ (2X)
dāl-bhāt mālphuā chaḍāvaiṅ (*or* lagāvaiṅ) (2X)
jo sakhī tipahariyā (*or* tijhariyā) jagāvaiṅ (2X)
kāṛ-chirauñji kā bhog lagāvaiṅ (2X)
jo sakhī sañjhariyā jagāvaiṅ (2X)
chaumukhdiyanā bātti jalāvaiṅ (2X)
jo sakhī ādhīratiyā jagāvaiṅ (2X)
tosak takiyā galaicā lagāvaiṅ (*or* bicāvaiṅ) (2X)
jo sakhī āṭho gharī (*or* paharī) jagāvaiṅ (2X)
Śiv kā bhakti amar pad pāvaiṅ, godī meṅ nandalālā khilāvaiṅ

2. (page 108)
uṭhu more hari jī bhaye bhinusaharā, dātuna khulā karauṅ/
karahu asnān

mākhan misri mukh meṅ dālo, tel phulel prabhu apatan kījīye
gangā jal asnān karāīṅ
kākar pāpaṛ aur guṛ mevā
itane ka hari jī tūṅ karuhuṅ kalevā (*or* karelā kaleva)
laciyā tamolin biṛā līyāaiṅ (*or* lagāvaiṅ)
sāj mālin gajarā pahirāvaiṅ
ārati mangal mādho jī kī

3. (page 109)

nahāi dhoy ke cale acche govind dekho (*or* dekhā)
hāth sone kā jhaṛiyā jal caṛāvat dekhā
hāth sone kā bāṅsurī bajāvat dekhā
goṛe sone kā pāyal, cuṭakāvat dekhā
hāth phūloṅ kī ḍaliyā phūl caṛhāvat dekhā
sīr sone kā seharā calakhāvat dekhā
pahire pitāmbar dhotiyā jhalakāvat dekhā
mukh pān kā biṛā chubhalāvat dekhā
naino kālī kājal lagavāvat dekhā
pauṅ sone kā kharaṛauṅ khuṭkāvat dekhā
haro govinda haro narāyan haro mere man kī cintā

4. (page 110)

har har vāsudevakī nande
dehuna candarāvati basu gangā dūāre
chīṭe cāval a kṛṣṇ ke pāṇī piyo kināre
Gaure gaure rām (*or* rāv) lāl rāī Damodar sāv (*or* sāṅ) lāl
lāī Damodar khīcarī maiṅ haṅs ke pūjū pātarī
tū khā Nārāyan khīcaṛī maiṅ pūjū terī kāyā
niranjan terī māyā
Sūdhā khol de kevāṛī Rādhā bāhare khaṛī
haro govinda haro narāyaṇ haro mere man kī cintā

5. (page 112)

ugat sūrajavā, ugat cakavā
gāuvā bandhana coṛ ke
mero svarg sundar dehu svāmī
tiriyā janam phal dījiye
nahāye kā phal dījiye
mere āvā gavā phal dījiyeṅ

baikuṇṭh vāsā dehū svāmī, apanā śaraṇ meṅ rākhiye,
mere āvā gavā phal dījiyeṅ
kachū āj kā kachū kāl kā, kachū aur ke din rāt kā
hare hare,
ram lalā kā sevā kariyoṅ, sevā karo bhagavān kā
ratn-siṅghāsan baiṭhī mātā, baiṭhī mātā
sakhin odan/orahūnā lāvatī; sakhin orahūnā, roj bāṛhe, roj bāṛhe
kāhū kī chotī, kāhū kī motī
le sūṭūkun, sūṭūkāvatī,
"mere lalanā kā kachū dosh nāhī, sakhī, śaṇ (jhagaṛā) macāvatī
bolāī lāo kuṅvar rādhā kuṅvar rādhā, sakhī kā sardār ko
sakhī, rār macāvatī. jāī bolāo kuṅvar rādhā
mere lalā kā ati śobhā nyārī."
le ūr kaṇṭh lagāvatī

6. (page 113)

hāth joṛ kar binavaiṅ nāth, binavaiṅ nāth,
tiriyā janm mat dehū hamār, dehū hamār
tiriyā janm hau, hīn hamār, hīn hamār, kaīse parichab caraṇa tohār, caraṇa tohār
tiriyā janm hau, nika tohār, nika tohār,
nit uth paricha huṅ caraṇa hamār, caraṇa hamār
hamare paṭukā tore tīr, tore tīr
ham ta nahāibai gangā tīr, pañcagangā tīr, benī mādhav tīr, maṇikarnika tīr,
assī ghāṭ par debai dān, debai dān,
gauvā kā poñch dhai kai utarav pār, utarav pār
bīc jamūn meṅ bole kāg, bole kāg
kṛṣṇ milan ta (*or* milāvat) hoi haiṅ āj, hoi haiṅ āj
ṭhāṛi rādhikā sagun vicār, sagun vicār
kṛṣṇa gayeṅ rādhā ke pās, rukmiṇi ke pās, satyabhāmā ke pās, tulsā ke pās
jis kī hai ratn-nyārī āṅkh

7. (page 114)

gangā hari manjan kījiye, mātā harī manjan kījiye
kaīsan gangā kaīsan pānī (2X)
kaīsan kṛṣṇ kī aṅcal joṛī, rādhā kṛṣṇ kī aṅcal joṛī

sāṅvar gangā nirmal pānī,
sāṅvar kṛṣṇ kī aṅcal joṛī, rādhā kṛṣṇ kī aṅcal joṛī
baṛhe gangā, baṛhe pānī (2X)
baṛhe kṛṣṇ kī ancal joṛī, rādhā kṛṣṇ kī aṅcal joṛī

8. (page 115)

ārati tulsā karauṅ tumhārī (2X)
maiṅ tose pūñchū ai rānī tulsā (2X),
ketor pitā kaun mahatārī (2X)
jaladhār pitā, dharat mahatārī (2X)
ṭhākur-jī kā prem piyārī (2X)
sīr par rahūṅ sīr chāyā karuṅ (2X)
mukh me jāye pavitar kāyā (2X)
yahīṅ guṇ bhaīlin prem pīyārī (2X)
lambī lambī ḍār hariya hari pātī (2X)
tulsā (*or* mātā) phūl caṛhai din rātī, mālā phūl caṛhai din rātī
chappan bhog lage harīyā ke (2X)
bin tulsā harī ek na mānaiṅ (2X)
jaisa jaisa tulsā let halorā (2X)
tasa tasa ṭhākur karaiṅ kalevā (2X)
madhu meva (*or* pañc mevā) pakavān mithāī (2X)
tulsā jī kā bhog lagāī, mātā jī kā bhog lagāī
jo sakhī tulsī-jī kī āratī gāvaiṅ (2X)
so vaikuṇṭh basera pāvaiṅ
janam janam suhāg pāvaiṅ, ridhi siddhī sab sampatī ghar āvaiṅ

9. (page 124)

jhulāo merī sajanī re śyām jhūlai palanā (2X)
kāheṅ kā tero banā palanā, kāheṅ lāgī ḍor
jhulāo merī sajanī re śyām jhūlai palanā
agare chandan kā banā palanā, reśm lāgī ḍor
jhulāo merī sajanī re śyām jhūlai palanā
jhulat-jhulat śyām macalī gayeṅ haiṅ
dudh na piye lalanā, god na khele lalanā
jhulāo merī sajanī re śyām jhūlai palanā
sāt sakhī din-rātan āveṅ, nazar lagāve lalanā, ṭonā lagāyeṅ lalanā
jhulāo merī sajanī re śyām jhūlai palanā
rāī-nūn, jasodā utāre, hasan lāge lalanā, khelan lāge lalanā

jhulāo merī sajanī re śyām jhūlai palanā
surāī-gaīyā kā dudh maṅgāyo, pīyan lāge lalanā, khelan lāge lalanā
jhulāo merī sajanī re śyām jhūlai palanā
je more lalanā ke palanā jhulāveṅ, debe jaṛāū kaṅganā
jhulāo merī sajanī re śyām jhūlai palanā
dūr khelan mat jāyo kanhaīyāṅ, roī mare terī maīyā
jhulāo merī sajanī re śyām jhūlai palanā
ekaī bhaurā lāl ke tū; ghāre hī khelo lalanā
jhulāo merī sajanī re śyām jhūlai palanā
pāṅv paijaniyaṅ kamar kar dhaniyāṅ, calan lage kachū aur
jhulāo merī sajanī re śyām jhūlai palanā

10. (page 125)

rastā ṭeke rahiyoṅ jī, baṅsī ke bajaīyā mero prāṇ liye jāy
kahāṅ gāye gaīyā, kahāṅ gāye gvāl, kahāṅ gāy baṅsī bajāvan hār
rastā ṭeke rahiyoṅ jī, baṅsī ke bajaīyā mero prāṇ liye jāy
van gāye gaīyā, van gāye gvāl, keśav gaye apne sasurāl
rastā ṭeke rahiyoṅ jī, baṅsī ke bajaīyā mero prāṇ liye jāy
āy gaīlan gaīyā, āy gaīlan gvāl
ajuhan āye kapatī nandalāl
rastā ṭeke rahiyoṅ jī, baṅsī ke bajaīyā mero prāṇ liye jāy
kā khaīye gaīyā, kā khaīye gvāl, kā khaīyeṅ apane madan gopāl
rastā ṭeke rahiyoṅ jī, baṅsī ke bajaīyā mero prāṇ liye jāy
ghās khaīye gaīyā, dudh pīhiye gvāl, mākhan miśrī khaīye mero madan gopāl
chote chote bālak, saṅvar svarūp
baṛī-baṛī ākhiyāṅ dekhat anarup
rastā ṭeke rahiyoṅ jī, baṅsī ke bajaīyā mero prāṇ liye jāy
mīrā ke prabhū giradhar nāth, pāī gaīlan darśan hoī gaīlan nihār
rastā ṭeke rahiyoṅ jī, baṅsī ke bajaīyā mero prāṇ liye jāy

11. (page 126)

kaho kaho sakhī govind kab milihaiṅ? (2X)
sāñjh nāhī milihaiṅ, savere nāhī milihaiṅ (2X)
govind kab milihaiṅ?
kaho kaho sakhī govind kab milihaiṅ?
āj nāhī milihaiṅ kal nāhī milihaiṅ (2X)

milihaiṅ ādhī rāt
kaho kaho sakhī govind kab milihaiṅ (2X)

12. (page 127)

kahale rām jī ke nahāyelā kartikī, ham nahāilā kartikī. kāhe khātir? ann khātir, dhan khātir, bharal bhaṇḍār khātir, apne suhāg khātir, apne baikuṇṭh khātir!

13. (page 128)

maīyā gūṛ sāttū avaro ghīv leḍḍū
jābo maiṅ kāśī banāras vidyā paṛan ke (2X)
kā karabā ai bābū gūṛ sāttū avaro ghīv leḍḍū
tūhārā je pitā bāsūdev, gharahī vidyā paṛhiyā ho
tūhārā je bābā nandabābā, gharahī vidyā paṛhiyā ho
kā karebā ai baruā gūṛ, sāttū avaro ghīv leḍḍū
tuhārā je bhaiyā balarām, gharahī vidyā paṛhiyā ho

14. (page 131)

uṭhaū mālin, maliyā jagāvelā; uṭhaū mālin, bhaīl bin sār re (2X)
akhiyān ughār jab dekhalī maliniyā; dvare śrī rām dūlhā ṭhār re (2X)
itanā dinā meṅ dūlhā kabahū na dekhalī
āj dvāre kaise ṭhār re (2X)
itanā din mā mālin lagan nahī rahal
āj kā laganiyā baṛā tej (2X)
rām ghar mālin uṭhelā śagunvā
raci raci mauriyā dehū re (2X)
raci mauriyā dūlhā ākhiyoṅ na dekhalī
ā raci mauriyā kā holā re (2X)
āj more rām kā bihā re
āge-pāche jaise mālin dilre ke melā; bicavā meṅ sīyā jī kumārī (2X)
aṅgane meṅ sohe sālī saharajiyāṅ
kohabar meṅ sīyā jī kumārī (2X)

15. (pages 132–33)

deś hī deś rājā ciṭhṭhiyā paṭhavalan (2X)
āj more rām kā bihā jī (2X)

ānan nevatī lā, cānan nevatī lā (2X)
kāśī viśeśvanāth ho (2X)
ākāś se sarasvatī nevatī (2X),
pātāl se śeṣ-nāg ho, ānan aīlan, cānan aīlan (2X),
kāśī viśeśvanāth ho
ākāś se sarasvatī jī aīlī, pātāl se śeṣ nāg ho (2X)
sajī baritiyā calalan rājā rāmcandar,
bhaṭavā lelā bela māya-jī
ham toke debe bhaṭavā caṛhane ke ghoṛavā
more āge sītā bakhān re.
kā ham sītā bakhānī ho, rājā rām candar
sītā sūrajavā kā jot jī (2X). rām se sītā hai baṛī sundar,
daśarath kul ojiyār jī
sajī baratiyā calalan rājā rām candar
ceriyā kalaś lele thāṛ jī (2X)
toke mai debe ceriyā sāṛī se cīrā, more āge sītā bakhān jī
kā ham sītā bakhānī rāmcandar
sītā surujavā kā jot jī; rām se sītā hai baṛī sundar, donahūṅ
kul ojiyār jī
sajī baratiyā calalan rājā rām candar
babhanā pothiyā lele thāṛ ho (2X)
toke mai deve bābhan sone ka janeūvā, more āge sītā bakhān
re
kā ham sītā bakhānī ho, rājā rām candar
sītā sūrajavā kā jot jī (2X). rām se sītā hai baṛī sundar,
daśarath kul ojiyār jī
sajī baratiyā calalan rājā rām candar
sālī sarahaj cheke lī dūvār jī
toke debe sarahaj gaj-motī haravā
more āge sītā bakhān jī, kā ham sītā bakhānī rājā rāmcandar,
sītā sūrujavā kā jot jī
rām se sītā hai, baṛī sundar, dūnahū kul ojiyār jī
more āge sītā bakhān jī. kā ham sītā bakhānī rājā rāmcandar,
sītā sūrujavā kā jot jī

16. (pages 133–34)

are mere kṛṣṇā ko koī mat dekho najariyā lag jāyegī
are kṛṣṇ tere jhārī kā cīrā kāno tere sūraj kī motī
cūnarī savāre sab sakhiyā najar lag jāyegī
are kalamī savāre sab sakhiyā najar lag jāyegī
mere kṛṣṇā ko koī mat dekho najariyā lag jāyegī

are gale sohe khāse kā jāmā kamar sohe gujarātī paṭukā
are jāmā savāre sab sakhiyāṅ, najar lag jāyegī
are paṭukā savāre sab sakhiyāṅ, najariyā lag jāyegī
mere kṛṣṇā ko koī mat dekho najar lag jāyegī
are pāṅv tere makhmal kā mojā (2X)
bainā tere kābul kā ghoṛā (2X)
are cābuk savāre sab sakhiyāṅ najariyā lag jāyegī
mehan savāre sab sakhiyāṅ najariyā lag jāyegi
mere kṛṣṇā ko koī mat dekho najar lag jāyegī
are kandhe sohe harivālā dolā, sej sohe raṅgavīlī lājo
pardā savāre sab sakhiyān najariyā lag jāyegī
are ghūṅghaṭ savāre sab sakhiyāṅ najariyā lag jāyegī

17. (pages 134–35)

jāī baīṭhe kauśalyā ke god, rāmchandra dūlhā bane (2X)
sīr sohe jārī kā maūrā (2X)
kalmī meṅ nāc rahī mor, rāmchandra dūlhā bane (2X)
jāī baīṭhe kauśalyā ke god, rāmchandra dūlhā bane (2X)
kāne sohe sūraj kī motī (2X)
bālā meṅ nāc rahe mor, rāmchandra dūlhā bane (2X)
jāī baīṭhe kauśalyā ke god, rāmchandra dūlhā bane (2X)
aṅg sohe kesariyā jāmā (2X)
caddar meṅ nāc rahe mor, rāmchandra dūlhā bane
jāī baīṭhe kauśalyā ke god, rāmchandra dūlhā bane (2X)
hāth sohe sone kī ghaṛiyā (2X)
kaṅganā meṅ nāc rahe mor, rāmchandra dūlhā bane
jāī baīṭhe kauśalyā ke god, rāmchandra dūlhā bane (2X)
pāv sohe makhmal kā mozā (2X)
sandal meṅ nāc rahe mor, rāmchandra dūlhā bane
jāī baīṭhe kauśalyā ke god, rāmchandra dūlhā bane (2X)
jāṅgh sohe kābūl kā ghoṛā (2X)
cābhūk pe nāc rahe mor, rām jī dūlhā bane
jāī baīṭhe kauśalyā ke god, rāmchandra dūlhā bane (2X)
saṅg sohe Janak (*or* sājan) kī betī (2X)
pardā meṅ nāc rahe mor, rām dūlhā bane (2X)

18. (page 135)

bidā nāhī karab ho, sītā mahārānī
sītā mahārānī ho, sītā mahārānī, bidā nāhī karab ho, sītā mahārānī
kev gaṅgā jamunā se jal bharī le aīheṅ? (2X) are kev more sīce phulvārī

bidā nāhī karab ho, janak dūlārī (2X), are kev more devatā ke
pūjā karihe (2X)
kevan mero pūjan sajāīyeṅ? (2X)
bidā nāhī karabeṅ, janak dūlārī (2X)
are, kev sakhī sang khelan jahiyeṅ? (2X) kev mero bābā
ghorahiyeṅ?
bidā nāhī karabeṅ Janak dūlārī (2X)
are kev more gharvā meṅ upar-nīce kariyeṅ? (2X) are ken
mero maīyā ghorahiye?
are kev mero nām ghorahiye
bidā nāhī karab ho, janak dūlārī

19. (pages 140–41)

mohan rasiyā tū banāras jaīyoṅ (2X)
bannī joge ho kaṅgan pākiṭ līyeṅ aīyo (2X)
pākiṭ meṅ le aīyo cāhe pars me le aīyo (2X)
palaṅg pe caṅh ke ho kaṅganā dhīre se pahanaīyoṅ (2X)
mohan rasiyā tū banāras jaīyoṅ (2X)
bannī joge ho ṭikavā pākiṭ lehale aīyo (2X)
pākiṭ meṅ le aīyo cāhe pars meṅ le aīyo (2X)
palaṅg pe caṛh ke ho ṭikavā dhīre se pahanaīyo (2X)
mohan rasiyā tū banāras jaīyoṅ (2X)
Bannī joge ho pāyal pākiṭ lehale aīyo (2X)
pākiṭ meṅ le aīyo cāhe pars meṅ le aīyo (2X)
palaṅg pe caṛh ke pāyal dhīre se pahanaīyo
mohan rasiyā tū banāras jaīyoṅ (2X)
bannī joge ho hār pākiṭ lele aīyo (2X)
pākiṭ meṅ le aīyo cāhe pars meṅ le aīyo (2X)
palaṅg pe caṛh ke ho haravā dhīre se pahanaīyo (2X)
mohan rasiyā tū banāras jaīyoṅ (2X)
bannī joge ho bichūā pākiṭ lele aīyo (2X)
pākiṭ meṅ le aīyo cāhe pars meṅ le aīyo (2X)
palaṅg pe caṛh ke ho bichūā dhīre se pahanaīyo (2X)
mohan rasiyā tū banāras jaīyoṅ (2X)

Chapter 4

20. (page 169)

bhaju man govinda, bhaju gopāl
haṅsi haṅsi rādhā pyārī pūchailī bāt

kṛṣṇa ke mathavā tilakavā kaīsan lāgal bā
kṛṣṇ kahalan sunā rādhā pyārī bāt, gaṅgā snān tilakavā lagī jāy
bhaju man govida, bhaju gopāl
haṅsi haṅsi rādhā pyārī pūchailī bāt
kṛṣṇa ke akhiyāṅ kajaravā kaīsan lāg
kṛṣṇ kahalan sunā rādhā pyārī bāt,
kalama uṭhāvat rośanāī lagī jāy
bhaju man govinda, bhaja gopāl
haṅsi haṅsi rādhā pyārī pūchailī bāt
kṛṣṇā ke muhavā lāl kaīsan bā
kṛṣṇ kahalan sunā rādhā pyārī bāt,
bhagat khilāvele pān mukh baīle lāl
bhaju man govinda, bhaja gopāl
haṅsi haṅsi rādhā pyārī pūchailī bāt
kṛṣṇ ke paūvā mahāvar kaīsan lāg
kṛṣṇ kahalan sunā rādhā pyārī bāt,
mehadī kā pātī aiṛī bhaīle lāl
bhaju man govinda, bhaja gopāl
haṅsi haṅsi rādhā pyārī pūchailī bāt
kṛṣṇ kā dhotiyā piyar kaīsan lāg
kṛṣṇ kahalan dhobiyā je dhotiyā badal liheṅ bāy
bhaju man govinda, bhaja gopāl
aitana vacan jab sūnalī rādhā pyārī
dhobiyā ke lehalī turant bulāy
sunu sunu dhobiyā hamro je bāt
kṛṣṇ ke dhotiyā badal kaīse jāy
dhobiyā kahalas sunā rādhā pyārī bāt
kṛṣṇ aur tulsā me ho gaīle bihā
bhaju man govinda, bhaja gopāl
aitanā vacan jab sunalī rādhā pyārī
bhitarā se hāni lehalī bajar kevāṛī
kṛṣṇ kahalan khola khola rādhā pyārī, bhajar kevāṛ
tulsā je hoīyeṅ dāsī tohār
bhaju man govinda, bhaju gopal

21. (page 170)

more pīchūvaṛvā lavaṅgiyā ke gachiyā,
lavaṅg cūvelā sārī rāt (2X)
lavaṅg-kaṭāī bābā palang salāvalan,
reśme bināval paṭīhāt ho (2X)

tāhī palaṅge sūtele dūlhā śrī kṛṣṇ dūlhā, tāhe pe rukminī deī rānī
ek or sūtele rādhe sa rukminī
bīcavā meṅ sūte śrī kṛṣṇ (2X)
tohase mai pūchilā e bahinī rukminī,
kaīsan damakiyā je āve (2X)
haṅsī-haṅsī kahele śrī kṛṣṇ jī batiyā,
tulsī sīrahanvā, bhaīlī thāṛ (2X)
tulsī damakiyā āvelā bās ho (2X), aihī avasar ham tulsī je paītī
jarī (*or* jaṛ) se kabārī ham letī (2X), jar se kabārī tulsī gaṅgā serahītū
chūṭī jaīt dūkhvā hamār ho (2X), jāhū tūhū ai rādhe, gaṅgā serahītū
kṛṣṇ kariheṅ snān (2X), kṛṣṇ caraṇvā hamahī chūī lihatī
jānam sūphal hoī jāī (2X), yahī avasar ham tulsī ke paītī
jar se kabārī leī āyī (2X), toharā ke ai tulsī jhakatī bhar saīyā
janam kā dūkh chūṭī jāī (2X), jāū dūhū ai ballī bharasaīyā jhokī dehatū
hoī jaītī māgh kī agnī (*or* agniyāṅ) (2X), maghavā a pūsvā pakeṛelā tusarvā
kṛṣṇ je tapiheṅ agīnī (2X), janam sūphal hoī jāī (2X)
Bolā śrī kṛṣṇ bhagavān kī jay!

Notes

Introduction

1. I will use the name "Benares" throughout the book since it is more familiar than "Varanasi" to many Western readers, while most Indian readers of this book will probably be familiar with both names. Diana Eck notes that the name "Benares" (also transliterated as "Banaras") is a corrupted form of "Baranasi," which is the Pali version of "Varanasi" (Eck 1982, 26).

2. The month is more properly written in Hindi as "Kārttik," from the Sanskrit "Kārttika." The Oxford Hindi-English Dictionary lists "Kārtik" (with one "t") as a corrupt form. But I have chosen to drop one of the "t"s and use the shortened form throughout the book because most of the popular literature available in Benares uses this shortened form.

3. The names of all informants in the book have been changed to help conceal their identities.

4. See also Caldwell 1999. In this work, Sarah Caldwell discusses very openly her own feelings of vulnerability and helplessness as a foreign ethnographer working in India.

Chapter 1. Kartik as a Sacred Month: The Kartik *Vrat* in Text and Context

1. Normal discrepancies between lunar and solar calendars mean that dates calculated by the solar calendar will not consistently correspond year after year to particular dates calculated by the lunar calendar. In addition, since the lunar year is about ten days shorter than the solar year, an intercalary month is inserted into the lunar year every two to three years to correct the discrepancy. When this happens the month of Kartik can fall quite a bit later than it does in years that are not intercalculated.

2. The full moon for which a month is named does not always appear in the asterism for that month each and every single year, but it never moves beyond the preceding or succeeding asterism (Freed and Freed 1964, 68-69).

3. These are known as the *amānta* system, in which months are counted from new moon to new moon, and the *pūrṇimānta* system, in which months are counted from full moon to full moon.

4. The Kartik Mahatmyas are not alone in praising themselves and their own meritorious powers. Lutgendorf notes that in general the Puranas "announce—frequently and often at considerable length—their own efficacy and the many benefits to be derived from listening to, reciting, or copying them or causing others to do so" (1991, 57).

5. The point when the sun leaves one constellation and enters another—the "cusp" of a zodiac—is called *saṁkrānti*. Each *saṁkrānti* is named after the zodiac into which the sun then enters (not the one that it leaves). While *saṁkrānti*s are primarily the basis of solar months—not lunar months, which are slightly shorter than solar months—each lunar month in the Hindu calendar is associated with a particular *saṁkrānti* and its corresponding constellation. Generally, months are associated with the last *saṁkrānti* to occur before the new moon in that month, which means that the sun enters into the Libra constellation during the one-month period leading up to the day of Kartik's new moon and is still in Libra on that new moon day.

6. This may seem puzzling, since the month of Kartik usually falls from mid-October to mid-November, but the autumnal equinox actually occurs around the twenty-first or twenty-second of September. The discrepancy in dates has to do with what is known as the precession of the equinoxes. In the Hindu calendar, the solar year is calculated as the time that it takes the earth to revolve once around the sun as measured with reference to fixed stars. A complete cycle of seasons, however, calculated from one vernal equinox to another, is actually slightly shorter than this. Hence there is a retrograde motion of the equinoxes in relation to the stars over time. The Hindu ritual calendar does not take into account this retrograde motion but calculates equinoxes according to the placement of the sun in relation to fixed stars that corresponded to the vernal equinox at the time, long ago, when the calendar was fixed. Over the years, the discrepancy between the true equinoxes—as measured by the length of days and nights at the equator—and the Hindu calendar's proclaimed equinoxes—as measured by the placement of the sun in relation to certain stars—has grown. The same is true of the solstices. Hence the solar transition that marks the winter solstice according to the Hindu calendar falls in mid-January; the vernal equinox, in mid-April; and the summer solstice, in mid-July.

7. "Fasting" in Hinduism encompasses a wide variety of food abstention practices, from complete abstention from all food and drink to abstention from a single type of edible product.

8. The importance of early-morning ritual bathing during the month of Kartik is lauded emphatically in the KMSP, which claims that such bathing

will enable one to escape torture at the hands of Yama, the Lord of Death, even if one undertakes such bathing casually, under compulsion, or unknowingly (3.24). Anyone, even a person defiled by thousands of sins, is said to be capable of obtaining spiritual liberation by bathing during Kartik (3.30, 4.78, 4.83).

9. The KMSP states that although one can bathe anywhere and in any type of water, it is best to bathe outside in a cold, publicly accessible body of water. Such bodies of water are ranked in terms of benefit: bathing in a well is the least meritorious, whereas one increases one's merit by bathing in a tank, lake, stream, or river, respectively (4.19–22). Although Benares is not specifically singled out, the text states that it is especially meritorious to bathe in a sacred place (*tīrtha*) or at a confluence of rivers (KMSP 4.23). Radha and Krishna themselves are said to have bathed in the Yamuna River in Mathura during the month of Kartik (KMSP 4.38).

10. The most well-known story of the Ganges's origin maintains that she descended from heaven to restore to life King Sagara's sixty thousand sons, who were burned to ashes by the fiery anger of the great Sage Kapila when they disturbed his meditations. To break her fall, Shiva caught the Ganges in the topknot of his hair, from which she flowed into India as a mighty river.

11. The KMSP states that bathing at Pancaganga in Kartik destroys instantly even a hundred thousand sins, and all of India's Hindu places of pilgrimage (*tīrthas*) are said to go to Pancaganga during the month of Kartik to bathe and purify themselves (KMSP 4.44–49). Shiva himself in his form as Vishveshvara, "The Lord of All," is said to take ablutions at Pancaganga during Kartik, along with Brahma and the seven oceans described in Puranic cosmology (Skanda Purana 4.2.60.136–37).

12. *Darśan* refers to an auspicious viewing of a deity or other conveyor of divine power (here the sky lamps) that has the ability to bestow blessings on the beholder. See Eck 1985.

13. See, for example, Padma Purana 7.24, 1.60.105ff, 1.61, and 6.23.

14. Diana Eck compares declarations of superiority in Mahatmya literature to what Max Muller called "kathenotheism," the praising and worshiping of one god at a time in which the deity of the moment is hailed as the best of all (1980, 81–82).

15. Many *vrat*s are, in fact, said to be conducive to both spiritual liberation (*mukti*) and worldly prosperity or well-being (*bhukti*). This is a fairly common formula.

16. Amla is a type of fruit. Amla and the Amla tree play important religious roles during Kartik (see chapter 2).

17. The Bindu Madhava temple is considered one of the most important Vaishnava temples in Benares. A sage and great ascetic named Agnibindu is said to have come to Pancaganga to eulogize Vishnu. Pleased with his devotion, Vishnu grants Agnibindu the boon that he will remain at Pancaganga for the sake of devotees and nondevotees alike. To honor Agnibindu, Vishnu takes a form at this *ghāṭ* that incorporates the names of both his devotee (Bindu) and his wife, Lakshmi (also called "Ma," "Mother") into his own name, which becomes Bindu Madhava (Skanda Purana 4.2.60.14ff).

18. For more on the relationship between celibacy, strength, and *śakti* in Hindu contexts, see Alter 1992.

19. This is an epithet of respect.

20. *Pītāmbar* is a type of yellow garment associated especially with Krishna.

21. Kirin Narayan (1997a, 50–58) has written eloquently about a different version of this story that a female storyteller in Kangra told her. On turning feces into gold, see also Wadley, 1986.

22. The cowherd boys or *gvāl-bāls* are Krishna's childhood companions and playmates when he is growing up in Braj.

23. Radha and Krishna's female friends and companions, the cowherdesses or *gopīs*, are often referred to as the *sakhīs*, female friends. For more on the *sakhīs*, see chapters 2 and 3.

24. The story of Radha and Tulsi's rivalry over Krishna recounted in chapter 4 is similar in structure to this story. Both narratives highlight the feelings of competition and envy attributed to the females who must share Krishna's affections and attention.

25. Cf. Sundara Kanda, ch. 27; Vana Parva, ch. 291, *śloka* 41.

26. Clothey (1982, 169–-70, 174) mentions a one- or two-day celebration called Tiukkarttikai that takes place in Tamil Nadu and represents the Krittikas's suckling and nurture of Karttikeya. J. N. Banerjea reports that women seeking progeny worship clay images of Karttikeya on the last day of Kartik month (Banerjea 1956, 364; cf. Rana 1995, 100), and in Bengal a fair in honor of Karttikeya is reportedly held on this day (Rana 100), supporting an association between Kartik's full moon period and the worship of Karttikeya. The Skanda Purana specifically recommends worshiping Karttikeya throughout the month of Kartik (I.2.34.99).

Chapter 2. Kartik's Religious Celebrations and the Churning of the Ocean of Milk

1. See Brahmanda Purana 4.9.31–47 and Devi-Bhagavata Purana 9.41. See Bedekar 1967, 14.

2. Beginning with the medieval period, Vishnu comes to be depicted as a mighty king dwelling in his heavenly court of Vaikunth, and while many versions of the story are told to explain how Indra became king of the gods, Vishnu's hegemony supersedes that of Indra and is more emphasized in some contexts. See Kinsley 1986, 27; Long 1976, 185.

3. The account of Alakshmi's marriage to Uddalaka reappears in a more elaborate version in the twenty-ninth chapter of the The KMPP.

4. In this version, the list of milk-ocean emergents includes Indra's elephant Airavata, the Kalpa or Parijata tree, the moon, Lakshmi, the white horse Uccaihshravas, Kaustubha, Vishnu in the form of Dhanvantari, and all divine medicinal plants.

5. Long (1976) notes that a popular Sanskrit stanza lists fourteen "jewels" that emerged from the milk ocean (181 n.19). This list includes twelve items frequently listed in Puranic versions of the churning myth plus Vishnu's conch shell and bow. Individuals in Benares who recited to me the items that they thought of as the "jewels" most consistently included Shri, nectar, the Parijata tree, Dhanvantari, Indra's elephant (or the King of the Elephants), Varuni, the divine horse, the Kaustubha jewel, the moon, the sun, the divine cow, and *apsarases*.

6. Lutgendorf (1991, 249–50) notes that to witness the retelling of the Lord's earthly adventures through some form of dramatic enactment is a way of tapping into divine, salvific power.

7. Kojagari is not a major holiday in Benares although it is celebrated there, particularly by devout Vaishnavas. Kojagari seems to be much more important, however, in nearby Bengal. See Mohanty and Nag 1998.

8. The KMSP refers to a story in which a child averts premature death when this lamp offering is made (9.21).

9. The Nirnayasindhu, for example, holds that this day is for people afraid of hell. The text instructs such individuals to light a four-wicked lamp and offer it to the fourteen hells, asking that the legacy of one's sins be destroyed. It also advocates proffering water offerings (*tarpaṇa*) to Yama, the Host of Death (NS 297–98).

10. Kane (5/1, 197) describes the four-wick lamps as offerings in memory of Naraka, and the KMSP claims that if one offers lamps to Naraka on this day, all of one's forefathers will be liberated from hell (KMSP 9.56).

11. The Brahma Purana's version of the Naraka story describes Krishna's fight with Indra over the tree at much greater length and depicts it as a fierce battle between Krishna and Indra's forces, which ends in Indra's submission to Krishna (Brahma Purana 94). The story is quite telling in its depiction of Krishna's victory, portraying Krishna—not Indra—as divine sovereign. The same theme reappears in the story of Govardhan described in this chapter.

12. The KMSP advocates an oil bath on this day, claiming that Lakshmi temporarily dwells in oil and in the Ganges, in water, so that bathing on this day is especially meritorious (9.31–33).

13. Skanda Purana 2.2.39.32–33, for example, cites Ashvin Purnima as Kaumudi, while the KMSP equates Kaumudi with Diwali (9.69ff; also Padma Purana 6.122.58–69). Kane suggests that the name of the Kojagari festival, which he cites as "Kojagara," is actually an abbreviated form of "*Kaumudī-jāgara*" (5/1: 291).

14. E.g., Gupte 1997, 37; Thomas 1971, 3; Gautam 1982, 176; Bharatiya and Brahmacari 1974, 153. It is also cited as the day of King Vikramaditya's coronation.

15. E.g., Brahma Purana 73; Kurma Purana 1.17; Vamana Purana 77, 92. See also KMSP, 9.49–60; 8; 10.4; Kane 5/1: 202.

16. Women are enjoined to provide a comfortable sleeping place for Lakshmi and the other gods on Diwali and then perform a ritual on Diwali

night to waken Lakshmi, in preparation for Vishnu's awakening later that month (KMSP 9.77–87).

17. E.g.,Bharatiya and Brahmacārī, 153; Gautam, 176.

18. See also Padma Purana 6.122.25–29.

19. See Handleman and Shulman 1997, 66. They cite more of the text than I am citing here and translate this passage slightly differently.

20. Like the story of Krishna's seizure of the Parijata tree described above in note 11, this story also establishes Vishnu/Krishna's dominion over Indra.

21. The Devi-Bhagavata Purana describes this day as a day for worshiping Surabhi, the divine cow that emerges from the ocean of milk in many of the churning narratives, claiming that Krishna himself worshiped Surabhi on this day (9.49). The KMSP describes this as a day when Lakshmi takes the form of a cow (10.22), and the Padma Purana claims that on this day Lakshmi in the form of a cow remained with Parvati during the dice game with Shiva (6.122.25).

22. Most textual sources conflate Govardhan *pūjā* and Annakut. In Benares, however, people seem to think of them as distinct from one another. Most Benarsis celebrate Annakut on the second day of Kartik's bright fortnight, not the first. Textual evidence, however, points to the first as the proper day, and some Benarsis celebrate it on the first.

In his research on Govardhan *pūjā,* Paul Toomey notes that Krishna is ultimately identified with both Govardhan and the piles of food offered to the mountain (1994, 24; 1992, 25). Charlotte Vaudeville, too, notes, "In the *Govardhanapūja* (sic) or *Annakūṭ* festival, Kṛṣṇa-Gopāl and the Lord of the hill are but one" (1991, 107). Krishna himself is said to declare in the Bhagavata Purana, "I am the mountain!" (*śailo 'smī,* 10.24.35).

23. See Hawley 1979 for more on connections between Krishna's victories over demonic forces, themes of cosmic renewal, and New Year's motifs.

24. See also Wadley 1989, 101.

25. See also Ramanujan 1994, 15–19. In another version of the story that my research associate, Sunita Singh, recounted to me, Yama decides to take the brother's life at the moment he is to put *sindūr* in his new wife's hair-part, which is a central part of the marriage ceremony. At that very moment, the sister runs up to her brother just as a star is falling out of the sky, headed right for him. She catches the star in the end of her sari (the *āṅcal*), fainting from the star's impact. When she comes to her senses, she explains to the wedding party that she had overheard Yama conspiring to kill her brother in this way, so she knew what to do to save him.

26. A *svarūp* is considered to be a form of the deity, not an actor. The *svarūp* embodies the deity for a temporally bounded period of time, while the performance is underway.

27. For discussion of the declaration of intention (*saṅkalp*) in *vrat* performance, see Pearson 1996, 66–67, 134–38, 167–68.

28. One Benarsi I spoke with postulated that originally Akshaya Navami was a day for cleaning and worshiping storage rooms so that they might remain full forever, and that only later was the goal of abundance reinterpreted as having to do with merit, not food grains.

29. For more on the *caturmāsa*, see McGee 1987, 729–31, 774–78. McGee also notes that the twelfth (*dvādaśī*) and full moon are also acceptable beginnings for the *caturmāsa*.

30. According to this narrative, the month of devotion actually begins on the eleventh of Ashvin's bright fortnight—that is, four days before Kartik even starts—and lasts until the day of Prabodhani Ekadashi, four days before the end of Kartik. The KMSP comments on the prescribed dates, proclaiming that devotees of different deities should bathe during different periods: Vaishnavas should observe the *vrat* from the eleventh of Ashvin's bright fortnight to that of Kartik's bright fortnight; Shaivas should observe it from full moon to full moon; and Shaktas, from the fourteenth of the Ashvin's bright fortnight to that of Kartik (KMSP 3.17–22). In Benares, some Vaishnava devotees follow the stipulations of the Kartik Mahatmya in counting the eleventh of Ashvin's bright fortnight as the beginning of the Kartik *vrat*.

31. In many contexts, the Goddess is said to embody Mulaprakriti, the primordial matter that constitutes the universe. This primordial matter consists of three parts or qualities—purity (*sattva*), activity (*rajas*), and lethargy (*tamas*)—with all existing forms constituted from these.

32. Tulsi is also said to be born from Vrinda's sweat (*sveda*) in Padma Purana 6.16.45. Vijaya Nagarajan (2000) notes that in many contexts, plants and trees are understood to absorb inauspiciousness, and that in situations of hardship a boy or girl might be married to a tree to enable the tree to absorb the inauspiciousness plaguing him or her. The symbolism surrounding Tulsi's divine marriage partakes of tree marriage symbolism, including removal of inauspiciousness and the restoration of auspiciousness.

33. The KMSP prescribes that one spend the day fasting, bathe at Pancaganga Ghat, worship Bindu Madhava in the evening, and then proceed to worship Shiva the next morning. It also advises performing the concluding rite (*udyāpana*) of the Kartik *vrat* on the day of Vaikunth Caturdashi (34.6).

34. The KMPP recounts the story of Vishnu's fish *avatāra* in conjunction with the Shankha narrative described earlier, in which Shankha attempts to steal the Vedas from the gods. Taking the form of a fish, Vishnu kills Shankha, leading to the restoration of the Vedas to the gods (KMPP 4.1–4).

35. The Devi-Bhagavata Purana claims that both Radha and Tulsi were born or were worshiped by Krishna on this night (9.1.152–53, 9.12, 9.50.42). One contemporary source describes Kartik Purnima as the birthday of both the Ganges and Tulsi, to which it attributes the offering of lights on this day (Tripāṭhī 1996, 296).

Chapter 3. Adoring Krishna at the River's Edge: The Practice of Kartik *Pūjā*

1. In John S. Hawley's research on *rāsa-līlā* performances in Braj, the term *rāsa-līlā* is also used to indicate both the *rāsa-līlā* episode itself and the entire *līlā* of Krishna's life enacted in liturgical drama. See Hawley 1981 and 1983, chapters 6 and 7.

2. To "meet with" someone of the opposite sex is a phrase used to indicate a sexual encounter.

3. I am grateful to Professor Richard Wolf of Harvard University for this insight.

4. Some newspapers of the Benares region also identify the groom as Krishna, not Vishnu (e.g., *Dainik Jāgaraṇ*, November 10, 1997). Holly Baker Reynolds (1978, 392–441) has documented a votive tradition from Tamil Nadu in South India that shares some common features with women's traditions pertaining to Kartik in Benares, including daily, predawn ritual bathing throughout the month in conjunction with devotion to Krishna. This votive practice takes place during the South Indian month of Markali, the Tamil equivalent of Margashirsh, which is the month that in North India occurs just after Kartik.

5. See Sered 1994, 120–21 for a discussion of this issue. Sered is suspicious of claims that women are concerned more with ritual than with theology, noting that the implication of this observation is "that ritual is somehow less noble, important, or sophisticated than theology" (120). Nevertheless, she concedes that in women's religions, "a strong emphasis on ritual is indeed typical." (121).

6. The refrain is not always repeated completely or in this order. Each line of the song is repeated twice.

7. One who is waking Krishna up at this time would, it is assumed, be doing so at the riverbank, since this is normally the time one would go to the river to perform one's morning ablutions.

8. *Pāpaṛ* is a type of thin, flat, crackerlike bread.

9. *Pān* is a mixture of betel nut, spices, and other additives rolled up in a betel leaf and chewed for enjoyment. Benares is particularly known for its excellent *pān*.

10. The epithet used here is "Madhava."

11. The epithet used here is "Govinda."

12. "Candravati" is probably a variation on the name "Candravali." Candravali is one of the *gopīs* of Braj and Radha's chief rival for Krishna's affection (Wulff 1984, 45; Garlington 1997).

13. Sudha is one of Radha's *sakhīs*.

14. Seymour (1999) distinguishes between upper- and middle-status families, where mothers tend to have more time to attend to their children, and low-status families, where working mothers might need to turn caretaking tasks over to other family members (e.g., a grandmother). As noted, from what I was able to discern, most women who participate in Kartik *pūjā* in Benares seem to come from middle- and upper-status families.

15. "Fruit" here indicates "result" or outcome.

16. Pancaganga and Manikarnika are, as noted earlier, names of *ghāṭs* in Benares; Beni Madhav is a local name for the Bindhu Madhava temple that sits atop Pancaganga Ghat.

17. It is unclear whether the term should be *āṅcal-joṛī, aṅcal-joṛī*, or *acal-joṛī*. In terms of its meaning, however, two of my most experienced informants were clear that the term refers to the mate to whom one is tied eternally and

immutably. Generally, the term would apply to the husband-wife bond as a unique and unbreakable joining of one male and one female.

18. Tulsa and Tulsi are used interchangeably as names for this plant-goddess.

19. Every line of the song is repeated.

20. The term for "earth" should be "*dharatī*"; it appears the final syllable has been dropped, probably for meter. The epithet "Thakur," "Lord," refers to Krishna or Vishnu.

21. Two different informants described the full list of associations between days of the week and deities (including planetary deities) to be worshiped on those days. These are: Monday, Shiva or the Moon; Tuesday, Hanuman or Mars; Wednesday, Mercury; Thursday, Vishnu or Jupiter; Friday, the Goddess; Saturday, Hanuman or Saturn; and Sunday, the Sun.

22. While the categories themselves are considered fixed and opposed to one another, however there is in fact "no consensus on what belongs to which category," with, for example, some individuals attributing to scripture materials that are in fact *laukik* (Parry 1985, 205).

23. Literally, "get me Krishna's shoulder." In Benares, corpses are carried through the streets on funeral biers that are supported on the shoulders of those carrying the bier.

24. Manikarnika Ghat is one of two cremation *ghāṭ*s in Benares.

25. This is an exclamation that conveys dismay.

26. Although laddus are usually associated with Ganesha, it is implied that the deity who intervenes in the story is Krishna.

27. I was unable to determine what this term means; none of my informants could explain it to me.

28. Or "stop the chariot" (*rath teke*). The epithet of Krishna used here is "Rahiyoñ-jī."

29. For another version of this song, see Singh and Amend 1979, 85.

30. "Bhāṭ"; this is the name of a bard caste that plays an important role in the marriage. Here the bard goes to greet the marriage procession.

31. An exclamation.

32. *khākhe* or *khāse kā jāmā*. According to one informant, this is a special type of clothing that grooms regularly used to wear. It is tight fitting on top but loose and broad on the bottom, and it was used to conceal the bride when *sindūr* was applied to her head. The *jāmā* was considered auspicious (*shubh*).

33. *Sej* is the decorated bed at the bride's conjugal home; it is decorated for the first night that bride and groom will spend together as husband and wife.

34. The *ghūṅghaṭ* is the cloth at the end of the sari that is used to hide or veil the face.

35. Some informants insisted that *mahī* refers not to buttermilk, but to lentils that are divided into two parts. Some Kartik votaries give up such lentils during the month.

36. *sāvan sāg, na bhādo dahī ai dahī, kuvār dudh na Kartik mahī ai mahī, sāsū jī kā lipanan, nanad jī kā pāṅv paṛī, goṛvā se goṛvā na dhohalī, rasoīyā meṅ baiṭh gayī, etana jap tap kaili śrī kṛṣṇ ke māairīya!*

37. The epithet used here for Krishna is "Mohan Rasiya." The epithet "Mohan" indicates Krishna's nature as divine "enchanter." The epithet "rasiya" points to his nature as an "enjoyer" or "taster" of the emotions associated with devotion. Each line of song text is repeated twice.

Chapter 4. Krishna, Kartik, and Hindu Women's Lives

1. Hawley (1983) also notes in the devotional poems of Sur Das, a sixteenth-century Vaishnava poet, permeability between the parental and amorous sentiments concerning Krishna.

2. Lit., "There will be a cosmic dissolution (*pralaya*)."

3. The story of Radha and Rukmini's rivalry over Krishna recounted in chapter 1 is similar in structure to this story even though the main characters differ. Both narratives highlight the feelings of competition and envy attributed to the females who must share Krishna's affections and attention.

4. *Bhaju man Govinda, bhaju Gopāl.* This refrain repeats throughout the song. For stylistic reasons, however, I have chosen to omit the repetitions.

5. Krishna here is indicating that a *pūjāri* (a ritual functionary) residing on the banks of the Ganges River put the mark (*tilak*) on his forehead in conjunction with religious activity performed at the river's edge. Such a mark would also be placed on the forehead at the time of marriage.

6. Chewing *pān* releases a red-colored juice that stains whatever it touches, especially the *pān*-chewer's mouth and teeth.

7. A *dhoti* is a type of cloth that is wound around around the hips; one end is passed between the legs and tucked in at the waist. The implication here is that Krishna is wearing his *pītāmbar*, a garment that the song implies is suitable for a groom to wear.

8. These are the months falling from roughly mid-December to mid-February.

9. Seymour (1999) cautions against over-emphasizing the centrality of the wife/mother roles in Indian women's lives. She notes that in the early years of marriage, the role of daughter-in-law often takes precedence over that of wife in a joint family setting. And later in life, when asked what gives them the greatest satisfaction, Indian women tend to speak more of being household managers and nurturers than mothers (98–99). Nevertheless, these other roles and responsibilities are contingent on marriage and motherhood.

Chapter 5. Kartik *Pūjā* Traditions and Women's Empowerment

1. I am grateful to fellow scholar Steven Heim who articulated to me this distinction between alternative and teleological discourses, both of which are often cited as "resistance," in a personal communication.

Raheja and Gold (1994) is an example of a work that, while commendable in numerous ways, seems to me to blur the line too much between these two types of discourse. In the conclusion to that work, the authors note that "poetic and ritual forms of protest can enable women to articulate a resistant stance and then to raise their voices when more practical forms of protest become possible" (187). I have two reservations about this claim. First, I would not use the term "resistance" to describe all the types of discourse discussed in that work and described as "resistance;" and second, I would not assume that voicing an alternative opinion about, for example, the relationship between female sexuality and birth-giving implies a repressed desire to protest against or change the social status quo. Indeed, when I used this book in a class in the late 1990s, the students who objected most to these sorts of claims were first- and second-generation Hindu and Jain women of Indian origin. These young women overwhelmingly felt that the authors were overstating their case.

2. For more on the relationship between Hindu goddess traditions and women's empowerment, see Hiltebeitel and Erndl 2000.

3. Gupta describes these as Western vs. Hindu concepts of power, but I find this dichotomy misleading. Hindu religion and culture embrace notions of physical and sociopolitical power, and Western religious notions of inner or spiritual power are not that different from those expounded in traditional Hinduism. "Secular" vs. "religious" might be a more helpful way of contrasting these differing concepts of power, although that distinction is certainly not absolute.

4. One reader of this manuscript chastised me for this assumption, noting that other Krishna devotional traditions are replete with examples of men assuming, for devotional purposes, the personae of female characters in the Krishna narrative, e.g., Radha, the *gopīs*, or Yashoda. But one needs to be careful about sloppily projecting examples from one group or tradition onto another group or tradition. The women among whom I worked were not necessarily familiar with such male devotional practices; indeed, not a single participant ever mentioned them to me. And many of the women I interviewed were very clear that they view Krishna devotion as a predominantly female enterprise.

Works Cited

Hindi and Sanskrit Sources

Bhagavata Purana

Śrīmad Bhāgavata Mahāpurāṇa, with Sanskrit Text and English Translation. 1971. Translated by C. L. Goswami. 2 vols. Gorakhpur: Gītā.

Bharatīyā, Rūpakiśor, and Kārṣṇi Raṇvīr Brahamacārī. 1974. *Bārahoñ mahīne ke sampūrṇ vrat aur tyauhār.* Mathura: Govardhan Pustakālaya.

Brahma Purana

Śrībrahmamahāpurāṇam. 1985 [1906]. Edited by R. N. Sharma. Reprint. Delhi: Nag.

Translation: The Brahma Purāṇa. 1985–1986. Translated by a board of scholars. Ancient Indian Tradition and Mythology Series, vols. 33–36. Delhi: Motilal Banarsidass.

Brahmanda Purana

Brahmāṇḍa Purāṇa of Sage Kṛṣṇa Dvaipāyana Vyāsa. 1973. Edited by J. L. Shastri. Delhi: Motilal Banarsidass.

Translation: The Brahmāṇḍa Purāṇa. 1983–1984. Translated by G. V. Tagare. Ancient Indian Tradition and Mythology Series, vols. 22–26. Delhi: Motilal Banarsidass.

Devi-Bhagavata Purana

Śrīmaddevībhāgavatam. 1919. Bombay: Veṅkaṭeśvara.

Translation: The Srimad Devi Bhagavatam [Devī-Bhāgavata Purāṇa]. [1921–1923] 1977. Translated by Hari Prasanna Chatterji

[Swami Vijnananda]. Sacred Books of the Hindus, vol. 26. Reprint, New Delhi: Oriental.

Dharmasindhu
The Dharmasindhu of Śrī Kāśīnātha Upādhyāya, with the "Dharmadīpikā" Hindi Commentary by Pt. Vaśiṣṭha Datta Miśra. 1968. The Kashi Sanskrit Series, 183. Varanasi: Chowkhamba Sanskrit Series Office.

Garg, Mukeś Kumār, editor. 1990. *Bārah mahīnoṅ ke vrat aur tyauhār.* Delhi: Pūjā Prakāśan.

Gautam, Camanlāl. 1982. *Bārah māsoñ ke sampūrṇ vrat evaṁ tyauhār.* Baroli: Saṁskṛti Saṅsthān.

Harivamsha
The Harivaṁśa, Being the Khila or Supplement to the Mahābhārata. Edited by Parashuram Lakshman Vaidya. 1969–1971. Critical ed. 2 vols. Poona: Bhandarkar Oriental Research Institute.

Translation: Harivamsha, Translated into English Prose from the Original Sanskrit. Edited and translated by D. N. Bose. Dum Dum, Bengal: Datta Bose.

Kartik Mahatmya
(1) Kārtik Māhātmya, with Hindi translation and commentary (from the Padma Purāṇa). N.d. Delhi: Dehātī Pustak Bhaṇḍār.

(2) Kārtik Māhātmya, with Hindi translation and commentary (from the Padma Purāṇa). N.d. Vārāṇasī: Ṭhākurprasād.

(3) Kārtik Māhātmya (Hindi Translation from the Padma Purāṇa). 1994. Vārāṇasī: Śri Ṭhākur Prasād Pustak Bhaṇḍar.

Kurma Purana
Kūrma Purāṇa, with English Translation. 1972. Edited by Sri Anand Swarup Gupta. Translated by A. Bhattacharya, S. Mukherji, V. K. Varma, and G. S. Rai. Varanasi: All India Kashi Raj Trust.

Mahabharata
The Mahābhārata. 1933–1959. Edited by Vishnu S. Sukthankar, S. K. Belvalkar, and P. L. Vaidya. Critical edition. 19 vols. Poona: Bhandarkar Oriental Research Institute.

Translation: The Mahabharata of Krishna-Dwaipayana Vyasa. 1973–1978. Translated by Pratap Chandra Roy. 2d edition. 12 vols. Calcutta: Oriental.

McGregor, R. S. 1993. *The Oxford Hindi-English Dictionary.* Delhi: Oxford University Press.

Narada Purana

Śrīnāradīyamahāpurāṇam. 1984 [1923 or 1924]. Reprint. Delhi: Nag.

Translation: The Nārada-Purāṇa. 1980–1982. Translated by G. V. Tagare. Ancient Indian Tradition and Mythology Series, vols. 15–19. Delhi: Motilal Banarsidass.

Nirnayasindhu

Nirṇayasindhu. 1996. Pune: Shri Venkateshwar.

Padma Purana

Padma Purāṇam. 1957. 2 vols. Gurumandal Series, no. 18. Calcutta: Manasukharāya Mora.

Translation: The Padma Purāṇa. 1988–1992. Translated by N. A. Deshpande. Ancient Indian Tradition and Mythology Series, vols. 39–48. Delhi: Motilal Banarsidass.

Ramanand Prakash (*Rāmānand Prakāś*). 1995 (November). Varanasi: Shri Math.

Skanda Purana

Skanda-Purāṇam. 1965. Gurumandal Series, no. 20. 2 vols. New Delhi: Munshiram Manoharlal.

Translation: The Skanda-Purāṇa. Translated by G. V. Tagare. Ancient Indian Tradition and Mythology Series, vols. 49–61. Delhi: Motilal Banarsidass, 1992–1997.

Tripāthī, Rāmpratāp. 1966. *Hinduoñ ke vrat, parv aur tyauhār*. Ilāhābād: Lokbhāratī Prakāśan.

Vālā, Dr. Rajanī, editor. nd. *Hinduoñ ke varṣbhar ke vrat aur tyauhār*. Delhi: Sumit.

Vamana Purana

Vāmana Purāṇa, with English Translation. 1968. Edited by Anand Swarup Gupta, translated by S. M. Mukhopadhyaya, A Bhattacharya, N. C. Nath, and V. K. Varma. Critical ed. Varanasi: All India Kashiraj Trust.

Varaha Purana

Varahapurāṇa. 1981. Edited by Anand Swarup Gupta. Critical ed. 2 vols. Varanasi: All India Kashiraj Trust.

Translation: The Varaha Purāṇa. 1985. Translated by S. Venkitasubramonia Iyer. Ancient Indian Tradition and Mythology Series, vols. 31–32. Delhi: Motilal Benarsidass.

Vishnu Purana

Śrīviṣṇupurāṇa. 1967. Gorakhpur: Gita.

Translation: The Vishnu Purāṇa: A System of Hindu Mythology and Tradition. 1961. Translated by H. H. Wilson. 3d ed. Calcutta: Punthi Pustak.

Other Sources

Abu-Lughod, Lila. 1990. "The Romance of Resistance: Tracing Transformations of Power through Bedouin Women." *American Ethnologist* 17/1 (February): 41–55.

Alter, Joseph S. 1992. *The Wrestler's Body: Identity and Ideology in North India.* Berkeley: University of California Press.

Archer, W. G. 1957. *The Loves of Krishna.* London: George Allen and Unwin.

Banerjea, J. N. 1956. *The Development of Hindu Iconography.* 2d ed. Calcutta: University of Calcutta Press.

Bedekar, V. M. 1967. "The Legend of the Churning of the Ocean in the Epics and Purāṇas: A Comparative Study." *Purāṇa* 9/1 (January): 7–61.

Bell, Catherine. 1992. *Ritual Theory, Ritual Practice.* New York: Oxford University Press.

———. 1997. *Ritual: Perspectives and Dimensions.* New York: Oxford University Press.

Brasher, Brenda E. 1998. *Godly Women: Fundamentalism and Female Power.* New Brunswick, NJ: Rutgers University Press.

Butler, Judith. 1990. *Gender Trouble: Feminism and the Subversion of Identity.* New York: Routledge.

Bynum, Caroline Walker. 1996. "Women's Stories, Women's Symbols: A Critique of Victor Turner's Theory of Liminality." Reprinted in *Readings in Ritual Studies,* ed. Ronald L. Grimes, 71–86. Upper Saddle River, NJ: Prentice Hall.

Caldwell, Sarah. 1999. *Oh Terrifying Mother: Sexuality, Violence, and Worship of the Goddess Kāḷi.* New Delhi: Oxford University Press.

Carman, John B., and Frederique Marglin. 1985. *Purity and Auspiciousness in Indian Society.* Leiden: E. J. Brill.

Carstairs, Morris. 1967 [1957]. *The Twice Born: A Study of a Community of High-Caste Hindus*. Bloomington: Indiana University Press.

Chodorow, Nancy. 1974. "Family Structure and Feminine Personality." In *Woman, Culture, and Society*. Edited by Michelle Zimbalist Rosaldo and Louise Lamphere, 43–66. Stanford, CA: Stanford University Press.

Clothey, Fred. 1982. "Chronometry, Cosmology and the Festival Calendar in the Murukaì Cult." In *Religious Festivals in South India and Sri Lanka*. Edited by Guy Welbon and Glenn Yocum. New Delhi: Manohar, 157–88.

Collins, Elizabeth Fuller. 1997. *Pierced by Murugan's Lance: Ritual, Power, and Moral Redemption among Malaysian Hindus*. DeKalb, IL: Northern Illinois University Press.

Craddock, Elaine. 2001. "Reconstructing the Split Goddess as Śakti in a Tamil Village." In *Seeking Mahādevī: Constructing the Identities of the Hindu Great Goddess*. Edited by Tracy Pintchman, 145–69. Albany, NY: State University of New York Press.

Derné, Steve. 1995. *Culture in Action: Family Life, Emotion, and Male Dominance in Banaras, India*. Albany: State University of New York Press.

Dimock, Edward. 1966a. *The Place of the Hidden Moon: Erotic Mysticism in the Vaiṣṇava-sahajiyā Cult of Bengal*. Chicago: University of Chicago Press.

———. 1966b. "Doctrine and Practice among the Vaiṣṇavas of Bengal." In *Krishna: Myths, Rites, and Attitudes*. Edited by Milton Singer, 41–63. Chicago: University of Chicago Press.

Eck, Diana. 1980. "A Survey of Sanskrit Sources for the Study of Vārāṇasī." *Purāṇa* 22, 1980: 81–101.

———. 1982. *Banaras, City of Light*. Princeton, NJ: Princeton University Press.

———. 1985. *Darśan: Seeing the Divine in India*. Chambersburg, PA: Anima.

Erndl, Kathleen. 1997. "The Goddess and Women's Power: A Hindu Case Study." In *Women and Goddess Traditions in Antiquity and Today*. Ed. Karen L. King with an introduction by Karen Jo Torjesen, 17–38. Studies in Antiquity and Christianity. Minneapolis: Fortress.

Falk, Nancy Auer, and Rita M. Gross. 1980. *Unspoken Worlds: Women's Religious Lives*. San Francisco: Harper and Row.

Feldhaus, Anne. 1995. *Water and Womanhood: Religious Meanings of Rivers in Maharashtra*. New York: Oxford University Press.

Freed, Ruth S., and Stanley A. Freed. 1964. "Calendars, Ceremonies, and Festivals in a North Indian Village: Necessary Calendrical Information for Fieldwork." *Southwestern Journal of Anthropology* vol. 20, no. 1: 67–90.

Garlington, William. 1997. "*Candrāvalī* and the *Caurāsī Vaiṣṇavan Kī Vārtā*." *Journal of Vaiṣṇava Studies* vol. 5, no. 4 (Fall): 187–200.

Geertz, Clifford. 1973. *The Interpretation of Cultures*. New York: Basic.

Gilligan, Carol. 1982. *In a Different Voice*. Cambridge, MA: Harvard University Press.

Gold, Ann Grodzins. 2000. "From Demon Aunt to Gorgeous Bride: Women Portray Female Power in a North Indian Festival Cycle." In *Invented Identities: The Interplay of Gender, Religion, and Politics in India*. Edited by Julia Leslie and Mary McGee, 203–30. New Delhi: Oxford University Press.

Griffith, R. Marie. 1997. *God's Daughters: Evangelical Women and the Power of Submission*. Berkeley: University of California Press.

Gupta, Lina. 1997. "Hindu Women and Ritual Empowerment." In *Women and Goddess Traditions in Antiquity and Today*. Edited by Karen L. King with an introduction by Karen Jo Torjesen, 85–110. Studies in Antiquity and Christianity. Minneapolis: Fortress.

Gupte, B. A. 1919. *Hindu Holidays and Ceremonials: With Dissertations on Origin, Folklore, and Symbols*. Calcutta: Thacker, Spink.

Haberman, David. 1988. *Acting as a Way of Salvation: A Study of Rāgānugā Bhakti Sādhana*. New York: Oxford University Press.

———. 1994. *Journey Through the Twelve Forests: An Encounter with Krishna*. New York: Oxford University Press.

Hancock, Mary Elizabeth. 1999. *Womanhood in the Making: Domestic Ritual and Public Culture in Urban South India*. Boulder, CO: Westview.

Handelman, Don, and David Shulman. 1997. *God Inside Out: Śiva's Game of Dice*. New York: Oxford University Press.

Hawley, John S. 1979. "Krishna's Cosmic Victories." *Journal of the American Academy of Religion* 47/2 (June): 201–21.

———. 1981. *At Play with Krishna: Pilgrimage Dramas from Brindavan.* Princeton, NJ: Princeton University Press.

———. 1983. *Krishna, the Butter Thief.* Princeton, NJ: Princeton University Press.

———. 1986. "Images of Gender in the Poetry of Krishna." In *Gender and Religion: On the Complexity of Symbols.* Edited by Caroline Walker Bynum, Stevan Harrell, and Paula Richman, 231–56. Boston: Beacon.

Henry, Edward O. 1988. *Chant the Names of God: Music and Culture in Bhojpuri-Speaking India.* San Diego: San Diego State University Press.

Hiltebeitel, Alf. 1990. *The Ritual of Battle: Krishna in the Mahābhārata.* Albany: State University of New York Press, 1990.

Hiltebeitel, Alf, and Kathleen Erndl, eds. 2000. *Is the Goddess a Feminist?* New York: New York University Press.

Hrdy, Sarah Blaffer. 1999. *Mother Nature: Maternal Instincts and How They Shape the Human Species.* New York: Ballentine.

Kakar, Sudhir. 1978. *The Inner World: A Psychoanalytic Study of Childhood and Society in India.* Delhi: Oxford University Press.

———. 1986. "Erotic Fantasy: The secret passion of Radha and Krishna." In *The Word and the World: Fantasy, Symbol, and Record.* Edited by Veena Das, 75–94. Beverly Hills: Sage.

———. 1990. *Intimate Relations: Exploring Indian Sexuality.* New Delhi: Penguin.

Kane, P. V. 1930–1952. *A History of Dharmaśāstra.* 5 vols. Poona: Bhandarkar Oriental Research Institute.

Kapadia, Karin. 1995. *Siva and Her Sisters: Gender, Caste, and Class in Rural South India.* Boulder, CO: Westview.

Khare, R. S. 1976. *The Hindu Hearth and Home.* New Delhi: Vikas.

Kidder, Louise H. 2000. "Dependents in the Master's House: When Rock Dulls Scissors." In *Home and Hegemony.* Edited by Kathleen Adams and Sara Dickey, 207–20. Ann Arbor: University of Michigan Press.

Kinsley, David. 1979. *The Divine Player: A Study of Kṛṣṇa Līlā.* Delhi: Motilal Banarsidass.

———. 1986. *Hindu Goddesses.* Berkeley: University of California Press.

Kumar, Nita, ed. 1994. *Women as Subjects: South Asian Histories.* Charlottesville: University Press of Virginia.

Kurtz, Stanley. 1992. *All the Mothers Are One: Hindu India and the Cultural Reshaping of Psychoanlaysis.* New York: Columbia University Press.

Long, Bruce. 1976. "Life out of Death." In *Hinduism: New Essays in the History of Religions.* Edited by Bardwell L. Smith, 171–207. Leiden: E. J. Brill.

Lutgendorf, Phillip. 1991. *The Life of a Text: Performing the Ramcaritmānas of Tulsidas.* Berkeley: University of California Press.

Marglin, Frederique. 1985a. *Wives of the God King: The Rituals of the Devadasis of Puri.* Delhi: Oxford University Press.

———. 1985b. "Types of Oppositions in Hindu Culture." In Carman and Marglin, *Purity and Auspiciousness in Indian Society,* 65–83. Leiden: E. J. Brill.

McGee, Mary. 1987. "Feasting and Fasting: The Vrata Tradition and Its Significance for Hindu Women." Th.D. diss., Harvard University Divinity School.

———. 1991. "Desired Fruits: Motive and Intention in the Votive Rites of Hindu Women." In *Roles and Rituals for Hindu Women.* Edited by Julia Leslie, 71–88. London: Pinter.

Menon, Usha. 2000. "Does Feminism Have Universal Relevance? The Challenges Posed by Oriya Hindu Family Practices." *Daedalus* 129/4 (Fall): 77–99.

Mohanty, Bidyut, and Dulali Nag. 1998. "Lakshmi and Alakshmi: The Kojagari Lakshmi Vrat Katha of Bengal." *Manushi* 104 (January–February): 9–11.

Mohanty, Chandra. 1988. "Under Western Eyes: Feminist Scholarship and Colonial Discourses." *Feminist Review* no. 30: 61–88.

Mukherjee, A. C. 1989. *Hindu Fasts and Feasts.* Second edition. Gurgaon: Vintage.

Nagarajan, Vijaya. 2000. "Rituals of Embedded Ecologies: Drawing *Kolams,* Marrying Trees, and Generating Auspiciousness." In *Hinduism and Ecology.* Edited by Christopher Key Chapple and Mary Evelyn Tucker, 453–68. Cambridge, MA: Harvard University Press.

Narayan, Kirin. 1992. *Storytellers, Saints, and Scoundrels.* Delhi: Motilal Banarsidass.

———. 1995. "How a Girl Became a Sacred Plant." In *Religions of India in Practice.* Edited by Donald Lopez, 487–94. Princeton, NJ: Princeton University Press.

———. 1997a. *Mondays on the Dark Night of the Moon: Himalayan Foothill Tales.* In collaboration with Urmila Devi Sood. New York: Oxford University Press.

———. 1997b. "Sprouting and Uprooting of Saili: The Story of the Sacred Tulsi in Kangra." *Manushi* no 102, 30–38.

Narayanan, Vasudha. 1985. "The Two Levels of Auspiciousness in Śrivaiṣṇava Ritual and Literature." In *Purity and Auspiciousness in Indian Society.* Edited by John B. Carman and Frederique Apffel Marglin, 55–64. Leiden: E. J. Brill.

———. 2000. "Diglossic Hinduism: Liberation and Lentils." *Journal of the American Academy of Religion* vol. 68 no. 4 (December): 761–79.

Newton, Niles. 1973. "Interrelationships between Sexual Responsiveness, Birth, and Breast Feeding." Chapter 5 of *Contemporary Sexual Behavior: Critical Issues in the 1970s.* Edited by Joseph Zubin and John Money, 77–98. Baltimore: Johns Hopkins University Press.

Northrup, Lesley A. 1997. *Ritualizing Women.* Cleveland, OH: Pilgrim.

Nussbaum, Martha C. 2000. *Women and Human Development: The Capabilities Approach.* Cambridge: Cambridge University Press.

O'Flaherty, Wendy Ḍoniger. 1980. *Women, Androgynes, and Other Mythical Beasts.* Chicago: University of Chicago Press.

Oxenhandler, Noelle. 1996. "The Eros of Parenthood." *New Yorker* (February 19): 47–49.

Parry, Jonathan. 1985. "The Brahmanical Tradition and the Technology of the Intellect." In *Reason and Morality.* Edited by Joanna Overing, 200–25. London and New York: Tavistock.

Pearson, Anne Mackenzie. 1996. *"Because It Gives Me Peace of Mind": Ritual Fasts in the Religious Lives of Hindu Women.* Albany: State University of New York Press.

Pintchman, Tracy. 1999. "Kārttik as a Vaiṣṇava *Mahotsav*: Mythic Themes and the Ocean of Milk." *Journal of Vaiṣṇava Studies* (7/2): 65–92.

———. 2003. "The Month of Kartik and Women Ritual Devotions to Krishna in Benares." In *The Blackwell Companion to Hinduism*. Edited by Gavin Flood, 327–42. Oxford: Blackwell.

———. forthcoming. "When Vows Fail to Deliver What They Promise: The Case of Shyamavati." In *Sacred Promises: Dynamics of Lay Religious Vows*. Edited by William Harman and Selva Raj. Albany: State University of New York Press.

Prasad, M. Madhava. 1998. *Ideology of the Hindi Film: A Historical Construction*. New Delhi: Oxford University Press.

Primiano, Leonard N. 1995. "Vernacular Religion and the Search for Method in Religious Folklife." *Western Folklore* 54, no. 1 (January): 37–56.

Proctor-Smith, Marjorie. 1993. " 'In the Line of the Female': Shakerism and Feminism." In *Women's Leadership in Marginal Religions: Explorations Outside the Mainstream*. Edited by Catherine Wessinger, 23–40. Chicago: University of Illinois Press.

Pugh, Judy F. 1981. "Person and Experience: The Astrological System of North India." Ph.D. dissertation, University of Chicago.

———. 1983. "Into the Almanac." *Contributions to Indian Sociology* 17, 27–49.

Puri, Jyoti. 1999. *Woman, Body, Desire in Post-Colonial India: Narratives of Gender and Sexuality*. New York: Routledge.

Raghavan, V. 1979. *Festivals, Sports and Pastimes of India*. Ahmedabad: B. J. Institute of Learning and Research.

Raheja, Gloria Goodwin. 1988. *The Poison in the Gift: Ritual, Prestation, and the Dominant Caste in a North Indian Village*. Chicago: University of Chicago Press.

Raheja, Gloria Goodwin, and Anne Grodzins Gold. 1994. *Listen to the Heron's Words: Reimagining Gender and Kinship in North India*. Berkeley: University of California Press.

Ramanujan, A. K. 1989. "Is there an Indian Way of Thinking? An Informal Essay." *Contributions to Indian Sociology* 23/1 (January–June): 41–58.

———. 1991. "Toward a Counter-System: Women's Tales." In *Gender, Genre, and Power in South Asian Expressive Traditions*. Edited by Arjun Appadurai, Frank J. Korom, and Margaret A. Mills, 33–55. Philadephia: University of Pennsylvania Press.

———. 1994. *Folktales from India*. Reprint. New York: Pantheon.

Rana, S. S. 1995. *A Study of Skanda Cult*. Delhi: Nag.

Reynolds, Holly Baker. 1978. "To Keep the Tāli Strong: Women's Rituals in Tamilnad, India." Ph.D. dissertation, University of Wisconsin, Madison.

Rocher, Ludo. 1986. *The Purāṇas*. A History of Indian Literature. Edited by Jan Gonda. Vol. 2, fasc. 3. Wiesbaden: Otto Harrassowitz.

Roland, Alan. 1988. *In Search of Self in India and Japan: Toward a Cross-Cultural Psychology*. Princeton, NJ: Princeton University Press.

Roy, Manisha. 1992 [1972]. *Bengali Women*. Chicago: University of Chicago Press.

Sanford, Whitney A. 1997. "Construction of Gender in the Aṣṭamāyalīlā." *Journal of Vaiṣṇava Studies* vol. 5, no. 4 (Fall): 163–86.

Sered, Susan Starr. 1992. *Women as Ritual Experts*. New York: Oxford University Press.

———. 1994. *Priestess, Mother, Sacred Sister: Religions Dominated by Women*. New York: Oxford University Press.

Seymour, Susan C. 1999. *Women, Family, and Child Care in India: A World in Transition*. Cambridge: Cambridge University Press.

Sharma, Brijendra Nath. 1978. *Festivals of India*. New Delhi: Abhinav.

Sharma, Ursula. 1980. *Women, Work and Property in North-West India*. New York: Tavistock.

Singh, Chandramani, and Ronald Amend. 1979. *Marriage Songs from Bhojpuri Region*. Jaipur: Champa Lal Ranka.

Smith, Jonathan Z. 1987. *To Take Place: Toward Theory in Ritual*. Chicago: University of Chicago Press.

Stacey, Judith. 1988. "Can There Be a Feminist Ethnography?" *Women's Studies International Forum* vol. 11, no. 1: 21–27.

Thomas, Paul. 1971. *Festivals and Holidays of India*. Bombay: D. B. Taraporevala.

Tiwari, Laxmi G. 1991. *A Splendor of Worship: Women's Fasts, Rituals, Stories, and Art*. New Delhi: Manohar.

Toomey, Paul M. 1986. "Food from the Mouth of Krishna: Socio-Religious Aspects of Food in Two Krishnaite Sects." In *Food, Society, and Culture: Aspects of South Asian Food Systems*. Edited by R. S. Khare and M. S. A Rao, 55–83. Durham: Carolina Academic Press.

———. 1990. "Krishna's Consuming Passions: Food as Metaphor and Metonym for Emotion at Mount Govardhan." In *Divine Passions: The Social Construction of Emotion in India*, 157–81. Berkeley: University of California Press.

———. 1994. *Food from the Mouth of Krishna: Feasts and Festivities in a North Indian Pilgrimage Centre.* Delhi: Hindustan.

Traina, Cristina L. 2000. "Maternal Experience and the Boundaries of Christian Sexual Ethics." *Signs* vol. 25, no. 2 (Winter): 369–405.

Trawick, Margaret. 1990. *Notes on Love in a Tamil Family.* Berkeley: University of California Press.

Underhill, M. M. 1921. *The Hindu Religious Year.* The Religious Life of India Series. Calcutta: Association.

Vaudeville, Charlotte. 1980. "The Govardhan Myth in Northern India." *Indo-Iranian Journal* vol. 22: 1–45.

———. 1986. Barahmasa *in Indian Literatures.* Delhi: Motilal Banarsidass.

———. 1991. "Multiple Approaches to a Living Hindu Myth: The Lord of the Govardhan Hill." In *Hinduism Reconsidered.* Edited by Günther D. Sontheimer and Hermann Kulke, 105–24. Delhi: Manohar.

Wadley, Susan. 1983. "The Rains of Estrangement: Understanding the Hindu Yearly Cycle." *Contributions to Hindu Sociology* 17/1: 51–86.

———. 1985. *Shakti: Power in the Conceptual Structure of Karimpur Religion.* New Delhi: Munshiram Manoharlal.

———. 1986. "The Kathā of Śakaṭ: Two Tellings." In *Another Harmony: New Essays on the Folklore of India.* Edited by Stuart H. Blackburn and A. K. Ramanujan, 195–232. Berkeley: University of California Press.

———. 1989. "Hindu Women's Family and Household Rites in a North Indian Village." In *Unspoken Worlds: Women's Religious Lives in Non-Western Cultures.* Edited by Nancy A. Falk and Rita M. Gross, 94–109. San Francisco: Harper and Row.

Weisskopf, Susan (Contratto). 1980. "Maternal Sexuality and Asexual Motherhood." *Signs* vol. 5, no. 4 (Summer): 766–82.

Wulff, Donna M. 1984. *Drama as a Mode of Religious Realization: The* Vidagdhamādhava *of Rūpa Gosvāmī.* AAR Academy Series 43. Chico, CA: Scholars.

Index

Abu-Lughod, Lila, 181
Agnibindu, 209*n17*
Akshaya Navami, 73–76, 212*n28*; offerings on, 74; pious acts and spiritual merit on, 73; ritual diagram for, 73, 74
Alakshmi, 49, 63; embodiment of inauspiciousness, 48
Amāvasya (new moon), 61
Amla, 74, 75, 209*n16*; birth of, 80; first fruits celebration, 75; as goddess, 75; theme of renewed fruitfulness and, 75–76; worship of, 75
Amṛta. *See* Nectar of Immortality
Ananta, 46, 47, 76
Annadev, 116
Annakut, 66, 212*n22*
Annapurna temple, 66
Ārati, 115
Ardhanarishwara, 175
Arjuna: brings Ganges River water to Bhishma, 33
Ashvini asterism, 55
Ashvin Purnima, 55; Kojagari and, 56
Assi Ghat, 96, 97, 99, 102, 137
Asterisms, 17, 42, 55, 208*n2*
Astrology: importance of planets in, 22; religious role of, 22–23
Auspiciousness: Amla and, 75; celestial cycles and, 21; churning of ocean of milk and, 46–49; climatic cycles and, 21; cultivation of, 27; defining, 20; Diwali and, 62; Kartik and, 20–23, 45, 50, 53, 54; levels and forms of, 20–21; marriage and, 49; moral/aesthetic, 21; Prabodhani Ekadashi and, 76, 77; reproductive, 21; restoration of, 50; ritual activities and, 21; ritual bathing and, 26; of sexual fluids, 86; sexuality and, 45; spiritual, 32, 78, 127; "this-worldly" values and, 21; time-bound, 53; transcendent type of, 53; Vaikunth and, 53; weddings, 45; well-being and, 45; worldly, 32–33, 127; worldly boons and, 45
Autumn Full Moon. *See* Sharat Purnima
Ayurveda, 47; Amla in, 76; change of season and, 16

Bali: 62, 63
Basil. *See* Tulsi
Basket Sixth. *See* Dala Chath
Bathing. *See* Ritual Bathing
Bell, Catherine, 145, 151
Benares, 207*n1*; Bhishmapancak tradition in, 33–44; Godauliya area of, 19; as pilgrimage center, 1; sacredness of, 1; Vishvanath Gali in, 19
Beni Madhav, 214*n14*; *see also* Bindhu Madhava Temple
Bhagavan, 94; observes Kartik bathing, 26
Bhagavata Purana: 51, 60, 69, 70, 84, 212*n22*
Bhaiya Duj. *See* Yamdvitiya
Bhakti, 98; stress on equality in, 149
Bharatīyā, Rūpakiśor, 73

173–74; in Kartik traditions, 54; of Tulsi, 78, 94, 130–42; Tulsi's as model for human marriage, 166–67, 175–76; of Vishnu/Lakshmi, 49
Maternalism: eroticism and, 155–66; in relation to Krishna, 12, 125
Maya: revives the demons, 84
McGee, Mary, 18, 23, 24, 25, 98, 99, 213n29
Menon, Usha, 181
Menstruation, 9–10
Mirabai, 93
Mohanty, Bidyut, 13, 211*n7*
Mokṣa. *See* Liberation, spiritual
Monsoons: fertility and, 27; season, 17
Months: Hindu, 17
Mount Govardhan, 64, 65
Mount Mandara: role in churning of ocean of milk, 47
Mukherjee, A.C., 57
Mulaprakriti, 80, 213*n31*
Muller, Max, 209*n14*
Muneshvari Devi. *See* Informants
Mūrti. *See* Icon
Myths. *See* Narratives

Nāgas, seize and drink poison, 47
Nag Nathaiya, 69–70, *70*
Nagarajan, Vijaya, 213*n32*
Narada Purana, 18; Krishna and, 57
Naraka, 60, 211*n10*, 211*n11*
Narak Caturdashi, 60–61, 82–83; celebrating Krishna's victory over Naraka, 60; liberation from hellish realms in, 60; lighting of special lights in, 60
Narayan, Kirin, 120, 170, 210*n21*
Narayanan, Vasudha, 20, 21, 111
Narratives: affecting relationships in the *pūjā* circle, 122–23; of Amla's origin, 76; appropriation of for organization of experience of self, 145; of Bali, 62–63; of Bhishma/Bhimsen, 36–40; of Buddha's wife, 31; of churning of ocean of milk, 12, 46–51, 86; classical vs. women's tales, 117; connection to cultural paradigms and familial arrangements, 155; on Dala Chath, 72; of Dandakara, 34; of Dhaneshvara, 32; of Dharmadatta and Kalaha, 31–32; ego-ideal identification and, 144; functions of, 144; of Ganesha, 116, *116*; of Ganges' origin, 209*n10*; of Govatsa Dvadashi, 58–59; instructive value of, 118, 119, 120–21; of Jalandhara/Shankhacuda, 79–82; in Kartik Mahatmyas, 30–33; of Kartik Purnima, 84–85; of Karva Cauth, 58; of Krishna, 39–40, 51–52, 60, 64–65, 69–70, 85, 167–68, 211*n11*; of Krishna, psychological interpretations, 155–59; on merits obtained by observation of Kartik *vrat*, 30–33, 119–20; orientation toward continuity of familial/spiritual identity and, 145; performative nature of, 123; of Prabodhani Ekadashi, 77, 79–82; principles of recounting during Kartik *pūjā*, 116–17; regarded by women as true, 118; of rivalry between Radha and Rukmini, 39–40; of rivalry between Radha and Tulsi, 167–68, 216*n3*; of Shiva and Parvati gambling, 65; of Surya, 72; transactions between humans and deities in, 120–21; of Tulsi, 119–20, 167–68; on Vaikunth Caturdashi, 83; as vehicle for women's commentary on own life circumstances, 121; *Vrat*-related, 120; worldly (*laukik*) vs. scriptural (*śāstrik*), 117, 118; Yama-Yamuna, 68, 69, 212*n25*; of Yamdvitiya, 67–68
Nectar of Immortality: 57, 58, 70; demons revived by, 84; emerges from ocean of milk, 46–49, 50; falls from moon, 55, 56, 57; *rasa* as, 85, 86
Newton, Niles, 162, 165
New Year: celebration of Lakshmi and, 50; Diwali as, 50; renewal of creation and, 51
Nibandhas: elucidation of Hindu laws/customs in, 18; Kartik-related material in, 18
Nirnayasindhu, 211*n9*; Kartik-related material in, 18; lamp lighting in, 28
Northrup, Lesley, 123, 153, 181
Nussbaum, Martha, 13

O'Flaherty, Wendy Doniger, 86
Oxenhandler, Noelle, 163, 165